Arteletra

Purdue Studies in Romance Literatures

Editorial Board

Íñigo Sánchez Llama, Series Editor
Elena Coda
Paul B. Dixon
Patricia Hart

Deborah Houk Schocket
Gwen Kirkpatrick
Allen G. Wood

Howard Mancing, Consulting Editor
Floyd Merrell, Consulting Editor
Joyce L. Detzner, Production Editor

Associate Editors

French
Jeanette Beer
Paul Benhamou
Willard Bohn
Thomas Broden
Gerard J. Brault
Mary Ann Caws
Glyn P. Norton
Allan H. Pasco
Gerald Prince
Roseann Runte
Ursula Tidd

Italian
Fiora A. Bassanese
Peter Carravetta
Benjamin Lawton
Franco Masciandaro
Anthony Julian Tamburri

Luso-Brazilian
Fred M. Clark
Marta Peixoto
Ricardo da Silveira Lobo Sternberg

Spanish and Spanish American
Catherine Connor
Ivy A. Corfis
Frederick A. de Armas
Edward Friedman
Charles Ganelin
David T. Gies
Roberto González Echevarría
David K. Herzberger
Emily Hicks
Djelal Kadir
Amy Kaminsky
Lucille Kerr
Howard Mancing
Floyd Merrell
Alberto Moreiras
Randolph D. Pope
Elżbieta Skłodowska
Marcia Stephenson
Mario Valdés

 volume 81

ArteletrA

The Sixties in Latin America
and the Politics of Going Unnoticed

Jason A. Bartles

Purdue University Press
West Lafayette, Indiana

Copyright ©2021 by Purdue University. All rights reserved.

∞ The paper used in this book meets the minimum requirements of American National Standard for Information Sciences—Permanence of Paper for Printed Library Materials, ANSI Z39.48-1992.

Printed in the United States of America
Template for interior design by Anita Noble.
Template for cover by Heidi Branham.
Cover image: "The texture of the old wall of large bricks/Alexmumu/iStock/ Via Getty Images" with modification by the Purdue University Press.

Cataloging-in-Publication Data on file at the Library of Congress

Hardcover ISBN: 978-1-61249-666-5
Paperback ISBN: 978-1-61249-653-5
ePub ISBN: 978-1-61249-654-2
ePDF ISBN: 978-1-61249-655-9

To Matthew John Phillips

Contents

xi Acknowledgments

1 **Introduction**
   ARTELETRA al vesre
     4 The Sixties in Latin America
     5 Casey, Filloy, and Somers
     9 Going Unnoticed
     11 Going Unnoticed in Cultural Markets
     13 Going Unnoticed and Avant-Garde Aesthetics
     16 Toward the Politics of Going Unnoticed
     26 Organization of the Book

29 **PART ONE**
   The Itinerary of Errant Palindromes

31 **Chapter One**
   On Errant Palindromes
     32 Crystalline Palindromes
     34 Reading ARTELETRA Against the Current

39 **Chapter Two**
   On Going Unnoticed
     40 Amid the Swirling Lights and Shadows
     44 Two Houses

49 **Chapter Three**
   On Unattended Details
     50 Amid Heaps of Scrap Metal
     52 A Weaponized Scorpion

57 **PART TWO**
   The Politics of Going Unnoticed

61 **Chapter Four**
   A Double Negative in Cuba
     62 *Lunes* and the Cuban Revolution
     65 An Unremarkable Intellectual
     67 Casey's Dissent

75 **Chapter Five**
   An Errant Allegory in Argentina
     77 Intruders in Argentine Politics
     80 Disagreeing with Plato
     86 Konsideransky's Ambush

Contents

91 Chapter Six
A Nude Woman in Uruguay
93 The Uruguayan Exception
95 Linke's Flight and Decapitation
100 First Encounter: Nataniel's Chains
100 Second Encounter: The People's Terror
105 Third Encounter: Juan's Dissent

109 PART THREE
The Aesthetics of Writing in Plain Sight

113 Chapter Seven
¡Ay, epopeyA!; or, Filloy's Gauchos at the Origins
114 The *Gaucho Jodón*
116 Dismantling the Original Gaucho
119 Proto and the Ochoas
124 A Gaucho by Any Other Name

127 Chapter Eight
¡Sometamos o matemoS!; or, Somers's Mandrake Syndrome
128 The Unsolvable
132 Enigmas and the Mandrake Syndrome
138 Immunity and Contamination

143 Chapter Nine
Supuso su puS; or, Casey's Wasted Narratives
145 Nineteenth-Century Trash
154 Getting Wasted
158 With and Through the Filth

165 PART FOUR
The Ethics of Being Perceived

169 Chapter Ten
Exposure through Dialogues
169 Being-With
171 And
174 Exposing Infinity

181 Chapter Eleven
   From Monodialogues to Pandemonium
   183   Monodialogues among Antagonists
   186   &
   189   Pandemonium
193 Chapter Twelve
   Aiding the Adversary
   194   A System of Unknown Dimensions
   195   Clean and Modern
   196   Rewriting Kafka
   198   From Enemies to Adversaries
203 Conclusion
   Re-ves la ARTELETRA
209 Notes
219 Works Cited
233 Index

Acknowledgments

The best part of finishing this book is being granted the space to thank many of the people whose guidance, collegiality, and friendship improved my work and sustained me throughout graduate school and in the years since.

Laura Demaría generously served as my dissertation director at the University of Maryland, College Park, where she taught me to be a much-improved reader and writer. Laura has been a guide and source of inspiration to develop my ideas and, importantly, to do so in dialogue with others. The constancy of her mentorship and friendship over more than a decade cannot be adequately expressed in words. Again and again, thank you, Laura.

I am indebted to the expertise and kindness of my professors over the years. Nancy Ryan, my high school Spanish teacher in West Virginia, not only taught me the joys of learning a second language but also made it possible for me to travel outside of the United States for the first time. At Gettysburg College, I had the pleasure of studying with creative and challenging faculty, many of whom opened lines of inquiry that continue to guide my research. Currie K. Thompson had the good sense to encourage me to study abroad in Mendoza, Argentina, and his courses and mentorship pointed me toward so many possibilities that I never knew existed. Steve Gimbel's imaginative courses still inspire my research and my teaching. For encouraging me to speak when I thought I had nothing to say, I also wish to thank: Gitte Butin, Nancy Cushing-Daniels, who will be missed, Eleanor Hogan, Mónica Morales, Paula Olinger, Alicia Rolón, Jack Ryan, and Miguel Viñuela. My friendship that began at Gettysburg with Leanne Tyler is one I will always cherish.

During my time at the University of Maryland, my gratitude goes to the faculty who taught and mentored me over many years. To Sandra Cypess for her unwavering support; to Mehl Penrose for his time and enthusiasm; and to Juan Carlos Quintero-Herencia for teaching me to "masticar" texts and ideas. I would also like to thank Jorge Aguilar-Mora, Peter Beicken, Carmen Benito-Vessels, Ernesto Calvo, Sergio Chejfec, Regina Harrison, Gwen Kirkpatrick, Manel Lacorte, Ryan Long, José María Naharro-Calderón, Eyda Merediz, and Saúl Sosnowski.

Acknowledgments

A number of friends in graduate school were the best companions during our years in Silver Spring. Thank you to Sofía Calzada-Orihuela, Laura Quijano, and Kathryn Taylor for being amazing friends in all senses of the word. To Randy Baden, who left us too soon, and Ted Clifford, thanks for the game and movie nights in College Park. For the great memories, thanks also to Sebastián Bartis, Elena Becerril, Elena Campero, Luis Charry, Carolina Gómez-Montoya, Norman González, Chila Hidalgo, Dory Hoffman, Amy Karp, David Libber, Chris Lewis, Goretti Prieto-Botana, Julia Tomasini, and Lisa Warren.

At West Chester University, a number of colleagues offered me their advice and support making it possible for me to complete the final manuscript while transitioning to a new city and a new job. Their collegiality and shared ethos are helping us build a stronger program. Thank you especially to Cristóbal Cardemil-Krause, Daniela Ciceri, Jelena Colovic-Markovic, Megan Corbin, Brigitte Goutal, Gloria Maite Hernández, Daniela Johannes, Margarete Landwehr, Joseph Moser, Metello Mugnai, Meg Niiler, Iliana Pagán-Teitelbaum, Innhwa Park, Fred Patton, Roxane Petit-Rasselle, Aliza Richman, John Rosso, Megan Saltzman, Ana Sánchez, Israel Sanz-Sánchez, Andrea Varricchio, Jerry Williams, and Dominik Wolff.

I also owe a debt of gratitude to the many members of the D. C. Area Theory Group who so graciously welcomed me into their lively debates. A special thanks to Manuel Cuellar, Laura Demaría, Todd Garth, Tania Gentic, Álvaro Kaempfer, Gwen Kirkpatrick, Silvia Kurlat Ares, Mariela Méndez de Coudriet, Núria Vilanova, Sergio Waisman, Brenda Werth and Griselda Zuffi. For welcoming me to the Southern Cone Studies Section of LASA, thanks to Fernando Blanco, Luis Cárcamo-Huechante, Leila Gómez, Gloria Medina-Sancho, and Cristián Opazo. For granting me time to discuss the works of Armonía Somers with her and for sharing many resources, anecdotes, and advice, thank you Cristina Dalmagro.

Colleagues at numerous conferences over the years have guided the manuscript's drafts through their generous questions and comments; thank you to all those who attended panels where I presented this work, including LASA, the Southern Cone Studies Section conferences in Santiago and Montevideo,

Acknowledgments

ACLA, KFLC, and at conferences at Tulane, Rutgers, and Dickinson.

Various fellowships, grants, and awards all made this book possible. At the University of Maryland, I would like to thank the Graduate School for an incredibly generous Flagship Fellowship that supported increased research time over five years, as well as a Summer Research Fellowship. The Latin American Studies Center funded a research trip to Argentine, Uruguay, and Chile in 2012. LASC also provided a grant to establish a working group, under the direction of Laura Demaría, titled "Aesthetics and Cultural Studies in Latin America: A Crossroads," during which I first studied a handful of texts quoted in the book. The Department of Spanish and Portuguese provided me with a scholarship during coursework and with the Ángel Rama Post-Proposal Fellowship to complete my dissertation. At West Chester University, the process of expanding my dissertation and rewriting it into this book was supported with a College of Arts and Sciences Support and Development Award in 2015, and a Research and Creative Activities Grant helped fund the publication of this book. Thank you also to the Latin American and Latino Studies Center for funding various conference trips during which I presented early drafts of this manuscript.

Early versions of some chapter previously appeared in publication. Parts of Chapter 7 were published under the title "Gauchos at the Origins: Lugones, Borges, Filloy" in *Variaciones Borges* 40 (2015): 133–52. Chapter 9 appeared as "Calvert Casey's Wasted Narratives" in *Revista Hispánica Moderna* 70.1 (2017): 19–35. The main arguments of Chapter 5 first appeared in Spanish under the title "La alegoría errante de la torre-cueva" in *Revista Iberoamericana* 82.254 (Jan–Mar 2016): 213–28. Many of the ideas of Chapter 10 appeared in Spanish in an edited volume on Armonía Somers as "La ética de exponerse en *De miedo en miedo* de Armonía Somers" *La escritura Armonía Somers. Pulsión y riesgo* (63–76).

To Joyce Detzner, and everyone at Purdue Studies in Romance Literatures and Purdue University Press, who helped usher this book from the proposal stage to its publication.

To my dear friends who first made Philly feel like home, Zachary Dutton, Alex Hamilton, and Arun Sethuraman, thank you most of all for the non-academic experiences and memories that will remain unwritten here.

Acknowledgments

Katherine Ann Davis is a friend like no other who always reminds me what really matters. She deserves a page filled with inside jokes about landlocked pirates.

Rocío Gordon not only has made each of my ideas better, but more importantly, she has always led the way and been with me through the good times and the bad.

To Ruskin and Eliot, our dogs.

To Mom, who always made it possible to create paths where none existed.

This book is dedicated to Matthew John Phillips, my husband, my partner in everything, the person who taught me how to love and what it means to be happy. He also read every page of this book, prepared the index, and has listened to me rehearse the ideas here for more time than anyone should be willing.

Introduction

ARTELETRA al vesre

> Estamos efectivamente sumergidos en una demanda
> de visibilidad total que parecería dejar fuera de lugar
> las prácticas críticas que buscan crear opacidades o
> refracciones, mostrar que no todos los cuerpos del
> sistema son translúcidos.
> Nelly Richard, *La insubordinación de los signos*

ARTELETRA, one of Juan Filloy's many palindromes, can be read from left to right and back again, as well as from the central letter out toward both ends, perfectly replicating itself in every direction (*Karcino* 199). This palindrome is composed of the Spanish words *arte* and *letra*, meaning "art" and "letter," respectively, or in my interpretation, "the art of writing." ARTELETRA, in this sense, becomes another possible way to say "literature." Yet, to conflate art and literature with the crystalline structure of palindromes at the start of a study on the Sixties in Latin America would be disingenuous. Since the historical avant-gardes, if not earlier, art and literature shatter consecrated forms. They continually break the rules that would constrict, contain, and order their fragmented parts within the space of a palindrome. Simply turning around to read this palindrome in reverse cannot illuminate a different reading of ARTELETRA, of the art and literature that, at best, leave only a trace of themselves and their politics in this invented word. Therefore, a linear reading of ARTELETRA, regardless of its directionality, cannot become a metaphorical heuristic for approaching the Sixties in Latin America or the underappreciated works of Calvert Casey, Juan Filloy, and Armonía Somers.

In order to catch a glimpse of what might be going unnoticed on the palindrome's glossy surface, I prefer to break its crystalline structure and read it *al vesre*. This phrase comes from Lunfardo,

Introduction

the late nineteenth- and early twentieth-century Argentine dialect with Italian roots that developed first among criminals and then gained popularity among the growing lower-middle classes in Buenos Aires. Lunfardo often appears in tango lyrics, and many of the words, including *zafar* (to get away with something, to get out of an obligation) and *trucho* (fake, shoddy) are commonly used today. *Vesre* is the Lunfardo word for a language game in which the syllables of common words are reversed or completely jumbled. For example, the word *tango* becomes *gotán*, but *amigo* turns into *gomía*. The word *vesre* is derived from the word *revés*, so the word that names this game also plays the game it names; it reverses the word *revés*, but it does so improperly. This game refuses the propriety of grammar and allows new words and ideas to be created through a process of disruption and reconstruction.

On the one hand, to read ArteletrA *al vesre* is to reverse the palindrome imperfectly. It is not to turn around and reveal what was always there to the light of today's knowledge nor to invert entrenched binaries. The past is never so perfectly uncovered, and the exclusive logic of binary thought must be rendered inoperative. Rather, to read and write *al vesre* is to break the palindrome's linear logic and rearrange its fragmented parts to create something different. In this sense, reading *al vesre* establishes a certain affinity with Walter Benjamin's assertion that the task of the historian is "to brush history against the grain" ("Theses" 257). Reading ArteletrA and the Sixties *al vesre* upends the perfect ordering of each letter in its place and opens new paths through highly structured and regulated spaces. Furthermore, it challenges the framing of biopolitical regimes of visibility and the essentialist narratives that undergird and seek to bring legitimacy to those structures. These new paths, detours, and thresholds through the literatures and politics of the Sixties, as I will demonstrate, unleash the potential to go unnoticed as well as the potential to engage with those who are going unnoticed without revealing them entirely under the pervasive light of knowledge and power.

On the other, to read Latin American literatures of the Sixties *al vesre* is, as this game is also called, to read *al verse*. First, the syllables of *revés* are flipped to form *vesre*, and then this re-organization slips even further through the metathesis of the "s" and the "r." Curiously, *verse* stands as a homophone in Spanish for a reflexive verb, "to see one another." However, to read these literatures *al verse* is not to illuminate them to one another. As Emmanuel Levinas argues, "To illuminate is to remove from being its resistance, because light opens a horizon and empties space—delivers being out of nothingness" (*Totality* 44). Rather, to read *al verse* is to rearrange different texts and set them in face-to-face encounters with one another that allow new dialogues to take place where partitions once stood. As the unnoticed protagonists I analyze in the works of Casey, Filloy, and Somers disrupt prescribed itineraries and wander off course, they stumble into others who are also going unnoticed. These unexpected encounters do not require each of them to fully reveal the essence of their identity to one another; rather, they enter into the difficult process of establishing dialogues with others who had been isolated behind walls or abandoned in large crowds. During these brief, unexpected encounters, the fictional protagonists I study seek the restoration of the potential to disagree—the defining characteristic of the political—and to find common ground, that is, to engage in what I call "the politics of going unnoticed."

At first glance, the politics of going unnoticed constitutes an oxymoron: politics is often defined as the struggle to be seen or heard within public spaces and governing institutions—in other words, to make the invisible visible. To go unnoticed would, in theory, necessitate a retreat from the political. However, becoming visible in the public sphere also subjects those bodies and ideas to the biopolitical and capitalist arrangements of space, constituting a potential trap for anything and everything illuminated within those structures. In the present study, politics will be defined not as the process of making visible but rather as the act of engaging in dissensus. In the works of Casey, Filloy, and Somers, going unnoticed becomes a means of evading the trap of visibility in order to restore the potential to disagree with institutional and everyday decisions. Those who go unnoticed encounter tools for dismantling essentialist narratives while moving toward the open, toward a field without norms, dividing walls, or the requirement to fully reveal oneself to the light of knowledge and power.

Throughout this book, I read the literatures and politics of the Sixties in Latin America *al vesre* and *al verse* in order to write different narratives of the era. My readings are not concentrated on the loudest voices and canonical figures of the Sixties nor on the disillusioned narratives that appeared immediately upon

Introduction

the era's violent closure. Instead, I establish a series of dialogues between these three untimely and underappreciated authors. The protagonists who inhabit their fictional worlds produce openings in the everyday that allow them to wander off course and render inoperative the binary structures of biopolitics (e.g., visible/invisible, pure/filthy, friend/enemy) that constantly divide humans from one another in the service of power and economic inequality. What was ignored in the Sixties for its apparent individualism demonstrates its radical commitment to forming better communities. As Casey, Filloy, and Somers imagine protagonists who go unnoticed, their texts confront and distort well-worn narratives from the nineteenth century to the Sixties, and they challenge the blind spots and limitations of each other, giving rise to new political, aesthetic, and ethical tools for thinking the densely populated crossroads of literatures and politics in the Sixties once more.

The Sixties in Latin America

Images of guerrillas and hippies, of university students and workers in the streets can appear today as relics of a by-gone era. From the perspective of a present characterized by the entrenchment of neoliberal economic policies; cultural and political globalization; the Left Turn, its subsequent recession, and the revitalization of fascist ideologies; the resurgence of indigenous movements; the transitions underway in Cuba after the Castros and in Venezuela after Chávez; and the technological innovations of the digital era, this distance between today and the Sixties can feel insurmountable.

At the same time, the literatures and politics of the Sixties opened spaces that continue to be inhabited throughout the Americas, and those archives have yet to be exhausted. The Sixties—written here with a capital "S"—serves as a shorthand for an era that exceeds the temporal limits of a decade. To begin in 1960 would already be too late, and to stop in 1969 would artificially truncate too many events and discourses. Óscar Terán underscores the flexibility needed to study this era that he names with the ungrammatical Spanish phrase, *los sesentas*, with an extra "s" on *sesenta* (*Nuestros* 11). Though Terán's study is of Argentina, tracing Peronism from the 1940s through the presidency of Arturo

Frondizi, it is possible to extend this notion of *los sesentas* as a temporal block throughout Latin America.

My own study establishes a dialogue among texts from this era while moving *al vesre* and *al verse* across various national and international contexts. This lapse of time begins, quite imprecisely, in the 1950s, with the military coup against Perón in 1955 and the successful overthrow of Batista in 1959. The Sixties was an era in which radical change in the world appeared as a historical necessity on the verge of materializing; therefore, according to a certain logic of the era, it was worth the armed struggle necessary to achieve it. Despite the big dreams of the Sixties, the reality was far from ideal. The rural and urban guerrillas fighting in Cuba to break free from neocolonial chains, for example, began to establish a Soviet-style regime under which they persecuted not only political dissidents but all those who were considered to be against the Revolution's values, whether they be critical artists, foreigners, or queer individuals.

Broadly speaking, the Sixties comes to a close at those moments when the potential for carrying out utopian projects appears to be lost. The Padilla Affair of 1971, for example, marked a moment when Castro's intellectual supporters from around the globe publicly declared their break with his regime. Another foreclosure took place when Juan María Bordaberry suspended the Uruguayan constitution in 1973 and enacted a regime of terror and violence that annihilated the Tupamaros and sought to suppress any remaining revolutionary sympathy among the general public. Of course, this is a hasty outline of the Sixties that is meant only as a point of departure for my particular reading of this era today. By reading the works of Casey, Filloy, and Somers, I follow their unnoticed protagonists as they wander off these most well-known paths and chart new itineraries throughout this era that provide a framework for different forms of utopian thinking outside of the violent, binary logic of success and failure.

Casey, Filloy, and Somers

Born to a Cuban-American family in Baltimore, Maryland, Calvert Casey (1924–69) lived in Havana between 1958 and 1965. He worked for *Lunes de Revolución* and *Casa de las Américas* before going into exile in Poland and Italy, and he published

Introduction

collections of his short texts at Ediciones R and Seix Barral: *El regreso* (1962), *Memorias de una isla* (1964), *El regreso y otros relatos* (1967), and *Notas de un simulador* (1969). He chose to live in the center of the revolutionary city and to publish in the centers of the cultural markets of the 1960s, documenting volunteers who labored in the Cuban countryside and discussing ways to improve Cuba's national arts, while crafting his own literature. Yet, he never occupied the center stage of the Revolution alongside Ernesto "Che" Guevara or Guillermo Cabrera Infante. After the founding of the UMAPs and the institutionalization of homophobia inside the Revolution, Casey fled Cuba, fearing future imprisonment for being gay. He continued writing for a few years but tragically committed suicide in Rome in 1969. Since his death, a number of his friends and colleagues, as well as more recent critics, have attempted revivals of his works. He has been the subject of special issues of the journals *Quimera* (1982) and *Gaceta de Cuba* (2009), many of his stories have been translated into English, and Jamila Medina Ríos has published two recent editions of his collected short stories in Cuba and in Argentina, respectively.[1] But during the Sixties, he received very little popular or critical attention.

From Río Cuarto, Argentina, Juan Filloy (1894–2000) is known as the "writer of three centuries" and the author of thousands of palindromes for which, according to him, he holds the world record. During his life, he wrote more than fifty novels, almost half of which remain unpublished today. His first novel, *Periplo*, appeared in 1930, and the last, *Decio 8A*, in 1997. Between the 1939 publication of *Finesse* and the 1967 re-edition of *Op Oloop* (1934), he worked as a judge in Río Cuarto and wrote numerous books that he refused to publish. Once he retired in the 1960s, he published consistently until his death. Among all of these short-story collections and novels with seven-letter titles, I focus on three texts published before the 1976 dictatorship, *Yo, yo y yo (Monodiálogos paranoicos)* (1971), *Los Ochoa* (1972) and *Vil & Vil (La gata parida)* (1975), as well as his lifetime collection of palindromes and essays on the art of writing them, eventually published in *Karcino: Tratado de palindromía* (1988). Most recently, his books are appearing in new editions in Argentina, but existing research has focused on his association with the historical avant-garde in the 1930s.

Armonía Somers (1914–94) is the pseudonym for the Uruguayan writer Armonía Etchepare. In 1933, she became a school teacher in Montevideo, gaining a solid reputation for her research in pedagogy. Her first novel, *La mujer desnuda* (1950), provoked an enormous scandal among the lettered elite of the Río de la Plata; they dismissed it as a poorly written pornographic text—based more on hearsay than on having read the novel that barely circulated at the time—and assumed the pseudonym was hiding a gay male writer. She continued writing and publishing short stories and novels with the prestigious Editorial Arca, including *Todos los cuentos. 1953–1967* (1967), *De miedo en miedo (Los manuscritos del río)* (1967), and *Un retrato para Dickens* (1969), among a number of other works over the following decades, yet her name never figures among the male-only list of Boom writers. In the 1960s, Ángel Rama began a revision of her critical reception, and since the 1970s, various waves of feminist criticism and studies on fantastic literature have set about to recover and study her dark and complex writings, particularly focusing on *Sólo los elefantes encuentran mandrágora* (written between 1972 and 1975, but not published until 1986). Currently, her archives are being organized by Cristina Dalmagro at the Université de Poitiers in France, and she is finally being translated into English.[2]

When one thinks of the Sixties in Latin America, these writers rarely come to mind. The literary-political arena became overcrowded with the manifestos and weapons of those who struggled to be seen and heard above all others; as a result, those who upheld threshold positions not wholly in line with more visible, powerful projects were all too easily cast aside as counterrevolutionaries and ivory-tower intellectuals, if they were paid any attention at all. Moreover, Casey, Filloy, and Somers are authors whose works do not even "belong together" in a traditional, canonical, or proper sense. These authors are from different generations. They were born in, lived in, and wrote about very different regions of the Americas, traversing North America, the Caribbean, and the Southern Cone. An identity-based approach to the authors would further divide them as queer, rural, and female writers, respectively, despite the expansive scope of their works that cannot be reduced to these categories alone. Their ideological positions do not cohere around a specific political party or movement. Even

Introduction

their aesthetic sensibilities vary drastically from one another: Casey's texts are brief and fragmented; Filloy's are perfectly and rigidly structured; and Somers's meander enigmatically across genres that range from the realist novel to horror and the fantastic. Thematically, they address a wide range of topics, from gauchos and rare diseases to the contents of sewage systems. I know of no record of conversations taking place between any of them, nor have I found evidence that they read one another's works.

Nevertheless, such disciplinary conventions are not the only possible means of constituting an object of study. By reading the literary-political arena of the Sixties in Latin America *al vesre* and *al verse*, the works of Casey, Filloy, and Somers can engage one another in dialogue. The encounters that take place in *ArteletrA* refuse any critical narrative that essentializes an origin or identity, and they reject a singular, linear arrangement of texts, discourses, and ideas. Instead, borrowing from Raúl Antelo, each new arrangement becomes subjected to "contaminaciones, desplazamientos, accidentes, reinterpretaciones y recontextualizaciones incesantes" (37). There never will be one totalizing narrative of the Sixties in Latin America that reveals everything to the light of knowledge. There can be only glimpses into the multitude of varying arrangements and rearrangements of materials and ideas, each time offering contingent, yet rigorous, narratives of the literatures and politics of the era that others in the future will disassemble and reassemble.

In my reading of the Sixties in Latin America, the fragmented, jumbled parts I study are the stories of unnoticed people and protagonists who turn away from the bright lights of literary and political institutions. Turning away is not a rejection of institutions, *tout court*, but a response to failing institutions that make no effort to engage with the unnoticed or their demands. Therefore, they seek positions within the heated polemics that raged throughout Latin America about the role of art and literature in the Sixties, but they are either hesitant to accept or openly disagree with widespread assumptions and normative values. Casey, Filloy, and Somers all imagine protagonists characterized by a quiet rebelliousness, by the desire to shy away from the spotlight, from overt political propaganda, and from choosing sides in the most visible political, aesthetic, and ethical debates of the era. By going unnoticed, their protagonists dissent without relying on the ancient binary between visibility and invisibility, or transparency and opacity, that continues to structure and define the political today.

Going Unnoticed

The anonymous narrator of Somers's *De miedo en miedo (Los manuscritos del río)* wants little more than to go unnoticed. At his job in a bookstore, for example, his boss remains silently perched on the second floor, a "lugar estratégico" that allows him to watch over everyone in the shop (12). The narrator feels trapped under the perception of other people who notice and scrutinize his every action. In one instance, he explains the extreme anxiety he feels even in the privacy of his own home when he and his wife decide to make love:

> Hay que hacerse el amor con cuidado a fin de no despertar a los de abajo, pues rechina el piso [...]. Y también cuidarse de los contiguos porque se escucha todo a través de estas paredes de mentira, que dejan traspasar los suspiros finales, el ruido del bidet, y si se tiene mala suerte hasta la vibración de los espermatozoides asediando al óvulo—añadí desde los puestos más altos de la exageración y la rabia contenida—. (40)

This combination of humorous exaggeration and rage underscores the fragility of the barriers that only appear to create distance and privacy in the modern world. The narrator lives isolated with his family in an old apartment building, making few connections with his neighbors who, nevertheless, can hear his every move. Given his rampant fear of germs, this partitioning into a clearly demarcated space is not the point of his critique, as it will be for some of the other protagonists I study; moreover, these floors and walls, he says, are built of lies. Every creak and vibration, even those sounds and movements otherwise imperceptible to the human senses, become amplified in this space. These partitions trap each of them in a particular place, while revealing their most intimate moments to the constant surveillance of everyone else. Going unnoticed for this narrator is not a matter of seeking isolation per se, nor does it require total concealment or stasis; more accurately, it is the process by which he seeks to evade the incessant surveillance of his neighbors, his boss, and the other anonymous people who scrutinize him in the crowded city. By going unnoticed, he seeks to reframe and even tear down these walls built on lies and to enter into dialogues with some of those kept on the other side, albeit imperfectly and for only a brief time.

As Gilles Deleuze and Félix Guattari have commented, "To go unnoticed is by no means easy. To be a stranger, even to one's doorman or neighbors" is a difficult task (279). In their analysis, going unnoticed takes the form of a becoming that moves between perception and imperception, or what they refer to as "zones of indiscernibility" (280). The protagonists I study, as in the case of Somers's narrator, do not hide behind masks or personas that would veil their true identities. Rather, they create temporary zones of indiscernibility, forms of movement along unexpected itineraries, wherein they will not be paid much attention by others. Though "Armonía Somers" is a pseudonym for Armonía Etchepare, her fictional characters are those who I consider to be going unnoticed. What goes unnoticed is the act, the subject, or the event itself presented or represented as itself, even though no one pays attention to its taking place or to its existence. Finally, the bodies of those who go unnoticed are visible in the sense that they are capable of being seen, yet they manage to create a temporary state during which little public light is shone on their bodies. When they pass by others, no one pays attention. When they speak out, everyone happens to ignore their voice. Still, they continue to move about and stumble into others with whom they can engage in dialogue along the way.

Going unnoticed involves an intentional desire to stay out of the public spotlight. These often-anonymous protagonists actively seek out shelters and refuges or attempt to hide and write in plain sight and to pass for something unworthy of further attention. Casey's many protagonists are closeted or secretive, both in terms of their sexuality and their general attempts to remain anonymous in public spaces. Filloy imagines, among others, a cave-dwelling writer and a quietly insubordinate military conscript. Somers's Rebeca Linke in *La mujer desnuda* and the anonymous man in *De miedo en miedo* seek quiet spaces where they encounter unexpected confidants in the countryside and in the city. Paradoxical as it may appear, this active gesture of going unnoticed is what allows me to form a dialogue among these three authors and their protagonists.

Going Unnoticed in Cultural Markets

According to a market logic, going unnoticed would be a failure within the publishing world, not an avant-garde gesture with political and ethical implications. Many of those who aspire to greatness, power, or prestige inadvertently go unnoticed, failing to succeed from the start. Even for those who do publish their works with a major press, there will be no guarantee of public or critical success. In my analysis, however, it should be noted that going unnoticed is primarily a status of fictional protagonists, not of the texts themselves, and that going unnoticed by writing in plain sight to perceive and be perceived by others is what allows Casey, Filloy, and Somers to exceed the reifying, but never totalizing, grasp of the cultural markets in which their texts and ideas circulate.

All three authors inadvertently went unnoticed despite being published in the heart of the Latin American and Spanish cultural markets that were responsible for the Boom and the circulation of more explicitly committed writers. Even though he was praised by Guillermo Cabrera Infante, Italo Calvino, and María Zambrano, Casey's works never enjoyed much renown in the Sixties, neither inside nor outside Cuba.[3] Filloy returned from his thirty-year editorial silence in the mid-1960s, publishing both with small presses in Río Cuarto and with Losada, a major press in Buenos Aires. Yet, he never rose to the status of someone like Macedonio Fernández whose works were recovered and celebrated during the era.[4] In Montevideo, Somers was published by Editorial Arca, a press that played "un papel fundamental en la legitimación de criterios estéticos nuevos e instancias de consagración en la literatura de las décadas del 50, 60 y comienzos del 70" (Dalmagro, *Desde los umbrales* 79). However, the current revival of her works is indebted primarily to the subsequent waves of prominent feminist critics from the late 1970s onward. There is no reason to believe that any of the authors under consideration here desired to have their works go unnoticed by reading publics, even as all three eschewed the public spotlight and wrote stories about those who go or desire to go unnoticed.

Though the leftist politics of the Sixties frequently make capitalism a major target, twentieth-century Latin American art and literature could hardly be characterized as independent of

Introduction

the market. However, it does not follow that what circulates in the market is fully co-opted by it. Brett Levinson demonstrates that the Boom was the most visible example of how literary culture navigated the rise and expansion of the global, mass marketplace (10–30). Further belying the notion that one totalitarian economic structure dominates global cycles of supply and demand while churning out nothing but propaganda for the masses, Luis E. Cárcamo-Huechante, Álvaro Fernández Bravo, and Alejandra Laera propose the term *mercado cultural* in order to study that which exceeds the horizon of consumption when considering the financing and circulation of art and literature. They recognize that cultural markets in Latin America are ubiquitous, but they also underscore the precarity of these markets, given their potential to fail at any moment due to global imbalances (11–13).

Furthermore, the cultural circuits of capitalist markets in the Sixties were not exclusively dedicated to distributing the commercially viable goods of mass production. Ángel Rama had previously developed the term *editoriales culturales* in order to emphasize this excess to profit-driven models for capitalist marketplaces. He references Spanish-language publishing houses in which the expanding networks of capitalist markets developed the means to finance less commercially viable works, generate publicity for them, and create greater access to them and other texts, including educational textbooks and bestsellers.[5] These *editoriales culturales* formed new, intellectually rigorous, and popular reading publics in Latin America, thus solidifying the necessary conditions for the success of the Boom (Rama, "El Boom" 66–70). To enter into circulation, cultural products inevitably pass through the markets tied to the culture industries, which leave their mark. Yet, cultural markets are incapable of reducing symbolic value merely to its use or exchange values. In sum, the influence between literature and cultural markets does not have to be read as a unidirectional, hegemonic force flowing from the markets to the texts, since texts can always be read *al vesre* and *al verse*, exceeding their sociopolitical or economic use value.

The works under consideration here were never invisible or hidden from public view in the Sixties. Casey, Filloy, and Somers published in the centers of the cultural markets, but their texts were often left unnoticed in the shadows of the bestselling Boom authors and other more explicitly committed writers. It might be tempting to explain their marginalized status as symptoms of homophobia, the cosmopolitan rejection of the provinces, or misogyny, respectively. That may factor to some degree into the equation. However, Casey was not closeted while working for *Lunes de Revolución* and *Casa de las Américas*. Filloy was praised by Cortázar in *Rayuela*. Somers was celebrated publicly by Ángel Rama, and eventually Mario Benedetti recanted his earlier criticism of her writing.[6] Studying these texts today does not grant them some sort of retrospective visibility in the Sixties, and the extent to which these texts have circulated or might become more commercially or critically popular in the future is of little importance to my analysis of the politics of going unnoticed. My primary object of study concerns the narratives about fictional protagonists who go or attempt to go unnoticed and the series of political, aesthetic, and ethical tools they develop along the way.[7]

Going Unnoticed and Avant-Garde Aesthetics

According to Julio Premat, the ideas that most resonate today, the ones that continue to generate "teorías, pensamientos y textos," are those related to "la vanguardia de los sesenta": "Al evocar el periodo se convoca, también, toda una efervescencia contestataria y se valoriza un *revival* posible de posiciones rebeldes multiformes" (60–61). At first glance, the concept of going unnoticed would appear to be at odds with an avant-garde aesthetics; this quiet rebelliousness that seeks out zones of indiscernibility could be interpreted as antithetical to the effervescence described by Premat. Nevertheless, going unnoticed is the process that restores the potential for the protagonists I study to engage in the avant-garde practices of dismantling and reconfiguring institutional and everyday norms.

In Latin America, the historical avant-gardes both critiqued the institutions of literature and the fine arts and created new forms for literature and art.[8] These new artistic practices were celebrated and financed by national institutions as part of their pursuit of modernization throughout the twentieth century.[9] For this reason, these destructions did not bring about the end of literary and artistic establishments—as Peter Bürger proposes in *Theory of the Avant-Garde*—but rather they provoked radical changes within, when not actually creating the first, national institutions, thus

Introduction

shattering the idea that the work of art could be isolated from political and economic influences.[10] Avant-garde aesthetics in Latin America cannot be defined primarily as anti-institutional or nihilistic; rather, they engage a deconstructive mode that both dismantles and renders inoperative long-standing barriers in densely populated spaces while building new institutions and tracing alternate itineraries through those same spaces. In the Sixties, Casey, Filloy, and Somers redeploy these avant-garde practices in order to dismantle reified binary constructs.

Many early critics—most notably, those of the Frankfurt School—sought to isolate avant-garde, or modernist, aesthetics in an autonomous realm. However, the vast bibliography on this topic proves that avant-garde gestures, popular cultures, and mass technologies all critically engaged with and transformed one another within capitalist markets. The works of Casey, Filloy, and Somers will be no exception to this. The historical avant-garde did not always make a clean break with preceding cultural forms. Benjamin explains that the historical avant-garde authorized a plethora of new techniques and possibilities for literature and art in general, many of which were derived from the formal innovations of photography, film, and radio—the technologies of mass reproduction and the culture industry (*The Work of Art* 19–55). In fact, Beatriz Sarlo argues that the sentimental narratives circulating in Latin American periodicals between 1917 and 1927—contemporaries of the historical avant-garde—kept alive supposedly outdated aesthetic forms borrowed from *modernismo* and late Romanticism; these provided habitual resources for marginal areas of high culture (*El imperio* 19–30). Furthermore, as Ana María Amar Sánchez demonstrates, Latin American writers throughout the entire twentieth century cited themes, styles, and entire works of popular or mass culture to attract larger reading publics before betraying those popular forms with innovative literary forms (11–37).

When considering literatures in the Sixties, the cult of novelty and originality associated with avant-garde aesthetics enters into conflict with what can be comprehended as an avant-garde tradition that plays out over the entire twentieth century and continues today. In this sense, the works of Casey, Filloy, and Somers cannot be interpreted as simple repetitions or copies of previous avant-garde gestures. Hal Foster insists that neo-avant-garde artworks be studied not for their novelty or repetition, but as demonstrative of the "deferred temporality of artistic signification" (8). He argues that the transformations and ruptures enacted and made possible by the historical avant-garde were not immediately understood or appreciated; only in retrospect was their impact felt, and it was not until the neo-avant-gardes that the historical avant-garde was first comprehended. In sum, Foster underscores a paradigm shift enacted by avant-garde works in which they overturn "any simple scheme of before and after, cause and effect, origin and repetition" (29). Neo-avant-garde works are those which comprehend, give artistic significance to, and act on the failures of chronologically earlier avant-garde gestures; they reconfigure other projects at their point of failure, but without the promise of emancipation or happiness inscribed in modernist aesthetic theories. There is no requirement that they make anything or anyone visible; rather, their creative deconstruction is what allows avant-garde gestures to recoup their political potential.

In studying the Sixties from today's point of view, it no longer matters which avant-garde project came first and which second, third, and so on. Establishing a chronology of ruptures in constant succession holds little meaning for the analysis of twentieth-century literature and culture. Writing on Cuban avant-garde aesthetics, including writers like Casey who went into exile and thus had to engage with national traditions from afar, Rafael Rojas argues that a major avant-garde undertaking after the Revolution required "una revisión del canon colonial y poscolonial" (18). In fact, Casey, Filloy, and Somers take up various failed projects and institutions of the past from a wide range of popular and literary styles and genres; in Chapter 3, for example, I analyze their engagement with nineteenth- and early-twentieth-century traditions, including the Romantic novel, the gaucho genre, and the family romance. These writers critique, dismantle, and repurpose past traditions that linger and reappear in the Sixties. In this sense, their texts engage in avant-garde aesthetics even though their protagonists seek these creative deconstructions through a quiet rebelliousness—an innovation in its own right considering the conspicuousness of many avant-garde gestures—well after the shocking disruptions of the historical avant-garde and alongside the roaring success of the Boom and the public demands of committed writers.

Introduction

Toward the Politics of Going Unnoticed

The crossroads of literatures and politics in the Sixties is a saturated space in which heated polemics threatened to consume every aspect of public life. Cold War politics situated Latin America at the heart of some of its most intense stand-offs as the United States and the Soviet Union sought to guarantee the supremacy of their respective regimes in the Western hemisphere. In addition, women and queer individuals, students and workers, all took to the streets in capital cities and in the provinces to demand radical transformations of their societies, governing institutions, and working conditions. However, Claudia Gilman contests this perception that everything was political and proposes a subtler description of the era, concluding that "más adecuado sería afirmar que la gramática característica de los discursos [políticos] fue antes excluyente que acumulativa" (32). Instead of reading the Sixties as an era in which everything was political, as if everything were included in this all-encompassing politicization, she recalls that such totalizing narratives are always the result of multiple exclusions. The internal debates between the Boom authors and other highly visible actors have become canonical anecdotes that structure our understanding of the Sixties in Latin America, but they do not always deactivate the binaries and multiple exclusions that relegated so many others to unnoticed thresholds during the era.[11]

In 1960, for example, Jean-Paul Sartre and Simone de Beauvoir visited Cuba like so many other committed intellectuals of the time. They had their photo taken with Fidel Castro and Che Guevara, where they appear slumped in the background behind the looming revolutionary figures. Based on this trip, Sartre published a series of essays that have been translated into English as *Sartre on Cuba*. Within the text, he rehearses the *mea culpa* that becomes typical of intellectuals on the revolutionary island. "I had misunderstood everything," he declares. "What I took to be signs of wealth were, in fact, signs of dependence and poverty" (12). Referring to a speech given by Oscar Pinos Santos on July 1, 1959, Sartre explains how the Cuban case taught him to reevaluate his prejudices:

> There is, said Pinos Santos, a sort of disease of the eyes called *retinosis pigmentaria* which manifests itself by the loss of lateral vision. All those who have carried away an optimistic view of

Cuba are quite sick. They see directly in front, never from the corner of the eye. [...] "Retinosis." The word escaped me. But for several days already I have misunderstood my profound error. I felt my prejudices vacillating. To discover the truth of this capital, I would have to see things upside down. (11; italics in original)

Sartre immediately narrates his experience as one in which everything he thought he knew would have to be reevaluated under the light of the Cuban Revolution. He quickly acquires what he understands to be a new, morally appropriate, and historically correct position regarding the Revolution. Juan Carlos Quintero-Herencia explains Sartre's proposition: "Al mirar 'correctamente' la Revolución, esta se presentará a sí misma translúcida ante su observador" ("'El regreso' de Calvert Casey" 387). Sartre claims to have overcome his ailment, inverted his point of view, and as a result, comprehended fully the political and economic reality of Cuba.

Yet, in my analysis, Sartre's Caribbean vacation is self-serving. His *mea culpa* and new way of looking—which was not actually new but rather the first time he looked at Latin America without a Eurocentric gaze—allow him to maintain his role as a leading intellectual of the global Left. The light of total knowledge has returned to Sartre's eyes through the good graces of the Revolution, thus shoring up his proper place in the center of the global intellectual scene. All he had to do was read upside-down, but never *al vesre* or *al verse*.

To Casey's anonymous protagonists, in contrast, the all-pervading lights of the Cuban Revolution do not simply reveal centuries of colonialism and dependency. In "Polacca brillante," they also facilitate discipline and persecution by subjecting any person and every thought to their totalizing gaze. At the start of the short story, the narrator finds the glowing remains of a cigar in his hotel room, and he suspects a secret officer is tracking his every move. Desperate to escape, he steps onto a deserted street on a freezing May night, possibly in Krakow, as he waits for his friends who will never arrive. Meanwhile, the narrator transforms from an observant subject into the scrutinized object of a local barber's eyes: "Inclinándome un poco, veo a través del cristal el montón de pelos rubios, castaños, blancos, que la escoba empuja lentamente. Cuando alzo los ojos, me doy cuenta de que el peluquero me

Introduction

observa por un gran espejo" (95–96). At first, he appears to be the one observing the actions of the barber through the window, but quickly this gaze is inverted in the large mirror. Now, even other locals are surveilling his actions and whereabouts. Whereas for Sartre the inverted gaze restores his power and prestige, for Casey's narrator this inversion subjects him to a surveillance apparatus supported by secret agents and collaborating locals.

"Polacca brillante" is one of the five stories collected in Casey's final book, *Notas de un simulador* (1969), that he published from exile. According to Ilan Stavans, the story deals "tacitly—and tactfully—with gays under repressive political systems" (xvii). This autobiographical interpretation is possible given that Casey's exile was almost certainly motivated by fear of incarceration for his sexuality. Many of his writings can be interpreted as queer critiques of the increasingly repressive Cuban state under Fidel Castro in the 1960s. However, such interpretations insert Casey's sexuality as the cause of the protagonist's exile, thus conflating the author with the protagonist. The text itself does not guarantee such a reading; details about the narrator's sexuality and the motives for his flight are never revealed on the surface of this text. In this sense, "Polacca brillante" makes a queer critique possible, but importantly, it exceeds that specific interpretation. In my reading, the revolutionary gaze threatens an anonymous person whose background information is never revealed; thus, the narrator could be just about anyone. Only an elite minority can occupy Sartre's position. The vast majority—queer individuals, yes, and also, the masses of the Revolution—will find itself subjected to this surveillance apparatus.

For a brief moment, Casey's narrator tries to dismiss his fears as simple paranoia, but he looks at the salon once more: "Detrás de la vidriera sudada, el peluquero me observa fijamente. Los ojos le brillan en la oscuridad. Embriagados por el perfume de las acacias los mirlos cantan en el parque inundado de luz. Atravieso las sombras espesas" ("Polacca brillante" 98). The barber is confirmed as a sinister figure, and the narrator recognizes he is on the brink of losing the potential to make decisions or to act in any manner other than submitting his body to their demands. "Seguiré caminando," he says, as his only option at the end of the story (99). He must attempt to go unnoticed within these dense shadows and flee along a path of his own invention if any potential for dissensus is to remain or be recovered. This is the start of the politics of going unnoticed.

The demand that all artists and intellectuals become committed reduces politics to a politics of visibility, but becoming visible does not have to be the defining characteristic of politics. Contemporary political philosophy, notably in the work of Chantal Mouffe, better defines politics as dissensus or disagreement between different individuals or communities. Without dissensus, Mouffe argues, "there is always the danger that this democratic confrontation will be replaced by a confrontation between non-negotiable moral values or essentialist forms of identification" (*Agonistics* 7). Therefore, the elimination of dissensus brings about the foreclosure of the radically democratic process. The pressing question is not how to eliminate the disagreements that allow democracy to prosper but rather how to engage in dialogue with an adversary without constructing them as an enemy to be vanquished. Strategies for achieving this ethical component of politics will be evaluated in the final chapter. For now, my point is that making someone or something visible is not the only means of engaging in politics. Dissensus can be achieved by any number of means, and the one under consideration here is by going unnoticed. In this sense, the politics of going unnoticed is not the oxymoron it first appeared to be.

In the following chapters, I study unnoticed protagonists who trace itineraries within saturated, politicized spaces wherein they stumble and bump into others who also refuse the demand to become visible. For this reason, the politics of going unnoticed is neither an *a priori* plan for revolutionary action nor does it align well with a politics premised on group identity. Instead of a frontal attack on institutions in order to secure a seat at the table, those who go unnoticed take a step back; they turn away from the institutions that have excluded them, even if they never manage to escape those institutions. The politics of going unnoticed begins at something like the everyday level, not necessarily before or below, but certainly in excess of politicized spaces, institutions, and everyday actions that seek to maintain a hold on these bodies. While going unnoticed, these protagonists register their dissent in order to reconfigure the foundational narratives that uphold those structures. As a result, they establish new forms of engaging in dialogues with those who have been abandoned in the shadows, with those who have been subjected to these totalizing lights, and even with those other people who have been aiding such totalizing regimes in their daily habits.

The politics of going unnoticed registers an uneasiness with identity politics, with the idea that one must first identify with a particular group in order to have one's demand for basic human rights and economic equality made visible in the public sphere. Identity politics has a direct tie to the various movements that gained traction in the Sixties, especially those related to questions of gender, sexuality, and race, and it has been successful in securing a place at the table for the disenfranchised in some instances. In no way is this book an attempt to deny that success; however, I put at stake here another option, another tool or tactic that can be deployed by those who never felt the burning glow of the public spotlight on their skin, by those who do not even desire to inhabit that place, by those who suspect that their institutions will never truly capitulate to their demands. Still, those who go unnoticed make political demands during their fleeting, everyday encounters with others, while wandering around where the light begins to fade and where voices are not so easily recorded.

From this particular position, those who go unnoticed recover the potential to deactivate the long-standing and unchallenged tradition in the Western canon that links politics, visibility, and knowledge, a tradition that unites diverse thinkers from Greek philosophy to contemporary political theory. In Plato's *Republic*, Socrates establishes the analogy that will relate the visible realm to the intelligible realm: the sun enables sight just as goodness enables intelligence. From this, he creates the metaphor of making truth visible: "Well, here's how you can think about the mind as well. When its object is something which is lit up by truth and reality, then it has—and obviously has—intelligent awareness and knowledge. However, when its object is permeated with darkness […] then it has beliefs and is less effective" (235–36). Plato ties light to knowledge within Western thought, superimposing the binaries of visibility/darkness, knowledge/ignorance, and morality/immorality.

For modern philosophy, both Descartes and Kant continue to explain the production of knowledge and its relationship to the public sphere through this metaphor. In the Third Meditation of *A Discourse on Method*, Descartes argues for the existence of

God by concentrating his attention on "the natural light" that is too easily obscured when "the vision of his mind" is "blinded by the images of sensible objects" (98). Descartes's skepticism allows him to return from these deceptive objects to perceive "the beauty of this light so unspeakably great," that of certainty, knowledge, and God (102). Concerned more with the public use of this knowledge, Kant expands the relationship between light and knowledge to the political in "An Answer to the Question: What is the Enlightenment?" He calls his moment an Age of Enlightenment—not yet enlightened—because men are just beginning to have the courage to make free use of their own understanding. As the light grows, Kant cautions that reason should be restricted to the public realm: "The *public* use of one's reason must always be free, and it alone can bring about enlightenment among human beings; the *private* use of one's reason may, however, often be very narrowly restricted without this particularly hindering the progress of enlightenment" (n.p.). An example he offers of this paradox is that of the soldier who must obey orders without questioning them, but who must also be free as a scholar to publicly critique the mistakes made by the military. Public debate, but not private insubordination, is the hallmark of the Enlightenment for Kant. This new light must be allowed to grow, as long as it is directed and kept within certain bounds.

Recently, Jacques Rancière's work has become a touchstone for contemporary cultural criticism interested in the politics of art and literature, but at its core remains this long-standing tradition of making visible that which is currently in the dark. Rancière defines aesthetic practices as those that question "the distribution of the sensible" (12). Their politics involve an intervention "in the general distribution of ways of doing and making as well as in the relationships they maintain to modes of being and forms of visibility" (13). Art and literature become political not by espousing the view of a particular party or movement, but rather by shining a light on the ways the sensible world is divided and shared, by making visible or heard the ideas and peoples whose appearance questions the current distribution of spaces and resources. This is another way of linking art and literature to identity politics. Despite their differences, these figures of Western thought uphold visibility as a goal to pursue and a necessary step for the production of knowledge and participation in politics.

Introduction

"Visibility," however, "is a trap," writes Foucault, although this sentence was not exactly a warning in the original context of the essay on Jeremy Bentham's Panopticon (*Discipline* 200). It functions as a description of how architecture eliminates blind spots from the cells used to partition and order either madmen, the condemned, students, or workers. Nonetheless, something ominous here spreads across the notion of making everything and everyone visible within the state, because perpetually visible bodies can be controlled through the techniques of discipline deployed within biopolitical regimes. At the end of his lectures from 1975 to 1976, Foucault sketches a transition from the theory of sovereignty—"the right to take life or to let live"—to that of biopolitics—"the right to make live and let die" (*"Society"* 241). The sovereign employs techniques of discipline "to ensure the spatial distribution of individual bodies (their separation, their alignment, their serialization, and their surveillance) and the organization, around those individuals, of a whole field of visibility" (242). The biopolitical regime embeds new technologies of regularization within those of discipline, including "the development of a medicine whose main function will now be public hygiene" in addition to "institutions to coordinate medical care, centralize power, and normalize knowledge" (244). Ultimately, biopolitics is an expansion of the technologies of power employed by the sovereign; instead of focusing on how to punish those who challenge the sovereign's authority, the primary goal of biopolitics becomes the perpetuation of life at the collective or species level. As a result, the individual bodies always visible under surveillance become little more than the bare, biological material that may be excluded, incarcerated, or killed, because their so-called impurity, degeneracy, or abnormality threatens the survival of the species as a whole. Therein lies the trap of visibility that the unnoticed protagonists I study do their best to evade.

As biopolitical regimes encourage the practice of making visible for the purpose of extending surveillance to the darkest corners of both public and private spaces, contemporary societies ordered by neoliberal policies and technologies demand and even celebrate total transparency, at least among the general public. Byung-Chul Han analyzes the current role of the public sphere, which does not function as Kant had imagined in the Age of Enlightenment. Han argues that politicians are no longer judged on their actions, but on how well they stage their performance, and as a result, the public sphere has become disconnected from civic duty:

> The loss of the public sphere leaves behind a void; intimate details and private matters pour into it. Publicizing a persona takes the place of the public sphere. In the process, the public sphere becomes an exhibition space. It grows more and more distant from the space of communal action. (35)

As it becomes easier to publicize even the minutiae of everyday life, only personas that mask identity actually come to light in the public sphere. Thus, Han argues, "Only depoliticized space proves wholly transparent" (7). Though identity politics allows newly visible constituencies to make political demands, the call for total visibility and transparency also can serve to co-opt all bodies within the state and the market, to prevent collective action that challenges the partitioning of spaces and the distribution of resources. In this sense, both visibility and the demand for total transparency are traps, especially for the already disenfranchised.

Nelly Richard critiques the incessant calls for total visibility and transparency: "Estamos efectivamente sumergidos en una demanda de visibilidad total que parecería dejar fuera de lugar las prácticas críticas que buscan crear opacidades o refracciones, mostrar que no todos los cuerpos del sistema son translúcidos" (*La insubordinación* 102). It is as if our dictionaries have become bloated with duplicity, and the only remedy is to trim the fat, to create a one-to-one correspondence between language and the real so that no complex body or idea can elude the structural and the everyday demands for normativity. The call to make visible the invisible has its place, but in this broader context, it becomes a too-narrow demand that requires literatures and politics to maintain a state- or market-centered focus, whereas both politics and literatures, both bodies and their representations, can and do exceed the state, the market, the nation, and even the identity group.

Similarly, Michel de Certeau refers to this demand as a "cancerous growth of vision" (xxi). He criticizes Foucault's structural analysis as incapable of taking into account how even consumers make errant paths through highly ordered spaces and institutions: "the trajectories trace out the ruses of other interests and desires that are neither determined nor captured by the systems in which they develop" (xviii). Bodies and language that refuse such transparency, that seek to create a place in the darkness, that accidentally or intentionally go unnoticed, will always exist even in the most rigidly structured societies. For my analysis, the difficulty now lies in locating the itineraries and discussing the politics of those who go unnoticed—those who seek complexity and errant trajectories in the everyday, those who leave a trace of themselves, but no clear or totalizing record in their wake—without revealing them to these disciplinary lights.

In order to analyze the works of Casey, Filloy, and Somers, I find it necessary to consider the critical language of scholarship that derives from this long-standing tradition. Otherwise, my own work could be subsumed under the idea of simply making those who go unnoticed visible, whereas I continually refuse to reveal fully the identities, motives, and ideologies of those who go unnoticed to the light of knowledge and power. In fact, I do not claim to have complete and unmediated access to such information; rather, I frequently signal the limits of what can be known about these unnoticed protagonists and construct my arguments accordingly. Part of this methodology requires me to avoid the critical vocabulary that relies on the metaphor of making something visible to refer to the production of knowledge. Unknown or complicated ideas and objects are often described with the following adjectives: in Spanish, *borroso, difuso, opaco, oscuro,* and *turbio*; and in English, blurred, faint, hazy, nebulous, obscure, opaque, and unclear. As a remedy, light serves as the metaphorical substance that allows one to produce knowledge in those dark places with the following verbal phrases: in Spanish, *aclarar, clarificar, echar luz sobre, elucidar, esclarecer, iluminar,* and *poner en claro*; and in English, to bring to light, to clarify, to clear up, to elucidate, to illuminate, to reveal, and to shed light on. Even when postmodern sensibilities praise the ambiguous, that work can be narrated as the process of making ambiguity itself visible. This critical vocabulary and the appeal of visibility is almost unavoidable in scholarship today, but it is not impossible.

The practice of going unnoticed begins to map out routes within these saturated spaces under constant surveillance in order to render inoperative the binary structures of biopolitics. Giorgio Agamben describes those who feel least comfortable with the standard practices of their community as being contemporary. To be contemporary is to divert one's attention away from dominant trends and to peer into the darkness of a given era. It is to look past that which is readily visible both to surveillance technologies and the everyday gaze. Unlike what Plato believed, Agamben explains that the eyes do not cease to act when light fades or disappears altogether. When light is absent, the off-cells in the retina become active: "When activated, these cells produce the particular kind of vision that we call darkness. Darkness is not, therefore, a privative notion (the simple absence of light, or something like nonvision) but rather the result of the activity of the 'off-cells,' a product of our own retina" (*Nudities* 13). Light is not necessary for vision and, by extension, the production of knowledge is possible well before something has been fully illuminated or revealed. For this reason, Agamben defines the contemporary as "the one whose eyes are struck by the beam of darkness that comes from his own time" (14). Contemporaries, therefore, do not get blinded or dazzled by the bright lights, but rather turn toward the shadows that swirl around them in order to seek out the darkness that others struggle to perceive or simply let pass unattended.

In my analysis, those who go unnoticed actively stumble *al vesre* and *al verse* through the darkness, and they will bump into others doing the same. Rather than making one another's bodies visible or translucent or banding together in a new identity group, those who go unnoticed produce an opening from which they can render inoperative the binary structures of biopolitics that constantly divide humans from one another. In *The Use of Bodies*, Agamben names the machines that continually erect these barriers as "the bipolar *zoè / bios* apparatus" (225). Such an apparatus makes recourse to scientific pseudo-concepts to create a form of political control over bare life in a generalized state of emergency by constantly pushing down, dividing, and excluding bare life. Moreover, he argues:

> If thought, the arts, poetry, and human practices generally have any interest, it is because they bring about the idling of the machine and the works of life, language, economy, and society, in order to carry them back to the anthropogenetic event, in order that in them the becoming human of the human being will never be achieved once and for all, will never cease to happen. Politics names the place of this event, in whatever sphere it is produced. (208)

Introduction

In the following chapters, those who go unnoticed seek to slow and eventually render inoperative the machines that incessantly produce binary thought, machines that serve only to erect barriers, prevent dialogues and disagreements, and legitimize violence. By going unnoticed and then becoming perceived, even if only temporarily, by others who also inhabit zones of indiscernibility, the characters I study restore the potential for disagreeing with the institutional and everyday demands for normativity without having to wait for a structural overhaul or a profound awakening of the people, since it is possible that neither will ever occur. Ultimately, these protagonists open new modes of interacting with others at the individual, everyday level of fleeting, chance encounters whether it be from a cabin in the woods or a dark, urban alley where such dialogues had been prohibited. Though they will not always be successful, they continually work to render inoperative these divisions that appear and reappear throughout ever-changing Latin American political landscapes without erecting new barriers in their wake.

Organization of the Book

In Part One, "The Itinerary of Errant Palindromes," I define "going unnoticed" as a challenge to totalizing narratives and hegemonic practices. Central to the totalizing discourses of the Sixties are the tropes of forming a univocal Latin American family and of constructing a revolutionary house, as in the Cuban journal *Casa de las Américas*. In contrast, I attend to the moments when language and bodies err from the preformed itineraries of the era. I begin with Filloy's essays on palindromes, in which these seemingly perfect constructions erupt from their crystalline confines. These errant palindromes serve as a metaphorical heuristic for approaching the improper paths of the characters in Casey's and Somers's narratives who go unnoticed around urban apartments and provincial manors and then stumble into abandoned individuals. Crossing the boundaries and thresholds considered appropriate in the Sixties will pose real dangers to these protagonists. In doing so, they begin the arduous task of opening paths toward a politics without violent bids for hegemony and moralizing demands.

In Part Two, "The Politics of Going Unnoticed," I advance a theory of engaging in the political without seeking visibility at the institutional level. In Casey's ignored essays from *Lunes de Revolución*—the journal that would be closed after the 1961 debate on *P.M.*—I demonstrate that he appears to follow the party line, while openly lamenting the limitations placed on Cuban intellectuals. Then, I analyze Filloy's "Yo y los intrusos" as an ironic retelling of Plato's "Allegory of the Cave" set in the "deserts" of Córdoba Province that challenges the notion of the ivory-tower intellectual. In *La mujer desnuda*, Somers's nude woman flees to the countryside on her thirtieth birthday—the age at which unmarried women in Uruguay were legally allowed to live alone. These real and imagined protagonists, or bare lives who can be cast out or killed with impunity, create spaces wherein dissensus—the defining characteristic of politics—becomes possible again, albeit briefly and at risk of danger.

In Part Three, "The Aesthetics of Writing in Plain Sight," I attend to what has always been apparent on the surface of hegemonic politics. I study Filloy's intervention into the gaucho genre, Somers's appropriation of the European family romance in novels by Charles Dickens and Enrique Pérez Escrich, and Casey's exploration of Havana's sewers and nightlife. Despite the differences in content, each author divests politicized traditions of their burdensome symbolic weight. Each chapter begins with a palindrome from Filloy's *Karcino*. The errant paths of these three palindromes connect Filloy to Somers and Casey by charting their movements from explicit toward subtler rewritings of nineteenth- and early twentieth-century texts. Along the way, the gauchos will be stripped of their heroic attire, the body politic will be exposed to infectious disease, and the people will revel in the filthy and the impure. Overall, essentialist myths that serve the interests of a ruling elite are rewritten by looking at the visible, yet unnoticed surface of political discourse in order to puncture and sully it.

In Part Four, "The Ethics of Being Perceived," those who go unnoticed must eventually be perceived by others; otherwise, going unnoticed would be a solitary, self-interested act. I contend that this exposure takes the form of an ethical encounter between radically different subjects with competing demands whose dialogue had been blocked by normative boundaries (e.g., good/evil, hero/villain, friend/enemy). I analyze the errant dialogues in Somers's *De miedo en miedo*, the "monodialogues" and "pandemonium" in Filloy's *Vil & Vil*, and the futility of playing by the rules in Casey's "La ejecución," a rewriting of Kafka's *The Trial*. In these texts, going unnoticed opens a space for dialogue and strives toward the construction of a coming community among subjects who now perceive one another as adversaries to be engaged, rather than as political enemies to be annihilated.

In the conclusion, "Re-ves la ArteletrA," I address the notion of failure that led to the widespread disenchantment of revolutionary politics and point toward the potential for utopian thought today. In the ethical encounter, it can be argued that those who go unnoticed fail to consolidate their politics into a power grab within existing institutions or to create new ones. However, the politics of going unnoticed is an attempt to prevent closures within the public arena; it locates and renders inoperative divisive, political paradigms by prying open thresholds between binary poles. What is left is the open. By reversing the title of the introduction, I end with a new type of commitment without dogma: to leave open even my own project so that it may be re-seen (*re-ves* means "you see again") or revised by others. Thus, going unnoticed provides a non-exclusive series of tools for opening paths toward a politics without hegemony and toward new forms of narrating and living in a community.

PART ONE

The Itinerary of Errant Palindromes

The Sixties in Latin America marks a paradigm shift in which the region's most well-known cultural and political figures imagined a number of totalizing narratives and charted clear courses for its cultural, political, and economic independence and modernization. The Boom authors—Gabriel García Márquez, Carlos Fuentes, Mario Vargas Llosa, Julio Cortázar—spoke as the universal voice of Latin American modernity by papering over the region's economic dependency with their cultural achievements as they aligned themselves initially with the Cuban Revolution. Armed revolutionaries became increasingly suspicious of, and even hostile toward, the most publicly committed intellectuals as they sought to incite a region-wide, if not global, revolution. Ultimately, these debates were overshadowed by the rapid escalation of state-sponsored repression against social actors as CIA-backed invasions and dictatorships erupted throughout the continent and secured the neoliberal restructuring of national economies. However, well before the failures of these totalizing projects, Calvert Casey, Juan Filloy, and Armonía Somers were writing about seemingly unimportant forms of language and bodies that went unnoticed in the Sixties. The protagonists to which they attend evade such totalizing gazes, either on purpose or by chance, allowing them to chart errant itineraries across the cultural maps of the era.

Central to the totalizing discourses of the Sixties are the tropes of forming a univocal Latin American family and of constructing a revolutionary house.[1] In her study of canonical scenes from the Sixties, Gilman explains the kinship ties that would promote the artistic and political activities of their clan across the continent and around the globe: "Los nombres más importantes de la ciudad letrada latinoamericana se alinearon con Cuba y trataron, en adelante, de consolidar un discurso homogéneo, manteniendo las diferencias y discrepancias dentro del ámbito interno de las discusiones familiares, mientras fue posible" (142). The Cuban Revolution became the catalyst for developing a regional identity that would demonstrate that Latin American politics and cultures are irreducible to the binary logic of the Cold War. Yet, among the discourses studied by Gilman, this oppositional identity could only be founded on the eradication of internal heterogeneity; in fact, she suggests that the terms "cofradía o hermandad" might be better than "familia," because these universals applied almost exclusively to heterosexual men (386). At best, these boys clubs of universal aspiration lasted until the Padilla Affair of 1971, at which point the majority of the Latin American leftist intellectuals and writers—with the infamous exception of García Márquez— publicly broke all ties with Castro's regime.[2]

Casey, Filloy, and Somers were not fully included within these family homes; being gay, from the provinces, and a woman, respectively, are likely causes for their exclusion. However, neither the authors nor their protagonists were truly outside of the spaces in which these debates took place, even if they went unnoticed within them. In what follows, I begin with Filloy's essays on palindromes in which seemingly perfect, totalizing constructions erupt from their crystalline confines. These palindromes chart the sort of errant itineraries taken up by the characters in Casey's and Somers's narratives as they move in and around urban apartments and a provincial manor, looking through the windows of these homes from the alleys and upending their precarious order that is only sustained through exclusion and inequality. While going unnoticed, they stumble into others who have been divided and isolated within the brightly lit family homes of the era. Evading the surveilling gaze of the sovereign, of governing institutions, and of the market, erring from preformed itineraries, and crossing the boundaries considered appropriate for political subjects in the Sixties will pose real dangers to these protagonists. There can be no guarantees that those they encounter along the way will join them in solidarity. However, going unnoticed becomes a first step toward opening new political, aesthetic, and ethical forms.

Chapter One

On Errant Palindromes

> *All history is written backwards*, writes Tony, writing backwards. [...] Yet history is not a true palindrome, thinks Tony. We can't really run it backwards and end up at a clean start. Too many of the pieces have gone missing; also we know too much, we know the outcome.
>
> Margaret Atwood, *The Robber Bride* (121)

Writing palindromes is not an easy task. It requires an obsessive, mathematical precision to construct intelligible words and phrases that read exactly the same from left to right as they do in reverse. In Margaret Atwood's *The Robber Bride*, Tony, a history professor, revels in writing and speaking words and phrases in reverse, as quoted in the epigraph. However, she also underscores the shortcomings of reading history, art, or literature too literally like a palindrome, favoring instead a plurality of vantage points in constant motion across archives and memories that are littered with debris, distorted beyond recognition, and punctuated with gaps and silences. As a framework for re-reading the Sixties in Latin America along these lines, I begin with Filloy's essays on palindromes and the art of writing them. In *Karcino: Tratado de palindromía*, Filloy's palindromes paradoxically relate to the writing of history as a collection of linear events that can be read not only forwards and backwards, but also *al vesre* and *al verse* in order to mobilize the avant-garde sensibilities that exceed and rupture those unidirectional narratives from within. As such, these errant palindromes will serve as a metaphorical heuristic for locating and analyzing the itineraries of those who go unnoticed within the cultural maps of the Sixties.

Chapter One

Crystalline Palindromes

Karcino is a collection of Filloy's palindromes, ranging from two to seventeen words long, that he wrote throughout his life. In the final section, titled "ArteletrA," Filloy even composes poems from his palindromes. He offers the following examples in different languages: "Never eveN"; "Roba saboR"; "Amor ¿bromA?"; "Madam adaM"; "Bon snoB"; "Luz azuL"; and "Amo idiomA," among many others (74–75). Filloy prefers to write them in capital letters to draw attention to them, since in some cases, a seemingly simple, yet unimportant, phrase might go unnoticed as a palindrome, such as "Acaso hubo búhos acÁ" (81). Some can be read as poetic aphorisms, as in the case of a seventeenth-century palindrome by John Taylor that Filloy references: "Lewd did i live & evil i did dweL" (49). Others may appear to be nothing more than quotidian language: "Dennis and edna sinneD"; or "Never odd or eveN" (49). Or as in one of Filloy's Spanish-language palindromes: "Eufemia, jaime fue … ¡Eufemia, jaime fue!" (101).

Yet, others tend to catch one's attention, begging to be noticed as the ingenious constructions they are. I have selected just three examples:

> Es re-mal eros en eso: relamersE (105).
> Aca, carolo adonis, amo la paloma … si no da olor a cacA (183).
> Ada, gorda drogada, di los nocivos a corola clay.
> y, al calor ocaso, vi consolidada gorda drogadA (195).

A single reading will always leave the palindrome unnoticed as such, but the capitalized letters or the comedic strangeness of these expressions is capable of provoking a reader into giving them a second or third glance. By reorienting my reading practices and moving in reverse, from a different threshold of perception, the palindrome can be perceived as such.

The Sator Square is a well-known enigma of Western cultures. Filloy describes it as "uno de los *jeux d'esprit* más intrigantes de todos los idiomas" (*Karcino* 59). The following is the Sator Square as reproduced in Filloy's treatise:

On Errant Palindromes

```
SATOR
AREPO
TENET
OPERA
ROTAS
```

The Sator Square is composed of four Latin words, *sator*, *tenet*, *opera*, and *rotas*, and the unknown word *arepo*, which is assumed to be a proper name but has no known, fixed meaning. As a multidimensional palindrome, the letters in this arrangement form a crystalline, closed structure when read from top to bottom and from left to right and then in reverse. Its earliest inscriptions have been dated to the first century C.E., and it has been found among Roman ruins and in Pompeii before the arrival there of Christianity. The Sator Square has been an object of historical and theological speculation for centuries, since it also forms an anagram for the phrase *Pater noster* that can be spelled twice crossing at the letter "n"; this formation leaves as its remainder two As and two Os, which are often interpreted as the alpha and the omega, the beginning and the end. However, its appearance in Pompeii challenges this possible Christian solution, and other partial interpretations attribute it alternately to pre-Christian, gnostic, Jewish, stoic, and even Satanic traditions.[1] Of course, not all of them can be correct.

Magical, miraculous, and metaphysical qualities aside, what is certain about this and other palindromes is that they challenge the reader's hermeneutical skills. As Rose Mary Sheldon demonstrates, there have been innumerable attempts at deciphering this potential cryptogram since the late nineteenth century by mathematicians, philologists, and theologians, but no one has yet to propose a widely accepted solution to the hidden meaning they all assume it must contain (233–87). What I find curious is how different intellectuals can be so skeptical regarding scholarly interpretations of the Sator Square made by others, yet these same scholars uphold the generalized belief that this is a puzzle with a hidden solution that has yet to be deciphered, despite all of the contradictions present in each of these "solutions." In the end, this may be nothing more than a clever linguistic game centered on a meaningless word, *arepo*. It may be an incidental enigma with no hidden meaning, from which so many interpreters extract only what they wanted it to contain *a priori*.

Chapter One

It is not my intention to pretend to have arrived at the definitive meaning hidden in the Sator Square or other palindromes. Instead, it is the process by which these enigmas and games go unnoticed as well as the process of noticing that which is inscribed on the surface of the palindrome that interests me as a method for analyzing the errant itineraries of the protagonists in the works of Casey, Filloy, and Somers. My contention is that Filloy's palindromes need some tending in order to be recognized in all their complexity and in their relation to the writing and reading of literary and cultural history. Otherwise, they remain unnoticed only to be dismissed as trivialities unworthy of further attention that remain locked within these linear arrangements.

Reading ARTELETRA Against the Current

Karcino includes two elegant and playful essays on the art of constructing palindromes. In addition to being a seven-letter word—all of Filloy's fifty-odd novels have seven-letter titles—the Greek word *karcino* has a particular relevance to palindromes. Filloy elaborates on his choice for the title in an interview with Mónica Ambort: "En griego, Karcino quiere decir cangrejo, animal que camina al sesgo formando zig zags, casi en la forma en que se leen los palíndromos" (*Juan Filloy* 27). The Greeks were quite fond of palindromes and had various words or phrases to name them; Filloy extracts the symbol of the crab, as he explains, from one of these phrases: *karkinike epigrafe*, or "the inscription of the crab." Another word used for "palindrome," Filloy explains, is the Greek *hysteroproteron*, which is the same as saying "lo posterior y lo anterior," and the word "palindrome" is a derivative of *palin dromos*, which suggests that these are words and phrases that "corren de nuevo" (*Karcino* 16).

Regarding this movement that flows in multiple directions, Filloy argues that palindromes exceed the strict linearity that is assigned to them:

> las letras son jánicas: presentan dos caras, una a la izquierda y otra a la derecha, manteniendo gestos, rictus y matices diferentes. Vale decir: una cara visible, orgullosa de expresar lo que ostenta; y otra cara secreta, exclusiva para iniciados en el culto esotérico de la palindromía. (13)

Filloy states that reading only in one direction unnecessarily limits what can be perceived. A narrowly logical, rational approach from a head-on perspective will always be confining and proscriptive; it will always limit one's perception to that which can be seen from only one place, to that which makes itself visible, whereas palindromes require a change in perspective in order to be noticed. For Filloy, to read only from left to right is to read only that which flaunts itself to that single point of view, while other subjects and objects remain out of focus or go unnoticed nearby. However, it should be noted that Casey's, Filloy's, and Somers's errant itineraries will not necessarily bring clarity to an obscure object or concept—revelation is not always possible or desired.

Filloy starts writing backwards, concocting strange phrases that can be read from different directions. The first reading, from left to right, is the common and visible reading, what Filloy's admirer Cortázar in *Rayuela* would call "la forma corriente" in the table of instructions, the reading that follows a sequential order (7). The second, from right to left, is that which occurs when one arrives at an end, limit, or blockage and turns around, finding exactly the same letters in reverse. Nevertheless, this is not the same reading as the first; this reading is the one that confronts the "cara secreta," which is not an invisible face, but rather the one already inscribed on the surface of the other that goes unnoticed at first glance (*Karcino* 13). What goes unnoticed is neither visible nor invisible, but rather in an indeterminate state located at the threshold of perception between those extreme categories.

By reading ArteletrA from the letter "L" toward the left and toward the right, the two-part, Janus-faced reading (from left to right and then from right to left) would appear to be stabilized and closed:

> La palindromía, por lo mismo que es jánica, es bífida, bifronte. Partida en dos, la frase se comide en ser UNA, sin embargo; porque, si una parte orienta, no es que la otra desoriente. Su condición bifronte asume entonces la de su logos unitivo; pues, al orientar con idéntico sentido lógico desde atrás, no implica que lo que orientó al principio se desoriente, ya que se cierra así la lectura doble de la misma locución. (19)

At this point, Filloy affirms that the palindrome does not unravel itself when read in reverse, nor is its core fractured when read from

Chapter One

the center toward the ends. Yet, I am not interested in palindromes for the ontological and epistemological stability that Filloy at first locates in these little, closed words that play autonomous games.

Still another approach to the palindrome goes unnoticed, one in which it exceeds and ruptures its supposed linearity. Filloy's palindromes are linear and precise. However, "art" and "letter," or "the art of writing, literature," the words inscribed in "ArteletrA," rarely conform to geometrical conceptions of perfection. At least since the historical avant-gardes of the early twentieth century, they tend toward that which infinitely opens and unfolds as opposed to that which closes in on itself. Cultivating this paradox, Filloy asserts that "[el] hábito de leer de izquierda a derecha" of Western culture has rooted itself into our ways of seeing the world:

> Vale decir que el lector se deja llevar por el rumbo de la mirada. De tal suerte, no va mentalmente contra la corriente escritural, no se empaca en ella ni se opone zurdamente al raciocinio. Esa propensión explica que pocas veces se detuvo a escrutar o auscultar el misterio implícito en las palabras del texto. (*Karcino* 25)

Filloy develops his theory of the palindrome into a metaphorical heuristic for reading any text by stubbornly, even haphazardly, refusing the effortless rationality and imposed limitations inherent in any unidirectional practice. By digging in his heels, turning around, and moving against the scriptural current, he immediately reorganizes his habitual thresholds of perception making it possible to catch a glimpse of that which has been going unnoticed within the current.

Without a doubt, this metaphor of turning against the current has an affinity with Benjamin's assertion that the task of the historian is "to brush history against the grain" ("Theses" 257). Unlike the easy back and forth reading of a palindrome, Filloy's now fluvial metaphor suggests the difficulty of wading upstream through moving waters. Reading against this current in order to attend to that which goes unnoticed in a given era becomes as difficult as the task of writing palindromes; however, it also involves a certain level of imprecision and unpredictability, of chance and guesswork. One's perspective changes drastically while moving in the opposite direction within the same space, and the force of any current is bound to prevent the one wading against it from retracing any original path with precision. In turning around, the original itinerary, if even known, will prove to be impossible to retrace, and a new, errant path can therefore be charted.

For my purposes, this space in which one can create itineraries comparable to those of Filloy's palindromes will be the Sixties in Latin America. The literatures and politics of this era can be approached from so many different perspectives. Though a true outside of these rhizomatic maps is unreachable and their general contours remain intact, the itineraries running across them can be continuously edited as the details found along the way move in and out of focus. Deleuze and Guattari define rhizomatic maps in the following manner:

> The map is open and connectable in all of its dimensions; it is detachable, reversible, susceptible to constant modification. It can be torn, reversed, adapted to any kind of mounting, reworked by an individual, group, or social formation. It can be drawn on a wall, conceived of as a work of art, constructed as a political action or as a meditation. Perhaps the most important characteristics of the rhizome is that it always has multiple entryways. (12)

In this manner, I propose to keep reading the complex dimensions of the Sixties as a rhizome that can be mapped, reworked, torn, or expanded, and entered from multiple points. The era can be studied from its periodicals and cultural markets; the Boom; the conjunction of politics and aesthetics; definitions of "internationalism"; Cold War foreign policy, dependency, and imperialism; constructions of gender, sexuality, and ethnicity; its protests, demonstrations, and violence; or its failures and the subsequent disillusionment of its social actors. Of course, these are only some the most visible landmarks of the Sixties in Latin America today. Joining these attempts to read the Sixties, I have chosen different entry points from which a series of seemingly unimportant and discontinuous lines of inquiry can come into dialogue, if only for the briefest moment.

Filloy's treatise begins with the rigid perfection of the palindrome. As these perfect structures burst apart, they produce new itineraries through that same space. In this sense, they are comparable to Deleuze and Guattari's lines of flight: "There is a rupture in the rhizome whenever segmentary lines explode into a line of flight, but the line of flight is part of the rhizome" (9). The line of flight is never an escape, but rather an unexpected path that moves in another direction. Similarly, the palindrome follows an errant itinerary as it flows again along an uncertain path that cannot be reduced to a linear, rigid movement between a fixed origin and a predetermined end, between the alpha and the omega. It is not an *ex nihilo* invention or a unique innovation, but rather a shift, an awry glance, and a subtle change of perspective. To read "ArteletrA," to read art, literature, or any form of cultural production against the current as if one were reading a palindrome, is to wander off course, to become errant, and to propose a reading from the perspective of that which had gone unnoticed despite being written in plain sight on its surface. Even when those who go unnoticed become perceived, this end should not be interpreted as a failure, but rather as having the line of flight cut off by another obstacle or blockage. As a result, new errant itineraries will have to be created, even if by someone else.

Chapter Two

On Going Unnoticed

The anonymous narrator of Calvert Casey's "Notas de un simulador" (1969) states the need to research abandoned, fragmentary, and almost unheard words, phrases, and texts:

> Debidamente investigadas, una frase, una palabra oídas al pasar, una carta abandonada sobre una mesa o caída de un bolsillo, fragmentos de la conversación escuchada en el breve trayecto de un tranvía, un cruce en las líneas telefónicas, pueden darnos espléndidas claves, tantos son los que sufren desatendidos. (51–52)

These bits of language slip in and out of perception as they get left behind or lost; they circulate briefly in public and private conversations but are of little importance to the passers-by who barely hear them. The happenstance interlocutors of these disconnected, fleeting, and untimely ideas and conversations pay little attention to them. As potential witnesses, perhaps they have arrived too early or too late to the conversation of which they are not a part, or perhaps they only notice their seemingly quotidian, unremarkable aspects and ignore them. For any number of reasons such remarks are left unattended, and anything they might communicate goes unnoticed.

For my purposes, it is necessary to avoid jumping to the well-worn argument that what is needed is simply to make these texts heard and visible, to restore them to some knowable, transparent, or transcendental realm. Rather, these fragmented texts belong to the everyday, to the quotidian practices and discourses overlooked by totalizing institutions while also evading, and possibly deactivating, their disciplinary organization. Everyday practices, as de Certeau argues, have "a certain strangeness that does not surface,

Chapter Two

or whose surface is only its upper limit, outlining itself against the visible" (93). Locating and analyzing these practices is not so simple, because what goes unnoticed is not always a complete and coherent text, discourse, or subject waiting in the shadows for a spotlight to pass by, illuminate it, and render it intelligible within governing institutions and social practices. Those who go unnoticed often desire or need to evade the tools of surveillance; in fact, their well-being and survival may depend upon it.

Amid the Swirling Lights and Shadows

Casey's narrator embodies the characteristics of these abandoned voices as he stumbles across the swirling lights and shadows of the city at night. Narrated in the first person, he recounts his surreptitious excursions. He provides palliative care to the dying, whether they be homeless or abandoned in a hospital, and he observes them in their last moments, taking great care to remember and narrate their passage from life into death. To avoid public suspicion, he tries to go unnoticed as he approaches these other abandoned characters he finds in the shadows. In section XVI, the narrator returns to his apartment, unsure how to react to the hostility of a man and woman who see him in a plaza taking care of a dying, young black man. They suspect this outsider of committing unseemly acts. Toward the end of the story, the narrator will be imprisoned for murder, because he was the unknown stranger last seen with this man and other dying people just before their death. His guilt or innocence cannot be confirmed in this first-person text, but the narrator has written this story from his jail cell as an attempt to set the record straight.

Going unnoticed, according to the narrator's version of the story, is not a matter of seeking isolation, but rather of stealth and camouflage, of hiding and writing in plain sight so that he may engage with these abandoned, sick, and dying people. Before his arrest, he explains how the music from the street fair outside his building seeps into his apartment, distracting him. Instead of joining the crowd, he climbs to the roof terrace where the noise from the fair did not reach: "Me sentí rodeado de silencio, calmado por la brisa apacible que venía del lado de la bahía" ("Notas" 80). The narrator, while hopping from one roof terrace to another and walking through the darkened outdoor corridors of neighboring homes, moves cautiously across and between lit spaces. In a sense, he attempts to step out of focus. He writes of this play of light and shadow not as a classic chiaroscuro with sharp divisions, but as a swirling of various colors, shades, and intensities through which he passes: "una luz sucia"; "la oscuridad era casi completa"; "una luz amarillenta me tiñó las manos"; "un fulgor remoto"; "un brillo pálido" (80). In these spaces, the lights are faded and distant. They cannot fully illuminate his body. They only offer quick glimpses as the lights flash across him.

Also mixing with these shadows and lights are sounds and silences that simultaneously flow through these spaces. The tranquil silence with which the scene begins is temporary, and the narrator moves in and out of earshot of other sounds: "el inesperado silencio" when the fair music suddenly stops; "el lejano clamor de la ciudad"; "Del pozo subían voces"; "Alguien tosió con una tos dura, una voz cantó; oí risas, más voces" (80). At this stage, he does not engage other people in dialogue; instead, silence interrupts the night, and within it echo bits of unintelligible sounds from distant people. The narrator who goes unnoticed clumsily navigates a complex, shifting field of lights and shadows and of voices, noises, and silences. He jumps over low walls that separate connected roof terraces, but he never passes from one clearly defined space of darkness, invisibility, or silence into another clearly defined space of light, visibility, and voice. Such sharply demarcated zones of perception are not to be found in this narrative and, in general, do not appear in Casey's fragmented writings. It is within such threshold spaces that he and others go unnoticed.

In all of the texts under consideration in this book, the underlying connection is the narration of a desire, attempt, or inadvertent experience of going unnoticed. This phrase, "going unnoticed," requires some pause in order to unravel the various forms it may take. By no means does going unnoticed require concealment or stasis. One may just as easily go unnoticed sitting alone in the middle of the woods or a desert as walking anonymously through a crowded, urban setting. Neither an origin nor a destination, it is a temporary state wherein one is not perceived or paid much attention by others, and this state can and will come to an end. Insofar as the "going" of the phrase "going unnoticed" necessitates some sort of spatiotemporal movement or duration, it names a process, a becoming, and a lapse of time during which a subject is not noticed and accrues potential energy. Even when this state comes to an end at a given point in time and space, the fact that one went unnoticed remains nonetheless significant, because the potential energy previously stored can be released upon emerging from this state.

Going unnoticed involves moving in such a manner as to be unobserved or overlooked by potential spectators who could perceive the unnoticed body or discourse if they were located in a different threshold. Going unnoticed occurs in the threshold between perception and imperception. By going unnoticed, one moves through what Deleuze and Guattari refer to as "zones of indiscernibility" in which only certain movements will be perceived while others will remain unobserved (280). The perception of movement is always dependent upon the viewer's position in relation to the movement or rest of others: "Movements, becomings, in other words, pure relations of speed and slowness, pure affects, are below and above the threshold of perception" (281). Movement is only perceptible from a specific threshold, from a position relative to that which is moving. Put in simpler terms, consider the following: while sitting on a moving train, the other passengers do not appear to be moving in relation to me, yet to someone standing on the station platform or watching the train from outside, all of the passengers including myself inside the train appear to be moving in relation to that viewer. As such, to perceive the movement of a body one must be situated in an adequate threshold of perception.

The connection between movement and perception is also, for Deleuze and Guattari, a matter of becoming. Avoiding metaphysical postulations about being, they define "becoming" as that which concerns the immanent relations of alliances that are set in non-linear motion within rhizomes:

> Becoming is a rhizome, not a classificatory or genealogical tree. Becoming is certainly not imitating, or identifying with something; neither is it regressing-progressing; neither is it corresponding, establishing corresponding relations; neither is it producing, producing a filiation or producing through filiation. Becoming is a verb with a consistency all its own; it does not reduce to, or lead back to, "appearing," "being," "equaling," or "producing." (239)

On Going Unnoticed

In my analysis, the process of going unnoticed is not a taxonomy; it refuses all rigid classification for establishing family ties, whether biological or fictional, as in the case of the lettered intellectuals of the Sixties in Latin America. Instead, going unnoticed is a process of becoming, of deactivating, and of opening up of those exclusive categories that operate through the logic of surveillance within the generalized state of exception to order and control bodies under the guise of bringing visibility and clarity to all.

Furthermore, going unnoticed cannot be reduced to imitation. Those engaging in this practice do not have an end goal of becoming like or becoming identical to something else, since at that point they would cease becoming and solidify into being or dissolve into a visible identity group that, although it may make some demands, can and will be co-opted by the state and the market. In contrast, going unnoticed necessitates the continuation of this movement that evades the stasis of identification. Once one stops moving, the thresholds of perception change immediately; one stops going unnoticed and can be perceived as similar or identical to something else, whether it be a friend or an enemy. Going unnoticed is moving perpetually with no *a priori* end or goal in sight, with no particular destination, transformation, transcendence, or *telos*. There are no guarantees about where these errant trajectories may lead, nor will those who traverse them be sheltered from violence, but those who go unnoticed do acquire the potential to disrupt and render inoperative the machines that continually partition humanity into opposing categories.

Moreover, there is no mask, no *persona*, and no pseudonym presented to a public as a purposefully distorted representation of one's identity behind which one goes unnoticed. Whereas pseudonyms and masks create an epistemological barrier by blocking access to knowledge or veiling truths about one's identity, the process of going unnoticed does not attempt to distort reality in favor of a falsehood, a lie, or a myth. What goes unnoticed is the act, the subject, or the event itself presented or represented as itself, even though no one pays attention to its taking place or to its existence.

Finally, those who go unnoticed are corporeal subjects, not ghosts or disembodied spirits who glide invisibly through spaces; they have bodies that interact with the swirling lights and shadows, the voices and silences, and the other human beings who surround them. Going unnoticed is a material practice. Their physical bodies are visible in the sense that they are capable of being seen, and all of those who go unnoticed will be perceived eventually. Yet, they manage to create a temporary state during which little public light is shone on their bodies. When they pass by others, no one pays attention. When they speak out, everyone happens to ignore their voice. Still, they continue to move about and stumble into others with whom they can engage in dialogue along the way.

More than a description of the place of these intellectuals and their written works in the political debates and cultural markets of the Sixties—although it is inseparable from these positions—going unnoticed involves an intentional desire on the part of their fictional characters to stay out of the public spotlight. These often anonymous protagonists actively seek out shelters and refuges, or attempt to hide and write in plain sight and to pass for something unworthy of further attention, albeit without masquerading as something or somebody else. This active gesture of going unnoticed is what connects the texts here and will be the primary focus of my analysis on the politics, aesthetics, and ethics of going unnoticed as I bring these authors into a dialogue that engages with and simultaneously exceeds their regional, national, and temporal contexts.

Two Houses

To return to the example with which I began this section, the anonymous narrator in Casey's "Notas de un simulador" stumbles across the lights and shadows, the sounds, noises, and silences of his city. As Florence Olivier explains, the entire narrative is structured around a spatial paradox between the "carácter abierto del espacio urbano" and "la abundancia de espacios cerrados" through which "la libre circulación y el confinamiento acaban por ser equivalentes" (214). Navigating this paradoxical space, opening thresholds between circulation and confinement, Casey's narrator manages to go unnoticed. The untimeliness of his actions, his evasion of the popular street fair, is precisely what allows him to open an errant itinerary within the same space but from a different threshold of perception. At first, his untimely actions go unnoticed by his peers, and he becomes capable of perceiving and engaging with others who have been abandoned in the nearby darkness where they struggle to communicate and survive.

While walking in the shadows near a neighbor's house, Casey's narrator stumbles across "una luz potente" coming from a bedroom ("Notas" 81). Under that light, an unexpected exchange takes place as the anonymous narrator notices a set of anonymous eyes noticing him. A sort of unequal symmetry takes place along the narrator's errant line of flight through the city:

> Por el hueco abierto que remataba la ventana, unos ojos me miraban fijamente. Me desplacé un poco para observar mejor el interior. La mirada me siguió hasta que desaparecí de su campo de visión, para volver a desplazarse conmigo cuando volví a entrar en él. Las sábanas ocultaban unos pies. El resto de la casa, a oscuras, permanecía en silencio. Volví a mirar los ojos abiertos bajo los párpados inmóviles. (81)

In their happenstance encounter, the narrator pauses along his errant itinerary. His otherwise unnoticed body steps in and out of the tiny threshold from which this other set of eyes can see him. He tries out a few different angles to remain unnoticed while peering into this house, but those eyes continue to find him as well.

What interests me is to read the house in Casey's story, which he wrote from exile after having worked for *Casa de las Américas*, in comparison to the metaphorical house that names that institution and its eponymous cultural journal and to the optical regime those institutions supported. In Cuba in the Sixties, *Casa de las Américas* played an important role in institutionalizing revolutionary discourses, which required constant intellectual reflection and participation. In *Fulguración del espacio*, Quintero-Herencia analyzes this journal and claims: "El poder institucional revolucionario armará una suerte de régimen óptico que llevará a cabo toda una peculiar espacialización del orden de lo real en la isla" (18). This optical regime is one that institutes specific "relatos morales e históricos" to which all those who appear under the revolution's all-pervading and supposedly all-seeing light must subscribe (18). This is to say that the idea of a Latin American "family" and homogenous group of intellectuals living in the "House of the Americas" is an invasive, even militarized demand inscribed within the logic of surveillance that is placed on those subjects who "siempre se sabrán tocados por esta luz y obligados a continuas definiciones y genuflexiones identitarias" (19). In retrospect, Quintero-Herencia cautions that this inward gaze and search for regional homogeneity should not be overemphasized. These highly visible spaces, debates, and discourses are never as monumental and homogenous as they purport to be; rather, the plurality of such an event is often forcibly homogenized and institutionalized under the harsh spotlight guided from a hegemonic point of view.

The house in Casey's story illuminates this other anonymous body with a harsh light; from this perfectly visible room, where everything can be seen, a set of eyes follow and keep watch over Casey's narrator. However, the fully visible person watching the narrator is barely mobile; in fact, the narrator's description of the other person's body closely resembles that of the other inanimate objects in the room. Under immobile lids, his eyes are practically dead, and as a reader, I wonder whether this person is even alive. He is not dead, but neither is he in a position to control other bodies and issue moral demands from within this house. His own surveillance power is severely curbed; he barely catches a few glimpses of the narrator when he steps in front of the window for a few seconds. As the only visible body in the only brightly lit room, the supposedly empowering lights of this house serve a disciplinary task—confining this anonymous man in his bed. The narrator continues along his errant route, stumbles, and once more, without consciously intending to return to this spot, finds himself seeing those eyes from the house: "Cuando volví a asomarme al patio, tropecé otra vez con la mirada inmóvil bajo la luz cegadora" ("Notas" 82). The house's all-pervasive light immobilizes the fully visible subject, tucking him in a bed in order to keep vigil over his actions. Paradoxically, he is included under the blinding lights of the revolutionary house—of the *Casa de las Américas*—but there he is abandoned, left completely alone, because the exact position of his fully illuminated, immobile, and impotent body is now known at all times.

Meanwhile, the narrator continues to go unnoticed, but he never locates a true outside of this house. He accidentally returns to it after walking along his errant path through the swirling lights and shadows. However, it is his errant itinerary that allows him to see this house and its lights from a different perspective and to slip out of its disciplinary gaze, albeit temporarily. More important than this degree of agency or mobility that he gains by going unnoticed, Casey's narrator makes the first step toward the type of ethical exchange that I detail in the final chapter. Over the next day or so, the narrator intentionally returns and exchanges glances with this person whose eyes ultimately "parpardearon con un saludo de despedida" (84). The narrator takes great care to go unnoticed by anyone else while he observes this fully illuminated, yet abandoned, person's last days in silent companionship. Though the narrator began by wandering around in the dark in order to escape the racket of the street fair and the hostility of his neighbors, he becomes capable of peering into the shadows and bearing witness to this lonely, dying person's last moments. He goes unnoticed and unintentionally begins to notice those who have been abandoned by, though not excluded from, the revolutionary house. The narrator briefly steps out of his threshold of imperception in order to accompany this other person. Though Casey's narrator and this dying man only exchange silent glances, others who go unnoticed will begin the even more difficult process of throwing these disciplinary institutions into complete disarray in order to deactivate their totalizing control.

Chapter Three

On Unattended Details

The first reviewers of Somers's *La mujer desnuda* (1950) presented her as a hermetic, unapproachable, even bad writer. Emir Rodríguez Monegal dismissed her for demonstrating an "obsesión erótica" and for creating "una prosa no muy transparente" (14). According to Mario Benedetti, she might one day become a good writer, but she "obstinadamente insiste en ocultarlo" ("Derrumbamiento" 102). It is not until a decade later that he recants his first judgment of her works, finally presenting her as a worthwhile Uruguayan writer.[1] Only Ángel Rama publicly defended her as a part of what he calls the Critical Generation within Uruguayan literature, whose most well-known writer is Juan Carlos Onetti. Rama praised the originality of her work, thus bringing credibility to it: "Todo es insólito, ajeno, desconcertante, repulsivo y a la vez increíblemente fascinante en la obra narrativa más inusual que ha conocido la historia de nuestra literatura: la de Armonía Somers" ("Insólita" 30). Nevertheless, his defense still marginalizes her works in relation to the national literary tradition of the 1950s and 1960s, calling her "un bicho tan fuera de serie que es imposible ubicarla con respecto a las restantes criaturas femeninas" ("Mujeres" 51). Rama's interventions simultaneously praise Somers's works for their uniqueness, but stop one step short of elevating her as the leader of a national vanguard, preferring instead to relegate her to the margins along with the other "feminine creatures" who were writing in the era.[2]

Perhaps these male critics feared the disordering effects that such a strange, fascinating literature would have on their national traditions. In conversation with Miguel Ángel Campodónico—one of the few interviews Armonía Somers gave during her life—he asks her opinion about this debate: "¿Su literatura es

Chapter Three

hermética o abierta? ¿Qué hay de cierto en esta controversia?" (239). To which she responds:

> Sí, concedo eso también, que mi literatura pueda juzgarse a veces como poco iluminada, y para algunos de difícil acceso. Confieso que a veces no comprendo que lo parezca, ya que por haber salido de mí tengo confianza de mano a mano con ella. Pero si alguna vez yo misma quedo atrapada en el cuarto oscuro de lo que he creado, un personaje, una situación, un desenlace, me doy a pensar que lo hice para salvar, para rescatar, para no inmolar a alguien o a algo en la excesiva luz del signo, y en la espantosa claridad que encierran todas las convenciones. (239)

Despite the varying value judgments made for and against Somers's narratives, she engages in an enigmatic aesthetic as a means of eschewing conventions. She actively avoids that which too quickly reveals its intentions, preferring instead to protect these characters and situations from being excessively illuminated. For Casey and Filloy as well, some things are best left amongst the swirling shadows and pale lights of an era in order not to be sacrificed to plain language or reined in by established social codes. A common thread uniting many of Somers's narratives—one that also allows me to bring her into dialogue with Casey and Filloy—is this search for those seemingly unimportant, forever unattended details that are unlikely to be found. In this chapter, I analyze two metallic metaphors, one in *De miedo en miedo (Los manuscritos del río)* (1965) and the other in "Muerte por alacrán" (1963), about unattended details that have the potential to throw a perfectly ordered narrative or family home into complete disarray. Though attending to these details will be a dangerous task, they can become the catalyst for rewriting the historical record and challenging a social order achieved through deception and violence.

Amid Heaps of Scrap Metal

In Somers's least studied novel, *De miedo en miedo (Los manuscritos del río)*, which I analyze in more detail in the final chapter, there is metaphor linking an avant-garde aesthetic and those who go unnoticed. The male protagonist works in a bookstore, and he has frequent conversations with a female customer. Both remain anonymous to the reader. They continue to meet and engage in long, meandering dialogues that range from the boredom of their lives to escapist fantasies and memories of the past. Their conversation turns briefly to a discussion of a non-existent novel. He says it would be a novel written by anyone at all, and it would be composed of bad drawings, used objects, trash, and photographs of people "en el momento de perder el orgullo, con la boca, las uñas y los ojos agarrados del aire al errar un pasamanos" (66). He continues to describe this novel:

> Quién sabe si con largos períodos en blanco, en los que se oyera como a las ranas de un pantano cada pequeño ser sin importancia en la explosión acompasada de su vida que nadie ha tomado en cuenta, pero que es suya y está llena de sus historias. Y que algunos solamente supiésemos traducir con el auricular bien ajustado. (66)

When read alongside the interview with Campodónico, the novel begins to delineate its own aesthetic, one built from random, worthless objects, images of people at their most embarrassing moments, and large, blank spaces. This novel would narrate the lives of seemingly unimportant individuals without building them into national myths, role models, or triumphant heroes. Instead, the rhythm of this coming novel would keep time with their trivial, banal lives. It would trace their everyday itineraries that otherwise go unnoticed. It would be the novel that, through trial and error, struggles to adjust the receiver to the settings that could tend to the unnoticed bits and pieces of their lives.

However, finding that setting, hearing those dialogues, and writing those narratives will not be a simple task. When the woman asks him how such a piecemeal, errant narrative could be read, he replies: "Pues con sacrificio, como quien buscase una pequeña tuerca entre montones de chatarra" (66). When read alongside Filloy's fluvial metaphor of reading and walking against the current, Somers's metallic metaphor points to the incredible difficulty, and also danger, of attending to that which goes unnoticed. For comparison, the English idiom, "Like finding a needle in a haystack," describes the futility of a particular undertaking, yet the needle is quite different from the surrounding hay, and with a magnet, one's chances of finding it drastically improve. In contrast, Somers's metaphor exponentially

Chapter Three

increases the difficulty of locating one specific screw among heaps of indistinguishable scrap metal, not to mention the inevitable cuts and scratches that would result from digging through the rusty, jagged heap of discarded scraps. When Somers's shards of scrap metal are dumped into the current of Filloy's palindromes, turning against that churning stream will also expose one's body to continual scrapes, lacerations, and even dismemberment.

A Weaponized Scorpion

The challenge of reading Somers's fiction lies in approaching her hermetic prose by engaging in the quite dangerous task of attending to the tiniest, most superficial details that store the potential for rendering inoperative the political machines of one's era with no guarantees about exactly where that process will lead. In my analysis, the scorpion that no one can find in Somers's terrifying short story, "Muerte por alacrán," represents this task. The story opens with the banal account of two delivery men driving a truckload of firewood to a provincial manor on a sweltering summer day—the thermometer reads 49°C. They sit in silence, interrupted by the occasional curse word, and out of pure boredom, the driver decides:

> desviar un poco las ruedas hasta aplastar la víbora atravesada en el camino alegrándose luego de ese mismo modo con cualquier contravención a los ingenuos carteles ruteros, como si hubiese que dictar al revés todas aquellas advertencias a fin de que, por el placer de contradecirlas, ellos se condujeran alguna vez rectamente. (109–10)

These men carry out their assigned task—delivering firewood to a wealthy family—while taking every opportunity to challenge even the simplest of rules and regulations along the route. They drive drunk and swerve across the lanes, but they are not motivated by an ideological or ethical position. They would break any rule for the pure joy of being disobedient, even those rules designed to get them to carry out a specific task by prohibiting said task. Though they strive to create their own itinerary, they settle for empty gestures. In this terrifying, suspenseful narrative in which the smallest, unattended detail will disorder hierarchies, uncover evidence of corruption, and result in death, these two men will not

On Unattended Details

become folk heroes or proto-revolutionaries. Everyone subjected to the economic interests of the wealthy family in "Muerte por alacrán" loses in the end.

Even as the loyal butler incidentally upends the country manor, the construction of a new political community will not take place just yet. What matters for my analysis at this point will not be a moral at the end of the story, but the inordinate power stored in and released from a seemingly unimportant detail over the course of the narrative. As Susana Zanetti has demonstrated, within Somers's short stories it is "el detalle muchas veces anodino que cobra una importancia inusitada" ("Arte de narrar" 6). Despite their stoicism and childish bravado, as the delivery men approach the mansion with its guard dogs, butlers, and maids in this suffocating heat, they are haunted by "algo de la dimensión de un dedo pulgar, pero tan poderoso como una carga de dinamita o la bomba atómica" ("Muerte" 110). This is how the narrator first introduces the image of the scorpion hiding among the firewood. Without a doubt, this small creature poses the greatest threat to every character living within this stifling environment.

As the men unload the firewood—a moment described as "la descarga del terror"—they move: "Del clima solar del jardín al ambiente de cofre de ébano de adentro" (111). The harsh, exposed gardens wither under the sun in contrast to the luxurious, protected rooms inside the mansion. The men unload the wood and, they believe, the unseen scorpion, meanwhile traversing the threshold that separates outside from inside, nature from culture, servant from master. Quickly returning to the truck in fear of the scorpion, they honk and shout a warning to the butler, as if in passing, about the threat hiding among the firewood. Their bodies, to borrow Jon Beasley-Murray's important differentiation between good and bad multitudes, do not "resonate and expand" forming a liberating challenge to hegemony, but rather become "dissonant bodies or bodies whose resonance hits a peak that leads to collapse" (247). These men drive off with a false sense of relief. In a surprise twist in the final sentences of the story, the scorpion appears inside the truck's cabin and prepares to sting one of them. Instead of working with the others, they try to unload this burden on them and flee. Perhaps they hoped it would wreak havoc on the wealthy owners, who only appear at the very end of this narrative, but they completely disregarded the threat it poses to the lives and well-being of all those other people like themselves who work on the estate. Their actions can only be interpreted as selfish.

At the very end of the story, the scorpion finally appears: "un bicho de cola puntiaguda iba trepando lentamente por el respaldo del asiento de un camión fletero, a varios kilómetros de Villa Therese y sus habitantes" ("Muerte" 122). As the scorpion crawls toward the "dos cuellos de distinto temperamento" of the delivery men, the narrator transforms the scorpion, through metaphor, into a sentient piece of military technology as it prepares its assault: "Nunca se sabe qué puede pensar un pequeño monstruo de esos antes de virar en redondo y poner en función su batería de popa" (122). The scorpion becomes metallic upon materializing, turning into a weapon of war, and this unattended detail threatens to destroy the lives of the two men who felt most at ease. This event is not morally justified within the narrative, and the politics and ethics that interests me here will not work toward justifying the men's actions or their death. What matters is that they never attended to this dangerous detail; they simply attempted to pass the burden onto others with whom they could have collaborated to ensure that everyone escaped this very real threat.

After the delivery men leave, the narrative shifts attention to the butler, and most of the story relates his frantic reaction to hearing the word "scorpion":

> Aquello, que desde que se pronuncia el nombre es un conjunto de pinzas, patas, cola, estilete ponzoñoso, era lo que le habían arrojado cobardemente las malas bestias, como el vaticinio distraído de una bruja, sin contar con los temblores del pobre diablo que lo está recibiendo en pleno estómago. (112–13)

Simply pronouncing this little word, "scorpion," with no empirical proof of its actual existence, is enough not only to send the fearstricken butler on a frenzied search of the entire mansion but also to transform the supposedly protective interior of the house into "el desafío de todos lados, y de ninguno" (113). This hierarchized house of an absent, elite family with its caste of servants who are subjected to a mandatory moral code is rattled by the possible presence of the scorpion. The butler imagines "Un millar de escorpiones" jumping from every piece of wood in the fireplace (118). Different objects in the manor even take on a new hue, "color alacrán" (115, 117). This tiny detail has turned into a full-fledged threat of violence and death that is ubiquitous yet undetectable.

Operating from a sense of duty, the butler commits to combing through every inch of the manor until he finds and eliminates this threat, even at risk of losing his own life. However, as he haphazardly sets out on this indoors hunting expedition, he upends the stately order of this provincial manor and ends up uncovering the secrets of all three members of the family. In this sense, Deleuze and Guattari's warning about the unpredictability of the line of flight holds true: "No one can say where the line of flight will pass" (250). Seemingly unimportant details, as in the case of this absent scorpion, store the potential "to rearrange the overall assemblage" (259). The butler rifles through the teenage Therese's bedroom, pulling out her intimates and reading through her diary as his own sexual fantasies play out in his mind. Later, he finds a secret hole in the wall with documents that prove that Günter, the master, built his fortunes through corruption; the father embezzled company funds by cooking the books, hid his assets from auditors, and manipulated the stock markets ("Muerte" 118). The butler also discovers the truth—"siempre sin relatar"—behind Günter's complicity in driving a man to bankruptcy and suicide, because this man had an affair with his wife (119). Finally, the butler goes into the wife's bedroom and spreads all of Günter's documents on her bed like "la carga microbiana de un estornudo" (121). His impromptu disruption of the family home contaminates this perfectly ordered space in which every person and thing is supposed to fall neatly into their assigned place.[3] By attending to this detail, as does the otherwise unimportant butler who becomes the protagonist of Somers's narrative, he destroys the filial relationship of the country manor and rearranges the overall assemblage, fragmenting and fracturing the order that had been imposed on all of these people even when the patron, the sovereign, or the state is not present.

In trying to protect his masters' lives and the disciplinary order of this house, the butler reveals their secrets, all because of one little word shouted by a stranger: "scorpion." While still in the wife's bedroom, the butler mutters to himself: "En realidad, eso de deshacer y no volver nada a su antiguo orden era mantener las cosas en su verdadero estado" (120). Margaret L. Snook interprets

Chapter Three

the butler's disruptions as primarily an attack on the institution of patriarchy: "his disruption of the mansion's order by playing master or dog challenge the patriarchal system from all sides" (n.p.).[4] Furthermore, I contend that the butler's futile search for an unseen scorpion that never left the delivery truck sets in motion the broader process of deactivating the rigid, corrupt hierarchies of the biopolitical order that violently controls the lives of all those connected to the manor, even those of the free-wheeling delivery men.

"Muerte por alacrán" ends with the scorpion's stinger poised to attack the drivers and the wealthy family walking into their upended manor. The aftermath of these events is excluded from the narrative frame, as in those horror films where the killer or malignant spirit is revived in the final shot, opening up the possibility for a sequel. Yet, there is no sequel to Somers's short story. As a reader, I am left spinning in this ambiguous space in which no one stands out as the hero and no justice triumphs over those corrupt individuals who might hide their secrets again and go on with their lives as if nothing happened. In the end, no utopian order is guaranteed in the wake of all this death and destruction. A politics and an ethics cannot be built from these selfish gestures and limited revelations. At this stage in my analysis, Somers's short story only begins to unfold the complexities and dangers of the unattended details that provoke drastic, errant itineraries through otherwise ordered spaces. There remains something enigmatic in Somers's gesture, because her narrative never reveals any underlying, potential ideology. For this reason, I insist that her works not be too hastily clarified and condensed into a visible political position, at least not yet. In the following chapters, those who go unnoticed will be able to take advantage of these seemingly unimportant, enigmatic, and unattended details that they encounter along their errant itineraries through the Sixties in Latin America as they use them to reclaim their ability to disagree with the political organization of their society and transform the aesthetic representation of their communities.

PART TWO

The Politics of Going Unnoticed

Going unnoticed begins as little more than an attempt to evade both the sovereign's gaze and the everyday demands for normative behavior. In the thresholds that open between the public and the private, visibility and invisibility, and democracy and dictatorship, bare lives can attempt to restore the potential for dissensus. During the Sixties, the politics of going unnoticed imagined by Calbert Casey, Juan Filloy, and Armonía Somers takes the form of disagreements with the more visible and audible politics of the era. In particular, each author writes about bare lives looking for a way out of the state of exception or for a way to disagree with the surveillance techniques of modern biopolitical institutions and societies by going unnoticed within them. In this section, I analyze Casey's essays on being a committed writer in the Cuban Revolution, as well as the seemingly unimportant protagonists in fictional narratives by Filloy and Somers who go unnoticed in order to engage in dissent and disagreement within a highly saturated public sphere.

Since the earliest Greek formulations, politics has been conceived as those matters that came into light within the *polis* where economic exchanges occurred in and around the *agora* in order to be subjected to debate for the good of the community. Jürgen Habermas explains that the Greek public sphere was the realm in which the unrestrained masters of a household came together to discuss matters of public or communal concern: "Only in the light of the public sphere did that which existed become revealed, did everything become visible to all" (4). Neither dependent upon presence in the city, nor seeking full visibility in the public sphere, the politics of going unnoticed would be meaningless within this classic framework.

Part Two

However, Habermas continues to trace the transformation of the public sphere through the twentieth century. In sum, he examines how the Greek division between the public and the private spheres loses its clarity. The two spheres infiltrate one another as the market economy grows and globalizes, as the State is called upon to intervene into private business transactions to ensure their success in a global market—though despised when it attempts to regulate labor conditions or environmental responsibility—and as the masses enter into political conflict and negotiate the competing messages circulating in the media and the culture industries (141–46). What interests me is not Habermas's intent to revive a rational-critical debate in the public sphere but his argument that the classic Greek divisions between private and public, between the visible and the invisible, do not adequately describe social, economic, and political relationships in the twentieth century.

Going unnoticed in the Sixties is not an act that takes place exclusively at the margins of political spaces nor in between different political spaces; one may go unnoticed just as easily near the perceived centers as in the margins. In fact, going unnoticed is not dependent upon an essential relation to either a margin or a center, concepts which are practically impossible to define in the wake of the debates on modernity, postmodernity, and peripheral modernity in Latin America.[1] Rather, the space in which the politics of going unnoticed takes place is better defined as the state of exception. In *Homo Sacer*, Agamben redefines the space of politics for the contemporary world: "Every attempt to rethink the political space of the West must begin with the clear awareness that we no longer know anything of the classical distinction between *zoè* and *bios*, between private life and political existence, between man as a simple living being at home in the house and man's political existence in the city" (187). The spatial binaries of political discourse are collapsed into a zone of indistinction, which prohibits the facile structuring of that which is inside or outside, communicable or incommunicable, voiced or silenced, of a particular judicial order or sovereign state.[2] Thus, Agamben shifts focus from these binary distinctions—to which must be added that of visibility and invisibility—to the human body that may be killed insofar as it is a body that is always already involved in a political order.

Politics of Going Unnoticed

This order is what Agamben calls "the state of exception," but he argues that it has become the norm for political organization even when the constitutional rule of law appears to be in place: "The state of exception is not a dictatorship (whether constitutional or unconstitutional, commissarial or sovereign) but a space devoid of law, a zone of anomie in which all legal determinations—and above all the very distinction between public and private—are deactivated" (*State of Exception* 50). In theory, these powers should only be invoked in times of great emergency when the sovereign must act paradoxically by suspending the law in order to guarantee the future of the law. However, Agamben locates variants of the state of exception as the foundation of modern constitutional states throughout the West. He chooses "state of exception" as the phrase to discuss what in German theory is termed *"Ausnahmezustand"* or *"Notstand,"* "state of necessity"; in the Italian and French traditions is called "emergency decrees" and "state of siege," as in "*état de siège fictif*"; and in Anglo-Saxon theory, "martial law" and "emergency powers" (4). Building from this analysis, Marina Franco and Mariana Iglesias have shown that the phrases *"estado de sitio"* and *"medidas prontas de seguridad"* have been used in Argentina and Uruguay, respectively, to name this type of juridical practice (92). Regardless of how they are named, the suspension of the law tends to be motivated more by an individual, a party, or a collective of governing bodies to secure their own sovereignty, both political and moral, than by the need to protect the constitutional foundations of a nation-state.

In my analysis, those who go unnoticed do so because they understand that the state of exception has become the norm and that there is no outside to which they might escape. Within the state of exception, their bodies become *"nuda vita,"* bare or naked life.[3] A bare life is not simply Aristotle's *zoè*, the animal-like human being who has yet to enter into public life or the political sphere, the one who remains silent and invisible. Instead, this form of bare life, which is irrevocably tied to a political order, takes the form of the *homo sacer*—the life that can be killed but not sacrificed, the body or, better yet, the person who may be abandoned by the law in the state of exception. Once abandoned, he or she may be killed with impunity. Since the normal rule of law has been suspended, his or her killing constitutes, "neither capital punishment nor a

Part Two

sacrifice, but simply the actualization of a mere 'capacity to be killed'" (Agamben, *Homo Sacer* 114).

Since the countryside is no longer a refuge from the political city, and the public-private divide no longer adequately describes social functions, then the following questions arise: To what extent can one engage in politics while going unnoticed in a crowded, urban center or in pseudo-isolation in the countryside? In what ways does going unnoticed restore the possibility of engaging in dissent without clamoring for a voice under the bright lights of the political arena? In what follows, I answer these questions by building a definition of politics as a means of engaging in dissensus within the overcrowded and saturated political environment of the Sixties in Latin America. Those who go unnoticed are not, or at least are not yet, the subjects who are interned in camps or killed with impunity, but they find themselves in incredibly vulnerable positions that at times lead to their exile, imprisonment, or death. Their politics will be founded on two irresolvable paradoxes: 1) the modern state of exception has become the rule that guides Western biopolitical relationships wherein the law is suspended in order to guarantee the future of the law and 2) radical democratic politics can only function as a never-ending tension between bids for liberty and bids for equality that must be guaranteed simultaneously from above and from below. Those who go unnoticed engage in politics by opening a place for disagreement within a highly saturated and inescapable political space. Along the way, they attempt to deactivate the divisive machines whose barriers serve only to order and control their lives.

Chapter Four

A Double Negative in Cuba

> Los últimos años de su vida fueron quizás un ejemplo doloroso de que en nuestra época es imposible "El no comprometerse."
> Calvert Casey, "El Premio Nobel y la muerte"

In 1960, Calvert Casey published "El Premio Nobel y la muerte" in *Lunes de Revolución*. The purpose of this article was to intervene in the international polemic that reappeared in the press after the death of Boris Pasternak, the Russian author of *Doctor Zhivago*, who won the Nobel Prize in Literature in 1958. In a rare moment of vehement disgust, Casey condemns the foreign press as a "terrible ámbito desfigurador" for having given such attention to a speculative debate about whether Pasternak truly deserved the Nobel Prize or whether, for the sake of Cold War politics, he was celebrated for his perceived critique of the Soviet Union ("Premio" 24). In particular, Casey is appalled that a somewhat mediocre writer, quietly composing a respectable novel, "de pronto se ve violentamente impelido a la arena política mundial, sin él esperarlo, ni jamás pedirlo, pues tal cosa evidentemente repugna a su naturaleza" (24). Casey respects Pasternak's desire to stay far from the violent bids for hegemony under the all-pervading lights of the global political arena, and this leads him to lament that today "es imposible 'El no comprometerse'" (24). This is an odd phrase for an otherwise genuinely committed writer to profess in Cuba in 1960. Though resolving this polemic is of little interest for my argument, Casey's double negative can serve as the entry point into the politics of going unnoticed. In this and other essays he wrote for *Lunes*, he develops an informal political theory with a radically democratic framework; incompatible with the totalizing politics that would dominate Cuba in the following years and decades, Casey's fragmented, discarded ideas would guarantee the potential for dissensus among friends and even so-called counterrevolutionaries inside the Revolution. However, in order to proclaim these ideas from within Cuba, he had to carefully construct an unnoticed threshold to evade the normalizing gaze of the Revolution. In this chapter, I take a slight detour from my analysis of fictional protagonists in order to consider how Casey constructed this threshold for himself while seeking recognition as a committed intellectual in the earliest years of the Cuban Revolution.

Lunes and the Cuban Revolution

Lunes was a *suplemento literario* to the Cuban newspaper, *Revolución*. *Lunes* appeared every Monday, and Guillermo Cabrera Infante served as the magazine's editor with Pablo Armando Fernández as its assistant editor. *Revolución*, edited by Carlos Franqui, was founded under the auspices of the Movimiento Revolucionario 26 de Julio (MR-26-7), the group led by Fidel Castro that carried out the failed 1953 attack on the Cuartel Moncada against Fulgencio Batista and later renewed their assault from the Sierra Maestra. Starting in 1959, the intellectual circle surrounding *Revolución* created new cultural markets; they operated a radio station, a television channel, a record company, and a publishing house, Ediciones R—where "R" stands for "Revolución." Casey published numerous short and seemingly inconsequential essays in *Lunes de Revolución* throughout its brief existence from March 23, 1959, to November 6, 1961. These included criticism on Cuban music, theater, dance, and opera; translations of essays on modern theater and acting techniques; and journalistic writings based on testimonies from men who fought during the Playa Girón/Bay of Pigs invasion and from volunteers who came from around the world to help build the Cuban Revolution.

Lunes provides an example of the degree to which free speech and even criticism of local realities were permitted temporarily by Fidel Castro, since those proclaiming such ideas were visibly connected to the mythical origin of the Revolution. "During its publication history," explains William Luis, "*Lunes* was a new and innovative supplement, and unlike previous magazines that were limited to a particular literary current, ideology, genre, or region, it provided a home for writers and artists from a range of positions and locations" ("Exhuming" 257).[1] Of course, such openness only remained possible for the first two years of the Revolution, during which the exact shape of its new institutions remained uncertain. After the suspicious explosion of the munitions freighter, *La Coubre*, on March 4, 1960, and the failed counterrevolutionary invasion of Playa Girón/Bay of Pigs in April of 1961—a full decade before the Padilla Affair—freedom of expression would no longer be guaranteed for the *Lunes* group. When they aired the documentary *P.M.* (1961), directed by Sabá Cabrera and Orlando Jiménez Leal, it became the subject of a heated debate regarding appropriate cultural expression. The *Lunes* group defended the documentary against the criticisms of the Instituto Cubano de Arte e Industria Cinematográficos (ICAIC). Controlled by the orthodox Marxists of the Partido Socialista Popular, the ICAIC was gaining favor with Fidel Castro over the MR-26-7, and the debate over *P.M.* formed part of a larger ideological struggle between the two groups seeking control of cultural production on the island. Ultimately, *P.M.* was censored. Five months after this polemic, *Revolución* and *Lunes* were closed, officially due to a shortage of paper, and Cabrera Infante and others from the *Lunes* group went into exile. The ICAIC became the State-sanctioned institution that would approve or censor Cuban film and culture, while *Casa de las Américas* assumed control with its eponymous journal, and the Unión de Escritores y Artistas de Cuba and the Consejo Nacional de Cultura were founded to ensure further unity in Cuban cultural production.[2]

The decision to censor *P.M.* was reached during a series of well-documented conferences in the Biblioteca Nacional José Martí on June 16, 23, and 30, 1961, during which Castro read his notorious speech, "Palabras a los intelectuales," and publicly pronounced the well-known phrase, "Dentro de la Revolución: todo; contra la Revolución ningún derecho" (n.p.). Castro is quite direct about the demand for total unity, while at the same time incredibly ambiguous in that he does not specify what does and does not pertain to the Revolution—the empty signifier *par excellence*. Thus, the topology of the Revolution acquires a legal and moral framework wherein those who are inside have rights and are good; everyone else is against the Revolution—

Chapter Four

a counterrevolutionary—and since they are still within the Revolution, their actions become legally inadmissible and morally reprehensible. Indirectly, Castro transforms Casey's lamentable double negative into a sovereign demand: it is impossible to not be committed to the Revolution.

With this speech Castro institutes a politics of consensus forged through censorship and the threat of juridical abandonment or death through legal means. In "On Absolute Hostility," Jacques Derrida interprets Carl Schmitt's definition of the political as the act of distinguishing between the friend and the enemy: "Even if no pure access to the *eîdos* or essence is to be had, even if, in all conceptual purity, it is not known what war, politics, friendship, enmity, hate or love, hostility or peace are, one can and must know—first of all practically, politically, polemically—*who* is the friend and *who* is the enemy" (116). Complex notions of the subject become irrelevant, because in such a definition of the political, a line is drawn to distinguish between visible friends and known enemies. Castro draws this line between those who are inside and those who turn against the Revolution's currents, between those who visibly and enthusiastically consent and those whose attitudes range from neutrality to active dissent. Castro's State is the arena in which that line is drawn, and he is the sovereign judge who draws that line. In this sense, the Cuban State assumes the form of a crystalline palindrome: within the Cuban Revolution, within the first, unidirectional reading everything is to be found; against the Revolution, or against the current of the Revolution's ideology, nothing and no one will be granted the legal or moral right to exist.

The ethos of the *Lunes* group and Casey's defense of Pasternak within that magazine suggest that another relationship to the political could have been possible in Cuba in the Sixties. What if, to borrow Derrida's phrasing, the political "were bound to an affirmation of life, to the endless repetition of this affirmation" (123)? Surely, this would be a difficult position to sustain within Cuba after 1961 when anyone adopting ideological positions ranging from neutrality to counterrevolutionary would be jailed, interned in the UMAPs, or killed.[3] After the closure of *Lunes*, Casey accepted a job writing for *Casa de las Américas* until 1965 when he went into exile.[4] Referring to the period around 1964 with the publication of *Memorias de una isla*, Medina Ríos maps a dense web of political and aesthetic debates as a context for reading Casey's works, and she argues that "las contradicciones entre él [Casey] y el *pathos* metafísico de la Cuba revolucionaria debieron tornarse arduas" (248). The challenge he faced as he navigated the Cuban Revolution along his errant path was to continually resituate himself as being inside the Revolution, allowing him to be accepted or, at the very least, to go unnoticed as a harmless, but willing participant. If he wanted to make claims about the path the Revolution should take, he would have to avoid being labelled as a counterrevolutionary given his already suspicious role as a gay intellectual from the United States who never bore arms. In what follows, I first analyze how Casey publicly and continually renewed his commitment to the Revolution among the diverse voices that composed *Lunes*; then I turn to the brief moments within a few of these texts where he deviates ever so slightly from the party line by interrogating Castro's definition of the political. In addition to his sexuality, I argue that Casey's exile in 1965 arises from his commitment to the politics of going unnoticed, which foregrounds the potential for dissensus and even respects those who do not agree as members of the community.

An Unremarkable Intellectual

In "Un ensayo oportuno" (1960), Casey takes up the habitual topic of writers in the Sixties: to analyze the state of the intellectual in the time of revolution and to provide a plan of action for his contemporaries. First, he appears to move along the current of the Revolution. Having lived much of his life in the United States, he could have been accused of having benefitted directly from imperialism; furthermore, as a gay man in a blatantly homophobic regime, the need to publicly assume his Cuban identity becomes all the more urgent.[5] In this essay, Casey favorably quotes Virgilio Piñera as a writer who had critiqued others who, under Batista's rule in Cuba, chose "refugiarse en el barroquismo o en el hermetismo" ("Ensayo" 13). While Casey does not name Lezama Lima directly, Piñera's reference to the hermetically Baroque writer and the Cuban journal *Orígenes* is certainly alluded to in this phrase.[6] Indirectly, Casey assumes the guilt of having remained neutral during the armed struggle, but he keeps his distance from those who might be slightly more guilty—assuming one can differentiate degrees of revolutionary guilt—as in the case of Lezama Lima and other members of the petty bourgeoisie. Casey constructs a space for himself somewhere between those who sought refuge and isolation in the aesthetic and those who took up arms to combat Batista's regime that subjugated Cuba to neocolonial powers.

Nevertheless, Casey knew this was not sufficient to earn the trust of the *barbudos*, nor did it meet the demands of the most public intellectuals and revolutionary figures of the era.[7] Toeing the party line, Casey confesses that he and other intellectuals only recognized their isolation and felt regret at not having participated directly in the armed struggle when they saw the Rebel Army arrive triumphantly in Havana: "El único sentimiento honrado que podíamos permitirnos al ver pasar a 'los otros,' a los hombres anónimos de las ciudades y el campo, a los que hasta ayer considerábamos la incolora e inculta medianía, era el de remordimiento y un enorme complejo de culpa, bajo el cual aún vivimos" ("Ensayo" 13). Here Casey freely offers his *mea culpa*; such statements became routine among Cuban intellectuals after 1959.

With this admission of guilt made public, Casey can then set forth an agenda for intellectuals in Cuba. The "timely essay" to which the title refers is a speech given by José Antonio Portuondo in 1938 that was republished in the anthology, *Los mejores ensayistas cubanos* (1959). The topic of Portuondo's speech, titled "Pasión y muerte del hombre," is the spirit of the revolutionary, Marxist man and, in particular, the role of the intellectual in relation to the masses. Portuondo outlines the failure of intellectuals to connect with the masses as a result of turning to irrationalism, which he defines as a rejection of the Cartesian method, that is, of a strictly logical, linear, technical, and empirical approach to interpreting the world (117–21). In order to combat the intellectual's solitude, Portuondo proposes he be "heroicamente razonable," but he must do so without handing himself over "al torrente de su tiempo que lo arrastra" (121). This rational intellectual, says Portuondo, must be humble, honest, and willing to recognize his own limitations, but he has a duty to continue to learn and to search for new ways of perceiving the world. However, Portuondo's intellectual still remains a heroic, vanguard figure leading the way forward. Ultimately, Portuondo believes intellectuals should "meterse desnudo en la pelea de los hombres y decirles con su voz lo que aprendimos, en los libros y en la vida, para que ellos lo hagan fructificar" (122–23). He insists that intellectuals—with whom he identifies—find a way to strip down their rhetoric so that the knowledge they develop may be used by the masses, thus gradually bridging the divide between the two groups.

Casey praises Portuondo's essay, stating it feels as if it had been written "para los hombres de 1960"; he builds from the laurels bestowed upon Portuondo in order to formulate and publicly declare his own position in this debate, while blending in to the crowd of public intellectuals ("Ensayo" 13). Alongside many of his contemporaries, he seeks a plan of action, without taking up arms, to at least partially suture the gap separating intellectuals like himself from the Cuban people. In order to do so, Casey turns to Portuondo's concept of the heroically rational, yet humble, intellectual and proposes that the first task of Cuban intellectuals be "expresar en términos de razón el sentido de la Revolución [...] construyendo nuevas formas" (13). Though intellectuals may not have participated in the armed struggle, their present use lies in translating and sharing knowledge about Cuba's colonial and neocolonial past, the struggle for liberation, the current obstacles, and the future goals of the Revolution to the Cuban masses. Casey concludes this brief essay with the following mission statement: "Aprender, formular las verdades de los hombres de pasión, servir, señalar los peligros, crear incesantemente, ayudar a mantener el frente ancho e irresistible de la Revolución: esos objetivos han de constituir la misión de los escritores en 1960 y en los años de la Revolución" (13). The revolutionary writer, therefore, must be heroic, humble, and honest, and his labor has to be at the service of creating, expanding, and defending the Revolution. In this sense, Casey's ideas are earnest, but not surprising, because they contribute little new substance to these debates. However, what Casey actually achieves in this banal essay is to position himself as one more run-of-the-mill intellectual going unnoticed among the consenting crowd.[8]

Casey's Dissent

From this unnoticed threshold, Casey acquires the potential to subtly introduce a politics founded not on forming a consensus through visibility, exclusions, and violence, but rather on dissensus. In *The Democratic Paradox*, Mouffe argues that dissensus is the only possible foundation for a radically democratic politics. In her analysis, the institutions through which consensus is reached (e.g., parliament or congress) and the institutions through which such agreements are guaranteed and enforced (e.g., police and armed forces) are not the ones that engage directly in the political (101).[9] Castro's sovereign demand and the legal and military institutions at his command fit her definition of consensus-building practices and institutions. In contrast, Mouffe argues that pluralist democratic politics should be seen as a paradox that does not need to be resolved through consensus-building or the construction of a homogeneous totality. The fantasy of transcending any point of conflict and resolving every debate would require the political choice to close democracy itself.

Nevertheless, Mouffe distinguishes pluralism from the sort of postmodern celebrations of all differences that end in a defense of relativism. She insists on upholding this difference to avoid arriving at a political process in which "relations of power and antagonisms are erased and we are left with the typical liberal illusion of a pluralism without antagonism" (*The Democratic Paradox* 20). She cautions against a form of multiculturalism in which the differences among identity groups are essentialized without giving recourse to the ways in which such differences have been historically and contingently structured via power relations founded on exclusion and oppression. When such antagonism is erased, a new consensus is constituted in which pluralism becomes the name that purports to celebrate cultural differences without modifying those power relations (20). Rather, in order to guarantee a pluralist democratic politics, the antagonism, difference, and dissent that constitutes this paradox must be upheld in order to guarantee the future of the democratic process.[10]

In *The Politics of Aesthetics*, Jacques Rancière similarly defines the political as dissensus, but his theory stands today as a reiteration of the classical Greek formulation by which politics derives from the necessary visibility of the act and the subject: "Politics consists in reconfiguring the distribution of the sensible which defines the common of a community, to introduce into it new subjects and objects, to render visible what had not been, and to make heard as speakers those who had been perceived as mere noisy animals" (25). This passage, via dissensus, from invisibility to visibility, from noise to speech, and from animal to man, is consistently upheld as the definition of politics throughout Rancière's work.

However, this successful passage to visibility and speech cannot be the case for the politics of going unnoticed, which always falls short of visibility and speech, whether on purpose or by accident. Rather, those who go unnoticed continually move toward a democratic politics that reopens the potential for dissensus wherever it has been blocked. For example, Casey's subtly deviant lamentation about the impossibility of not being committed is practically ignored within Cuba before and after his exile, and I contend that this is because he situates himself in an unnoticed threshold among all the other committed intellectuals. The politics of going unnoticed begins with dissent and disagreement, but it does not require the transcendental passage into visibility nor does it constitute a retreat into complete darkness. Going unnoticed opens the potential for disagreement for those who can be discarded at any moment because of their perceived irrelevance. Thus, this politics allows the unnoticed to disagree with their own abandonment without first having to agree to participate fully in the institutions that have excluded them and are likely to imprison or execute them long before they would grant them visibility and a voice.

Lunes organized a series of round-table discussions about the political role of literature with writers who had travelled to Cuba. As only one voice among various participants, Casey occasionally interjects in these dialogues with a defense of the right of the unnoticed to dissent. I am particularly interested in the conversations with Pablo Neruda in December 1960 and with Nathalie Sarraute in September 1961, two months before *Lunes* would close. Both of these invited authors advocate for artistic freedom, rejecting State-prescribed forms similar to Zhdanovism and socialist realism, and their ideas correspond with the positions taken by the *Lunes* group in general. Despite the rivers of ink used to explain, defend, and debate the role of the revolutionary intellectual, and despite the generally accepted sound bites that are incessantly repeated in these highly visible debates, the intellectual's role remains quite imprecisely defined. By situating anti-dogmatism at the center of this debate, as many intellectuals struggle to do in these first years of the Revolution, they simultaneously defend their right to free, artistic experimentation and subject themselves to potentially harsh criticism and persecution dependent upon a rapidly changing geopolitical environment. As long as these intellectuals had good faith in the Revolution's commitment to an open process, this would not be perceived as a problem. Unfortunately, the *Lunes* group was among the first to be attacked when disagreement was declared to be counterrevolutionary.

In the conversation with Neruda, Casey asks him if he thinks he has succeeded in overcoming "el problema de la comunicación oral con el pueblo en un alto nivel" ("*Lunes* conversa con Pablo Neruda" 40). Casey's preoccupation with establishing a dialogue with the people without simplification takes precedence, and he seems to have found in Neruda a model for traversing that distance between the foreign-born intellectual and the Cuban people. Neruda deflects the question, saying the people will have to answer as to whether or not he was successful. Instead, he decries dogmatism in literature and in politics, which he defines as "una visión parcial de la vida y de los acontecimientos. Una visión única, determinada y que no puede ser alterada" (41). Neruda defends remaining open to an exploration of artistic expression as long as this expression is committed to engaging the people in dialogue, and his ideas are generally supported by Casey and the *Lunes* group. This commitment to dialogue will come to characterize the ethical implications of the politics of going unnoticed, but such an open, unbounded exploration would not be permitted in Cuba after Castro's decree in 1961.

Casey is listed as one of the participants in the conversation with Nathalie Sarraute—alongside Lisandro Otero, Manuel Díaz Martínez, Guillermo Cabrera Infante, Heberto Padilla, César Leante, Pablo Armando Fernández, Rine Leal, Natalio Galán, and Edmundo Desnoes—but each question, unlike in previous conversations, is asked anonymously. This editorial change is not explained in the article, but their refusal to name names might be explained as a hesitation on part of the *Lunes* group to be perceived as operating against the Revolution while inside it, since it was published just months after Castro's "Palabras a los intelectuales." During the conversation, Sarraute repeats what has been a fairly common and vague talking point: the need to represent concrete, local situations instead of universal theories and to create new aesthetic forms that correspond with the new ideas and situations of the era (Casey, "Diez escritores cubanos"

4). What particularly is of interest for my discussion of Casey is how Sarraute goes beyond the concrete cases; she says: "Pretendo captar aquellas cosas, pequeños incidentes, muchas veces banales que están en el límite de la conciencia y que pueden ser lo más importante" (3). This emphasis on that which is seemingly minor or unimportant, on that which is left unattended and goes unnoticed, becomes in my analysis a curious point of dialogue between Sarraute and Casey. For both, a writer can tell the story of that which goes unnoticed, of voices heard in passing and of the abandoned fragments of a text thrown into the sewers, and still be a committed intellectual.

At the very least, both Sarraute and Casey conceive of a fruitful, non-neutral relationship between the writer and the Revolution while telling these stories. In making such claims, however, they have begun to walk along an errant path of their own invention that starts to turn against the currents of the Revolution. In the few moments Casey speaks from within the crowd of intellectuals, he promotes commitment to revolutionary ideology, but he also defends the possibility of exploring that which is barely perceived both in public and in private. His dedication to what Sarraute locates at the limits of consciousness might come dangerously close to a defense of a European, bourgeois aesthetic obsessed with individualism or irrationalism that proves to be of little use for indoctrinating or raising the collective, revolutionary consciousness of the people; even if it were useful, it still might be too hermetic or enigmatic to engage in direct communication with the people, since the people—yet another empty signifier bandied about by so many in Cuba at the time—are often spoken of as a homogeneous group who can only understand simple, direct language with little to no complexity. Writing about that which goes unnoticed already appears in an indistinct zone on the threshold between commitment and autonomy, and Casey commits primarily to the arduous task of representing the unnoticed without forcing them into a homogeneous "people" who speak in a single, visible voice to offer their consent. At this point, the politics of going unnoticed takes place within a space no longer conceived as an autonomous public sphere, and it opens toward a radical democratic politics that recognizes but does not essentialize difference, while guaranteeing the right to dissent. By opening and unfolding the political space within which such

Chapter Four

differences and antagonisms can be weighed against one another, this politics will continue to challenge instances of hegemony and other power relations that construct barriers between individuals within their own communities.

But none of this would be compatible with the politics, aesthetics, or ethics of the Cuban Revolution after 1961. Within the context of this chapter, it is now possible to better understand Casey's defense of Pasternak in "El Premio Nobel y la muerte" with which I began. Casey frames his analysis with a reminder that he is a committed intellectual and that any other stance is unacceptable in revolutionary times: "Para nosotros, comprometidos, la actitud pasiva, neutral, no comprometida, de Pasternak, es contraproducente, incluso dañina, pero la respetamos" (24). Following the party line, Casey assumes a certain authority to extend his individual voice as the one who can speak in the plural—"nosotros, comprometidos." As a critique of imperialist propaganda, Casey's vehement outburst could be justified as a completely committed position as long as he distances himself from a figure like Pasternak; however, Casey veers off course, assumes the voice of the sovereign, and authorizes the other unnamed, committed intellectuals to invite Pasternak into the fold. From within the logic of a politics of consensus, a writer like Pasternak who refuses to actively create and support a revolution should be considered its enemy just as much as those who actively seek to block or destroy it. Nevertheless, Casey defies this logic and concludes that all committed intellectuals in Cuba can and do respect Pasternak's passive attitude: "pero la respetamos."

Casey continues along this errant path in the concluding, disjunctive paragraph of the essay in which he further slips into an emotional outcry against a cold, unjust, and painful world:

> Pero lo terrible había sucedido. Un artista modesto, silencioso, que no aspiraba más que hacer su obra, buena o mediocre, limitada o de aliento, se había visto atrapado en medio de la furia, fríamente utilizado por unos, e injustamente alocado por otros. Los últimos años de su vida fueron quizás un ejemplo doloroso de que en nuestra época es imposible "El no comprometerse."
> ("El Premio Nobel" 24)

Recognizing the ambiguities of Pasternak's position, since he never publicly declared his politics, Casey laments the painful example proving that such a solitary life and literature is now impossible, because it leaves one's works too open to be manipulated within the public sphere. The double negative with which Casey expresses the current state of affairs for intellectuals—the impossibility of not being committed—registers a closure in the public and the private spheres. It is no longer possible, Casey claims, to maintain an apolitical stance, even when living in a peripheral, isolated area. Being committed is now a demand, a requirement of the Sixties. And Casey finds this utterly painful and regrettable.

Casey never directly states that he would have preferred to live like Pasternak, modestly creating his work in silence; nevertheless, his description of Pasternak's desires and aspirations almost perfectly describes so many of Casey's own protagonists: modest, quiet individuals of mediocre talent seeking to stay out of the public spotlight. His "original sin," as Guevara would have it, has resurfaced. But precisely because of his genuine confessions as a committed intellectual, which in 1960 were sufficient to at least generate a precarious trust between the *barbudos* and the intellectuals, his line of flight goes unnoticed. Paradoxically, Casey's public declarations allow him to be swallowed up in the seemingly homogeneous mass of intellectuals in the Revolution from which he writes his essays and his fiction that seek to restore some sense of individuality to the otherwise homogenized "people"; Casey steps onto the public stage under the light of the Revolution and becomes indistinguishable as an individual, thus opening the possibility for him to disagree with the party line. Pasternak's isolation has the opposite effect; in trying to hide in the periphery and avoid public, political statements, he attracts even more critical attention to himself. From this unnoticed deviation from the party line, what is at stake in Casey's essays is the politics of going unnoticed that he will attempt to disseminate from within the Revolution. For at least a few years, Casey's public image makes it possible for him to write in plain sight along a dissenting, temporarily unnoticed itinerary and still be offered a job at *Casa de las Américas* after *Lunes de Revolución* was closed.

Chapter Five

An Errant Allegory in Argentina

Quite similar to Pasternak, and in stark contrast to Casey, Maximiliano Konsideransky lives alone in his inverted, subterranean tower located somewhere in the provincial lands outside of Río Cuarto, Argentina, and he refuses any and all external contact. Konsideransky is the main character in one of Juan Filloy's "monodialogues" entitled "Yo y los intrusos" from the short story collection *Yo, yo y yo (Monodiálogos paranoicos)* published originally in 1971.[1] He resides alone in order to contemplate the starry skies as he hides himself from all forms of social interaction. At first sight, he might appear as emblematic of the ivory-tower intellectual who severs all ties with the real world in pursuit of higher knowledge. However, in what follows, I analyze Filloy's short story as an ironic rewriting of Plato's "Allegory of the Cave." Through this irony, Filloy's text pries open a threshold for the politics of going unnoticed to take place within a highly saturated political space.

The narrative begins when a man arrives at Konsideransky's front door asking to see the inside of his house and, at the very least, for water for his mule. This provokes Konsideransky's extensive monodialogue in which he explains his state as "un hombre póstumo" who must not be disturbed ("Yo" 129). Konsideransky tries to dismiss his visitor, a reporter with a bunch of new-fangled electronics, but when asked why he has created this refuge, he replies with the following sermon:

> Ya no hay distancias ni discreción. Eso es todo. Antes el mundo ponía muros de distancia y discreción para proteger la intimidad. Ahora no. Siete infames intrusos se han lanzado al abordaje de la felicidad del hombre: el Miedo, la Moral, la Propaganda, la Política, el Cine, la Radio, la Televisión ...

Chapter Five

> Actúan sueltos o en pandilla, desquiciando, mortificando, o trucidando al ser inerme, al *zoon politikon* que pulula en campos y ciudades. Felizmente, ya estoy inmunizado a su influencia deletérea. ¡Libre! ¡Libre en la autonomía de mi soledad! ¡Libre en el goce de mis sentidos! ¡Libre de la despersonalización forzada que embiste por doquiera. (135–36; italics in original)

Konsideransky desires to isolate himself and create a semblance of freedom from these seven infamous intruders. However, his so-called freedom is only gained through isolation and immunization. Aristotle describes such a man in *Politics*: "But he who is unable to live in society, or who has no need because he is sufficient for himself, must be either a beast or a god: he is no part of a state" (Book I, Part II, n.p.). Konsideransky feels he lives up to this definition: standing at 2.7 meters (8'10") tall, he claims to be his own god, priest, faithful worshipper, temple, martyr, shoemaker, tailor, and interlocutor ("Yo" 130–38). He has even sworn off sexual encounters with others: "Me hice entonces onanista: *self-made man*" (137; italics in original). His self-sufficiency is impressive, although no mention is made of how he procures foodstuffs given that he needs thirty percent more than the average man to survive, according to his own calculations (129). He has dedicated his life to restoring the barriers that would allow him privacy, because he believes he has sealed himself away from the seven intruders, or the all-pervasive public sphere and the all-consuming biopolitical relations of the modern state of exception.

The cave-tower is Konsideransky's *magnum opus*, the most recent iteration of an experiment in architectural design that could provide him with a refuge from the overwhelming politicization of his era. Previously, he had attempted to live in the Argentine Pampas, but he found them to be adorned with parrots ("orlas de loros") and was annoyed by the public cries of the roosters ("pregones de gallos") that invaded his desire for silence ("Yo" 137). Then, he moved to "un promontorio en medio del mar," but the flying fish seemed to be "espiando [su] soledad," not to mention the unrelenting waves "golpeando [sus] nervios" (137). Finally, he claims to have found complete solitude within "la desolación y el desierto" of Córdoba Province (133). Now standing at the entrance to his refuge and lecturing the reporter, he launches into a didactic sermon in which his cave-tower becomes an allegory for the need for silence, isolation, and self-contemplation away from the seven infamous intruders—Fear, Morality, Propaganda, Politics, Film, Radio, Television. However, Konsideransky talks without paying attention to the reporter, who is recording and transmitting everything he says back to a radio station in Río Cuarto to be disseminated around the country without his consent (152). He attempts to shelter himself from the seven intruders, but by erecting even more barriers, he creates his own disciplinary cell and facilitates his own surveillance. His masterpiece proves to be as porous and insecure as his former abodes. Thus, the cave-tower is divested of its potential to be read only as a literal allegory. In my analysis, the cave-tower becomes the crossroads for a series of earnest and ironic allegories that pry open various binary divisions of the Argentine political landscape of the Sixties; in that opening, the politics of going unnoticed can take place.

Intruders in Argentine Politics

By reading the list of seven intruders like a palindrome from left to right and back again or by starting in the middle toward both sides, an allegorical reading of Filloy's text centers Politics in the Sixties as the essential intruder, since after all, everything had become political. For my purposes, the capital "P" in "Politics" also can be read as signifying "Peronismo" as the essential intruder in the Argentine political landscape. Throughout the entire period that spans the triumph of Juan Domingo Perón in 1946 to the start of the dictatorship in 1976, the political landscape of the country shifted dramatically and in numerous directions. Silvia Sigal maps the reactions of the Peronists to the Cuban Revolution during the era. At first, many intellectuals equated the fall of Fulgencio Batista to the overthrow of Perón, and as such, many Peronists and leftists were immediately reticent to support Castro. Nevertheless, Sigal traces the varying readings of the Cuban Revolution between 1959 and 1961 that come to identify Castro with Perón, and as a result, "Cuba devino puente entre izquierda, nacionalismo y peronismo" (201). What is curious about this retrospective reading of Perón after the Cuban Revolution is that it transforms Peronism, for some, into its Argentine analog and acquires characteristics that it never had, "forjando la metáfora: el socialismo nacional y el peronismo revolucionario" (202). Of course, this rereading of Peronism by the Peronist youth, who moved toward a revolutionary Marxism made most visible by the Montoneros, provoked a discrepancy with Perón himself and the older generation of Peronists who moved toward the right.[2]

Various faces of Peronism and its various proscriptions and resurgences permeate Argentine politics throughout the Sixties. Despite all of the conflicting and rapidly changing ideologies, Maristella Svampa recalls that Perón's return in 1973 appeared to many groups "como condición necesaria para cualquier transformación social y política, y aún aquellos sectores que no tenían ningún interés en 'peronizarse,' consideraban que sólo su retorno haría posible la pacificación nacional" (389). For my purposes, analogous to the way that there was no outside of the Cuban Revolution after 1961, only an inside and an against, there appeared to be no true outside of Peronism in Argentina. I do not mean to say that there were no other alternatives or dissenting groups in Cuba or Argentina. There were plenty. Rather, the Cuban Revolution and Peronism occupied such highly visible political spaces in their respective countries that it becomes difficult to locate a place to establish a dialogue that does not grapple with those ideologies to some degree. In the most literal, perhaps even simplistic, reading of Konsideransky's cave-tower, he builds this refuge in order to contemplate a politics that is not directly engaged with Peronism.

Nevertheless, three significant contradictions arise from reading Filloy's text as an allegory within the context of my analysis. First, many other major political movements existed in this era in Argentina without direct ties to Peronism. Mónica B. Gordillo demonstrates that in the year 1969, in particular with the Cordobazo and the Rosariazo, the non-Peronist worker protests in the provinces transformed into "rebelión popular" that resulted in the downfall of General Onganía's dictatorship in 1970 (348). Only later did the Montoneros, who did not exist at the time of the Cordobazo, begin to engage in acts of urban guerrilla warfare. These workers, who were not associated with the Montoneros, generally rejected those tactics: "las estrategias armadas aparecían como ajenas a su experiencia y necesidades de trabajadores" (366). Any consideration of the social protests and armed guerrilla groups in this era must take care to distinguish between the different demands and tactics of these heterogeneous groups, not all of which were invested in Peronism nor located in the capital city.

Second, the politics that Konsideransky develops in his cave-tower conflicts with the politics of going unnoticed. Konsideransky hides underground where he cultivates his own political movement: "el yomismo" ("Yo" 146). A first translation of *yomismo* might be "Me-ism," which focuses on the benefit and development of the only person in this party of one. Also, "yo mismo," written as two words, translates literally as "I myself," and it emphasizes the isolation, the purported self-sufficiency, and even the self-indulgence of such a movement. Konsideransky explains that this neologism serves as an alternative to "anarquista" (146). Furthermore, I understand this as an attempt to differentiate himself from any other already named political philosophy, whether it be socialism, communism, liberalism, libertarianism, or even Peronism, Leninism, Trotskyism or Maoism. Though he only speaks of *yomismo* as a political movement, this word also invokes the endless "-isms" created to name the aesthetic movements of the historical avant-gardes (e.g. *creacionismo* and *ultraísmo*). Ironically, his aesthetic sensibilities seem more in line with those of the hermetic ideal of pure art and autonomy cultivated by Latin American *modernismo* than by the self-proclaimed apocalyptic ruptures of the avant-gardes.

The pun created by turning the phrase "yo mismo" into the homophonic name of Konsideransky's own politics and aesthetics challenges the literal reading of this text. He believes he is making his own, individual party, which he would share with no one: "no divido con nadie mis ideas políticas" (146). He does not use the verb *compartir*, but rather *dividir*. The verb *compartir* does not seem to be a part of his extensive vocabulary. To share would be to include others in his movement, which does not interest him; to split his ideas would be, even worse, to break the unity of his individualism, of himself. Yet, any "-ism" always implies a program or a manifesto that, in theory, can be adopted by others. In choosing *yomismo* over something like "Konsideranskismo," a term which could make it more uniquely his, he unwittingly names his political movement in such a way that it can be easily appropriated by someone else. In fact, anyone in the world could adopt *yomismo* as the name by which they elevate their personal opinions into a theory or movement. Thus, Konsideransky is not to be taken seriously, and I prefer to read the politics of *yomismo* ironically, as yet another impossible and unviable political movement for the Sixties.

Third, I find it tempting to draw the parallel between Maximiliano Konsideranksy, the fictional character, and Filloy, the writer. Filloy lived and worked as a judge in Río Cuarto, a city in Córdoba Province, during a period of prolonged silence after the publication of his first works in the 1930s. Though Filloy continued writing in isolation, he returned to publishing in the cultural markets in the 1960s.[3] His short story, "Yo y los intrusos," could almost be read as an idealized, fictional autobiography of the life Filloy might have preferred to live—isolated in an unknown cave-tower in the Argentine provinces. But there is one major difference between Filloy and Konsideransky: Filloy comes out of his isolation and self-imposed editorial silence of his own will and is interrogated by the police in 1976 for the novel *Vil & Vil* that was immediately censured under the new regime, whereas Konsideransky fails to isolate himself within his cave-tower. When the reporter at his door admits he recorded and transmitted their conversation to a radio station that would broadcast it nationally, Konsideransky unleashes a caustic series of insults as the final words of the short story, calling the reporter "hijodeputa," "imbeciloide," "gransodomita," "vómitonegro," and "semendespárrago," among many other inventively offensive phrases (152–53). Konsideransky's fears about the intrusions of the mass media, as it turns out, were well-founded.

Disagreeing with Plato

Overall, this cave-tower fails to isolate him from the seven intruders; when read superficially this allegory would only serve to reinforce the worn-out and historically inaccurate tropes that Peronism was the only politics in Argentina and that intellectuals were either committed to a politics in the street or they were hiding in their isolated, ivory towers. Therefore, I propose to read the allegorical nature of "Yo y los intrusos" *al vesre* and *al verse*, flipping its parts around in order to have them face one another in a new arrangement. As an errant allegory, Filloy's text opens a place within the highly saturated political space already occupied by the various Peronist groups, their so-called internal enemies, the endless list of other Leftist groups, including Marxists, Leninists, Trotskyists, and Maoists, and their political adversaries in the Armed Forces, the Catholic Church, and elsewhere.

An Errant Allegory in Argentina

Reading "Yo y los intrusos" as an errant allegory of the cave-tower raises the question of its relation to Plato's "Allegory of the Cave" in *Republic*. Plato's allegory is one of three interrelated narratives by which Socrates illustrates the transcendental path from the darkness of the likenesses, shadows, and reflections, toward the light of the Good that generates Truth. Leaving the cave and eventually looking at the sun is an allegory for the process of illuminating the intelligence that is necessary to create a community founded on consensus, the Republic. It relies on linear logic, moving from point A, the cave, to point B, the sun, and back again. The light of the sun, as an analog for the Good, guides the philosopher-king toward reason and logic, which will be at the service of him and the legislators as they reign over the Republic.[4] This paternalistic attempt to illuminate the truth for those still chained in the cave is comparable to the task set for the revolutionary intellectuals of the Sixties who sought to make their knowledge communicable to the people. Since Plato, visibility, light, and consensus-building have been set at the heart of the political; without the light of the Good that all are able to perceive, the Republic cannot pass from becoming into being. However, I am not interested in creating such a passage. Going unnoticed, as I have argued, is a form of becoming, a perpetual, everyday movement through various thresholds of perception that does not aim to transcend from invisibility to visibility. It is simply an errant passing, and its politics will arise along this dimly lit path. What I contend is that Filloy's allegory takes a detour from the Platonic text to pry open the essentialized binaries that structure the Greek text and every politics that derives from it.

In *"Khôra"* Derrida interrogates the allegorical qualities of Plato's writings and their totalizing impetus. He argues that *Timaeus* is nothing less than a "general ontology" that "includes a theology, a cosmology, a physiology, a psychology, a zoology" (103). Its encyclopedic scope claims to situate all things, all "mortal or immortal, human and divine, visible and invisible things" (103). Similar to the unchained prisoner in the "Allegory of the Cave," *Timaeus* is constructed as a text that acquires and displays total knowledge. In contrast, what interests Derrida is establishing that the Socratic dialogues written by Plato only succeed in taking the first of many "backward steps" whose *telos* is, in actuality, nothing more than a *mythos*, a fictional origin only accessible through writing ("*Khôra*" 125).⁵ The rational order imagined by Plato is actually a mythical fiction employed to establish a foundational narrative for the Republic that masks an originary void. Derrida enumerates these short fictions that narrate this mythical origin from one to seven (a curious coincidence with Filloy's obsession with the number seven); the first fiction is the dialogue in the *Timaeus*, and the second fiction, "the conversation of the evening before," can be, without saying it must be, Plato's *Republic* and *Politeia* (121). In Derrida's assessment, the Platonic texts actually remain within a space between the origin and the end, between its *mythos* and its *telos*, endlessly rewriting myths and fictions that only supplement the lack of an origin and the lack of an end.

Derrida makes it possible to read Plato's texts outside of Platonism's linear logic, direct analogies, and referential allegories. Thus, the Platonic text, once Derrida is finished with it, becomes an errant fiction. He divests the allegory of its truth-bearing analogies and referentiality and turns it into a fictional text that drifts toward myth. The possibility of transcendence from the visible realm to the intelligible realm, from becoming to being, gets lost in the space opened by this errant writing—the space called "*khôra*." Derrida chooses not to translate the term "*khôra*" because of its semantic density and the irregular ways in which it has been translated by others. He considers it to be a space or a receptacle that opens a gap between *logos* and *mythos*, while articulating the link between them. *Khôra* never possesses what it receives nor does it have a referent in the world: "And in fact, *khôra* will always already be occupied, invested even as a general place, and even when it is distinguished from everything that takes place in it. Whence the difficulty [...] of treating it as an empty or geometric space" (109). *Khôra* opens a place in an already occupied space, but it becomes different from that space even while sharing it; once this opening is located, Derrida is able to read it as the element that ironically undermines Platonism's foundations from within, as that which disagrees with the formerly closed and populated space. *Khôra*, this opening in an already occupied space, is what interests me as the threshold from which the politics of going unnoticed can take place.

At this point, I propose reading Filloy's "Yo y los intrusos" as an errant allegory of the cave-tower, as a rewriting and an opening of Plato's text not unlike the one carried out in Derrida's text, but without passing through Derrida (Filloy's short story was published in 1971, a contemporary of Derrida's 1968 essay "Plato's Pharmacy" and well before his 1987 essay "*Khôra*"). In my analysis, Filloy's errant allegory underscores its own fictionality not only by deviating from the historical reality of Argentina in the Sixties, but also through irony when read alongside Plato's classic text. The cave-tower is not intended as a prison for its inhabitants; this is Konsideransky's refuge from the outside world. This underground fortress, or temple to himself, is built like an upside-down tower that he ascends by going further underground: "Me precipito para arriba hundiéndome en ella. Tengo mis raíces en el aire. Soy un árbol invertido" ("Yo" 133). Instead of leading directly from the depths toward the outside sun, this cave-tower is structured like one of Filloy's palindromes. It is built around "la escalera caracol, por la cual subo y bajo yo, sube y baja mi pensamiento, lo mismo que un destornillador helicoidal. Sin moverme, es obvio, en ninguna faena inútil" (135). This obsessive back-and-forth, spiraling movement in the darkness is so obviously pragmatic for Konsideransky, but it is not so easily perceived as a useful task by everyone else. Unlike the philosopher-king's sovereign aspirations, Konsideransky only desires to stimulate his ability to think and to listen to the echoes of the rocks that surround him as he cultivates silence and solitude. He makes no gesture toward opening his reflections to anyone else, and he certainly is not volunteering his time to promote or document social change. These would be useless tasks for him.

At other moments in the narrative, Filloy's text undermines its own analogically didactic qualities. First, the geometrical perfection of the cave-tower would correspond to the crystalline structure of Filloy's palindromes; however, Filloy's short story opens with an extended four lines of ellipses, and it closes with an unnecessary ellipsis after an exclamation mark: "tu panegírico! ..." (153). While the palindrome is a closed set of perfectly balanced letters that start and end at precise points, exactly like the lesson in Plato's allegory, "Yo y los intrusos" is left open at the beginning and the end. The contrast between the enormous ellipsis at the beginning and the short one at the end throws off the symmetry. These ellipses become indefinite openings toward a before and an after of the plotline that impede the closed, linearity of the

Chapter Five

crystalline palindrome and the classic allegory. Thus, the text acquires the fluidity of an errant palindrome.

Second, the text ironically recreates the structure of a certain branch of testimonial literature that became increasingly popular in the Sixties. The text begins and ends with Konsideransky outside of the cave talking to the reporter. It is written entirely as a long dialogue without the intervention of a third-person narrator. As such, it can be interpreted as the transcription of the reporter's recordings, which had been broadcast ("radiotelefoneada") back to a station in Río Cuarto (152). This story is narrated as an eyewitness, first-person narrative of Konsideransky's life, his politics, and his surroundings. However, he represents the exact image of the bourgeois intellectual obsessed only with his individuality and his elitism. As such, Konsideransky is the last person who would be considered the ideal subject of the sort of testimonial literature that was celebrated in the Sixties. According to John Beverley's classic formulation of the *testimonio* as a genre, the subject must be an underdog who struggles against the status quo, and the text should have an "efecto metonímico," that is, the individual who speaks should be speaking not as an individual but as a voice for the entire community (12). In contrast, Konsideransky speaks only for himself. He does not have the desire or the political urgency to seek the assistance of other intellectuals to tell the world about his story. Despite its formal similarities, this text in no way contains the content frequently documented through *testimonio*, as in the case of Casey's testimonies from soldiers who fought at Playa Girón/Bay of Pigs, or in that of those about the violence committed in the Sixties during events such as the Cordobazo and the massacre at Tlatelolco, or later, as a result of state terrorism and death squads.

Since Konsideransky's biography and the details of his cave-tower are only available to the reporter through the mono-dialogue, the reader of the recorded monodialogue is even one step further removed from it, only having access to the broadcast text. Yet, nothing in the text explicitly claims that the reporter does not believe Konsideransky's story. It is transmitted as a text that upholds a reading pact based on journalistic credibility. Testimonial literature similarly operates as the story of an apparently true, lived experience that could, at least in theory, be verified empirically.[6] In contrast, Konsideransky's cave-tower is a space whose existence can only be verified through his monodialogue, which is to say that it can never be verified empirically. Konsideransky's monodialogue generates a fictional *testimonio* divested of its explicitly referential, verifiable content.

Third, Konsideransky is also dragged up and out of the cave-tower similar to the unchained prisoner in Plato's allegory. Konsideransky is compelled to open the belly-button shaped door when the reporter intrusively arrives at his refuge, but he comes out of the cave to find, not the realm of the intelligible and the light of the sun, but that which forms his ideal world: "la desolación y el desierto" ("Yo" 133). The exterior world surrounding his cave-tower appears to him to be completely empty. Since his name, "Konsideransky," as he explains to the reporter, is etymologically related to *considerare*, which means "contemplar atentamente las estrellas," this deserted landscape is the perfect space where he can contemplate the stars in the night sky while completely alone (138). His surfacing purposefully falls one step short of contemplating the sun in the Platonic text, yet another deviation, and he remains literally at the threshold of his dark cave as he stares at the night sky.

Finally, Konsideransky never reaches Plato's ideal end point, and his return to the cave-tower will not be a journey that seeks to free the other prisoners chained to the wall; he returns only to complete solitude. However, his solitude is belied by a simple detail that he neglected to take into account when constructing his refuge. There is a road that leads through the mountains, directly to his cave-tower. The reporter at one point notes that he was able to ask for directions from another man who lives in the province. The road that leads to the cave-tower serves as the one remaining trace of the line of flight taken by Konsideransky into the Argentine "desert"; his home would have been practically impossible to find if it were not for this path tying his refuge to the provincial city. In this sense, Konsideransky seems to have read the nineteenth-century narratives of the Argentine provinces as a deserted landscape too literally, and he neglected to erase the trail leading to his home. The Argentine "desert" was, of course, already populated by indigenous civilizations, and their land was violently conquered by 1879 during the genocidal Conquest of the Desert.[7] By the mid-twentieth century when this story takes place, numerous cities, ranches, industries, and tourist destinations stretched across the country's interior. It is only Konsideransky, and not Filloy, who believes that the provinces are a deserted space. Ironically, it is the trace Konsideransky left, the path leading to his front door, that leads the reporter directly to his refuge. Whether he desired it or not, Konsideransky's trail created a path that others could follow when he went wandering into the Argentine provinces. Whereas the reading of the cave-tower as allegory would suggest a real desire to construct such a refuge, the narrative turns against the current of Konsideransky's literal enunciations. This errant allegory does not serve as a direct analogy for Konsideransky's explicit ideas and desires; rather, it serves as an allegory for what is only suggested through irony—that there is no such desolate desert, no isolation, no escape, and no transcendence made possible, even with the construction of a cave-tower in the Argentine provinces.

Konsideransky's Ambush

In this errant reading, the politics of going unnoticed acquires the potential to pry open a space between the binary division that simplistically opposes democracy to dictatorship. Peronism was proscribed from the electoral process during two interim, pseudo-democratic regimes—Arturo Frondizi (1958–62) and Arturo Illia (1963–66). Following the victory of the Peronist Héctor Cámpora in 1973, Perón returned to Argentina and secured his third electoral victory, serving as President until his death in 1974. A series of *coups d'états* interrupted these governments in 1955, 1962, 1966, and 1976. Franco and Iglesias detail the difficulty in sustaining a division between democracy and dictatorship during this period in Argentina. First, they show how Argentina's 1853 Constitution already included within it a version of the state of exception—*el estado de sitio*—that could be implemented in the case of external attack or internal commotion. Already under Perón in the 1940s, there were important antecedents to the various laws and "security" measures that would allow for the suspension of the state of law; these became ever more prevalent over the next three decades and were used to justify the 1976 dictatorship (Franco and Iglesias 104). Then, as Cold War pressures came to affect the decisions made by the Armed Forces and the constitutional governments, exceptional measures were seen as the necessary solution to combat both the return of the proscribed Peronists and any other revolutionary ideological positions. All of this, Franco and Iglesias contend, "implicó la identificación entre defensa nacional y seguridad interior y se instaló una concepción bélica del mantenimiento del orden interno" (105). In 1974, Perón established the *Ley de Seguridad*, which was used to combat Marxism, both internal and external to Peronism. These exceptional means were framed by the increasing militarization of the country, in part as a response to the existence of armed guerrilla movements, which aided the Armed Forces in presenting themselves as the necessary, legal response to the threat against national security and in justifying the brutal repression with which they crushed both Peronism and the leftist opposition in 1976 (106). Thus, after considering the various "security measures," Presidential decrees, and military operations that characterize what can be called the Argentine state of exception in the Sixties, it becomes necessary to reframe the binary opposition between democracy and dictatorship.

What, then, is the politics of Filloy's errant allegory? *Yo, yo y yo* was first published in 1971, and there are many parallels to be drawn with the cultural and political landscape of the Sixties in Latin America. The reporter in "Yo y los intrusos" is perplexed by Konsideransky's selfish desire for total isolation and opulence, "no habiendo guerras a la vista ni otros riesgos inminentes" ("Yo" 135). The reporter's naïve statements about the relative peace and stability of the times suggest he is caught up in the euphoria of the era. The collection of short stories was published only two years after the Cordobazo of 1969 and takes place in the outlying regions of Córdoba Province, a time and a place that could barely be described, especially in retrospect, as one without past, present, or foreseeable violent conflicts and confrontations. Certainly, the reporter should have been aware of the imminence of Cold War politics throughout all of Latin America, whether it be in the form of the Cuban embargo or of the CIA's intrusions into almost every country of the region. The reporter, more realistically, seems to be among those who unquestionably championed the need for intellectual commitment during the Sixties and radically opposed any form of autonomous, isolated, or socially useless intellectual activity. In my analysis, this reporter could be among those who contributed to the disfiguring and monstrous foreign press that Casey vehemently attacks in his essay on Pasternak.

Ultimately, the reporter's statement is not justified at any moment in the text; in contrast, Konsideransky uses this naïve claim to launch into the sermon on freedom quoted at the beginning of this section. He decries "este bastión de protesta perenne" against a wide range of topics, from isolation to socialization (136). Then, he offers an extensive list of the ideologies and power brokers that motivated his search for solitude:

> —¡Libre de los grupos de presión y de los grupos de interés! ¡Libre del imperialismo de los poderes de hecho! ¡Libre del gobierno invisible de la plutocracia universal! ¡Libre de la tercera cámara, que constituyen las fuerzas armadas! ¡Libre del cuarto poder de la prensa; del quinto, del clero; del sexto, de los sindicatos; del séptimo, de los estudiantes; del octavo, de los burócratas; del noveno, de la ciudadanía aborregada por los partidos; del décimo, del cretinismo ambiente! ...
> —¡ ... ! ("Yo" 136)

Konsideransky undermines the reporter's optimism about the future by mapping all of the political forces that collude, albeit indirectly, to subdue the citizenry, those *zoon politikon* in both the cities and the countryside, while struggling violently among themselves to establish hegemony over the others. Konsideransky's sermon traces the pressures and power brokers of his time from which he seeks refuge. For him, the world is becoming too mechanized as "the powers that be" attempt to create masses of trivialized human beings with no genuine emotional connections between them. These power brokers, which he organizes into ten groups that include the State, the military, the Church, labor unions, and students, certainly correspond to the major competing voices that came into visible political conflict in the Sixties. The rigorously structured rhetoric of Konsideransky's sermon to the reporter—who only responds with emphatic silences—belies its seeming improvisation. This is the speech of a man who has rehearsed these words over and again in isolation. Konsideransky has been going unnoticed in his cave-tower, lying in wait until he could ambush someone with his monodialogue. Filloy's text registers its dissent with the political and cultural organization of the era while refusing to make choices when only offered false dilemmas; this cave-tower pries open a space between all of these competing ideologies, but it does not pretend to transcend the particular debates of the era in some ideal, autonomous cave-tower.

The politics of going unnoticed is not Konsideransky's *yomismo*. His cave-tower text can be read as one that makes claims about a politics in the Sixties, but only when read as an errant allegory, as one that states its claims through irony. Ultimately, Konsideransky's defense of isolated intellectual practices and autonomous art becomes a comic proposition. The politics of going unnoticed, then, is not the creation of such an autonomous, individual political movement. Even Konsideransky cannot guarantee his position as *yomismo*'s only leader and member, especially after the story of his secret cave-tower and his secret political party is broadcast nationally by the reporter. Not only is it impossible to not be committed, as Casey regrettably explains, but as Filloy's errant allegory suggests through irony, it is also impossible to locate an autonomous space for both politics and aesthetics in the Sixties. In the end, the cave-tower is neither the Platonic cave nor the intellectual's ivory tower, but the space that opens in the already occupied fictional deserts of the Argentine provinces from which one can disagree with the limited options structured around fictional binaries in order to imagine alternatives that have the potential to deactivate them.

Chapter Six

A Nude Woman in Uruguay

Armonía Somers's *La mujer desnuda* was first published in 1950 in the journal *Clima*, but it was not made popularly available until 1966 when it was republished by Arca. In an interview with Campodónico, Somers explains that the National Library purchased almost all of the copies of the first edition of *La mujer desnuda*, and the director of the Library had sent them around the world: "Es decir que *La mujer desnuda*, realmente, no se difundió en Montevideo, la revista [*Clima*] fue para ciertas élites y la separata fue adquirida por la Biblioteca. De tal manera, la novela siguió siendo un mito, porque se hablaba de ella pero muy pocos la conocían" ("Diálogo" 255). Though Somers was outright rejected as a serious writer for having written a supposedly pornographic novel, only a few people actually read it when it first appeared, and it went almost completely unnoticed internationally. In this chapter, I analyze how Somers's nude woman attempts to restore her own potentiality for dissent and disagreement while going unnoticed in the context of Uruguay.

La mujer desnuda opens with a grotesque, fantastical scene. On her thirtieth birthday, Rebeca Linke flees from her family home in the city to a cabin she bought in the woods. There she takes off her only article of clothing—an overcoat that allowed her to travel unnoticed by train—reaches for a dagger, and cuts off her own head: "La cabeza rodó pesadamente como un fruto. Rebeca Linke vio caer aquello sin alegría ni pena" (18). At first, it might be argued that Linke has become hysterical and overreacted to an early mid-life crisis, only to be relieved in an affectless state, her death. However, the first sentence of the novel establishes the banality of this day: "El día en que Rebeca Linke cumplió los treinta años, comenzó con lo que ella había imaginado siempre, a pesar de una secreta ilusión en contra: la nada" (15). The day seemed to be of little importance, one in which nothing ordinary nor extraordinary would occur. The narrator further describes the day as "apenas como un aburrido bostezo de verano igual a tantos" (15). This stands in direct opposition to the decapitation scene that follows this opening frame, but what is certain is that her thirtieth birthday, on an otherwise meaningless day, becomes the symbolic catalyst for her to open a line of flight. As Deleuze and Guattari sustain, "We can be thrown into a becoming by anything at all, by the most unexpected, most insignificant of things" (292). Such a seemingly minor, everyday event is all it takes to send Linke down this errant path.

The fourth paragraph registers a second beginning for the novel. Linke steps out of the spotlight and almost disappears from sight: "Todo empezó así, entonces: que ella fuese retrocediendo inconscientemente en un escenario vulgar y desapareciera de la vista" (*Mujer* 15). There is an uncertainty in these actions, and the narrator hesitates to tell them as fact. Moreover, the narrator frequently slips in and out of Linke's consciousness, at times narrating her thoughts as if they were shared by the narrator, at times commenting on the events of the story as if from an omniscient perspective. As Marjorie Agosín explains, the entire novel is written "como una serie de monólogos circulares donde la realidad exterior y la interior emergen entrelazadas" (586). In this second beginning in which the distinction between inside and outside, self and other, is lost, Linke begins to create an opening in her life by going unnoticed of her own volition.

Similar to Konsideransky's cave-tower, Linke's cabin establishes certain resemblances with Plato's "Allegory of the Cave." Once she arrives at the little house, she removes her overcoat and falls into a sort of trance under the moonlight that filters through the blinds, "el rayado blanco y negro" (*Mujer* 17). The light of the moon creates the effect of prison bars that simultaneously cover and expose her nude body, symbolically imprisoning her in this cabin. As with Filloy's cave-tower, this narrative is not a simple reconstruction of the Platonic text. The prisoner in Plato's allegory is unchained by some unnamed source, whereas Linke breaks her own symbolic chains. She remembers that she has a small dagger, "una obra de arte," tucked inside a book that will be apt "para decapitar a una mujer prisionera" (18). This small work of art will become the means by which she attempts to produce a clean break with the past and free herself, but she does not plan to return to her cabin as in the Platonic text, nor does she desire to hide from the world. Here Linke produces an opening in an already occupied space—a national political context characterized by patriarchal restrictions on women's bodies and by the state of exception—and from that opening, she will step out into the world as a nude woman, a bare life, who has recovered her potentiality to engage in dissent and disagreement.

The Uruguayan Exception

Uruguay was known as the Switzerland of South America in the first half of the twentieth century, ever since the Partido Colorado's candidate, José Batlle y Ordóñez, became President. The country's strong, two-party democratic institutions were celebrated in contrast to its surrounding neighbors, Argentina and Brazil, who had engaged each other in war in the nineteenth century for control of the Banda Oriental, as Uruguay was known in Spanish, or the Cisplantina, as it was known in Portuguese. By the end of World War II, Uruguay was praised internationally for its economic growth and stability, which were dependent upon the regulations made by the Welfare State.[1] Despite the differences with the Cuban Revolution and with Argentina's frequent alternations between democracy and dictatorship, Uruguay's so-called model democracy also made frequent recourse to the state of exception—known in the 1830 Constitution as *medidas prontas de seguridad* in case of external attack or internal commotion—since the beginning of the twentieth century (Iglesias 132).[2] Between 1946, the year in which Batllismo consolidated its power under Luis Batlle Berres, and 1973, the year in which the Armed Forces began the dictatorship known euphemistically as "el Consejo de Seguridad Nacional," the *medidas prontas de seguridad* were increasingly invoked as a political strategy oriented toward maintaining the sociopolitical order dominated by the two ruling parties, the Partido Colorado and the Partido Nacional. This two-party state felt the need to reaffirm its centrality and superiority over "cualquier colectivo social—tanto patronal como asalariado—que pretendiera erigirse en representante de intereses sociales específicos por fuera de instancias controladas por ellos" (148). The Uruguayan state invoked these exceptional measures

Chapter Six

in order to guarantee the transition between the two parties to the exclusion of any others.

With the growing tensions of the Cold War, the "threat" invoked in order to justify recourse to this Uruguayan variant of the state of exception became, first, Communism and, later, the armed urban guerrillas known as the Tupamaros. Abril Trigo argues that in Uruguay the Cuban Revolution "destapó los demonios y los echó a andar por las calles de nuestra gris Montevideo" (186). As he contends, the possibility of a political revolution exposed many tensions that had been hidden behind the apparently peaceful, two-party democracy, and it is in this context that the Movimiento de Liberación Nacional-Tupamaros (MLNT) attempted to alter the status quo by making frequent reference to Uruguay's nineteenth-century civil wars. The MLNT, Trigo writes, "le lleva a recordar [a los detentadores del *statu quo*] que la guerra civil fue el recurso habitual del pueblo uruguayo en la primera mitad de su vida independiente. Que los mismos partidos tradicionales, hoy vocingleramente pacifistas, fueron los protagonistas de aquellas 'patriadas' en las cuales nacieron" (205). The Tupamaros, in this sense, evoked a strange mixture of national history with a revolutionary present as they visibly and violently rebelled against the traditional parties, but they would not succeed. For Trigo, the Tupamaros attempted "salvar los restos del naufragio," those of the sinking Uruguayan state, rather than provoke a more profound revolution (206).

By July of 1970, the violence had escalated, and on April 15, 1972, the recently elected Juan María Bordaberry declared a state of internal war—a state of exception—and suspended the Constitution. As Thomas C. Wright explains, approximately six hundred Tupamaros were captured and one hundred killed by July 15, 1972, but the counterinsurgency measures were not dropped, leading to labor unrest, political protests, and allegations of military involvement in death squads and brutal treatment of prisoners. In reaction to this popular unrest, and not just to the existence of urban guerrilla cells, "Bordaberry acceded to the gradual militarization of his government until the culminating coup of June 1973, when he closed congress and municipal governments and began to rule by decree with a military-civilian cabinet" (101). Under this more generalized state of exception, which by 1973 was no longer shrouded in democratic robes, the

Tupamaros were quickly eliminated by the militarized state that remained in power until 1985.

Linke's Flight and Decapitation

La mujer desnuda predates the dictatorship by over two decades, but the democratic state's recourse to the state of exception stretches over this entire period. On the one hand, it is possible to read Linke's cabin as an attempt to go unnoticed within this generalized state of exception. On the other, Linke's ability as an unmarried woman to legally abandon her home on her thirtieth birthday provides a more concrete reference to a specific legal context within the Uruguayan state. As María Rosa Olivera-Williams argues, Linke's dependency refers to the Uruguayan Civil Code in operation in 1950 that constructed an eternal dependency for all women, considering a woman to be "'incapacitada' para abandonar la casa de sus padres si no se había casado—sujeto que no había alcanzado la mayoría de edad—hasta los treinta años" (32). This patriarchal partitioning of all female bodies made possible by this particular Civil Code within the generalized state of exception becomes a more specific point of contention for Linke. Toward the end of the novel she explains what she was thinking as she chose to run away:

> Que yo diera en mirar a los demás en la forma cómo serían otros treinta después, con las voces cascándose, el pellejo colgado que ellos se estiran a veces con los dedos para crearse un segundo de ilusión, el sexo con los verbos ya sin conjugar, y el miedo de morir desprevenidos al acostarse cada noche. (*Mujer* 95)

After seeing these aging guests and imagining living the next thirty years just to end up like all of them, she decides to take advantage of the legal freedom she has finally been granted in this patriarchal society. At the first moment it becomes legally possible to do so, she flees to the cabin.

Briefly, Linke experiences her flight and decapitation as a clean break with the past: "Empezó desde ese instante a acaecer el nuevo estado" (19). Nevertheless, Linke does not stage a protest, found a guerrilla army, or fight to overturn the laws that created eternal dependency for all women; up to this point, she does not

Chapter Six

contest the biopolitical organization of the Uruguayan state in any meaningful way. She waits until she has been legally permitted to leave, flees in the night, sits alone in her cabin, and cuts off her own head. When read in the context of national politics in this era, it becomes difficult to establish an allegorical reading of *La mujer desnuda* that would lead to any relevant political or social change. Suspecting the inefficacy of her actions, the narrator asks a rhetorical question: "¿Era posible que el mundo deslizante se hubiese solucionado así, de un golpe seco?" (19). The unwritten answer would be in the negative. Her flight and decapitation will not produce a clean break with the past. There can be no escape, because there is no outside; there can be only the possibility of opening an errant path within the cultural and political maps of the era.

Linke's decapitated body decides, by unexplained means, it is time to return to the world. She eventually stands up, picks up her severed head, places it on a pedestal, and takes "algunos pasos atrás buscando el efecto en la penumbra" (21). Somehow, her body without eyes or ears is capable of observing her decapitated head as if it were a sculpture on display in a poorly lit museum. Then, she becomes scared: "Vio de pronto con terror que la hemorragia persistía, y que el rostro empalidecido mortalmente clamaba por su sangre" (21). The non-existent eyes from her body see her dying head, and her non-existent ears hear the demands it makes of her. She decides that now is the time to restore her head to her body: "Se hacía, pues, impostergable volver a lo anterior, tornar a echarse el pensamiento encima, construir de nuevo el universo real con las estrellas siempre arriba y el suelo por lo bajo, según esquemas primitivos" (21). What was experienced at first as a radical break becomes unsustainable; she must reconstruct the spatial configuration of the stars above and the earth below, of a world that functions according to a Cartesian notion of physical space and a Newtonian physics of predictable interactions between objects in that space. After experiencing a fantastical form of audio-visual observation that does not pass through the ears or the eyes, she labels those classic paradigms as primitive, because they are based solely on empirical observations of the visible, audible world. She then picks up her head and puts it on "como un casco de combate" (21). The wounds quickly heal themselves, restoring her ability to see and hear through her eyes and ears. Now geared up, she prepares to set back out into the world, completely nude.

Her decapitation will not produce a definitive rupture with the state of exception or the paternalistic world in which she lives. From the cabin where she finally goes unnoticed under the paternalistic gaze of her family and of the Civil Code, Linke acquires the potential to engage in dissent, a potentiality that previously had been obstructed. In "On Potentiality," Agamben studies Aristotle's *Metaphysics* and *De anima* to consider the relationship between *dynamis* and *energeia*, potentiality and actuality. In Agamben's reading of Aristotle, *energeia* or actuality corresponds to the light, whereas *dynamis* or potentiality corresponds to darkness. However, Agamben argues, when one sees, one actualizes one's potential for sight, that is, for the perception of light: "when we do not see (that is, when our vision is potential), we nevertheless distinguish darkness from light; *we see darkness*" (180–81; italics in original). In this perception of darkness when light is absent, there is still the potential for sight even though one is not actually seeing. Linke comes to see the darkness of her situation, the nothingness, "la nada," that takes over the day of her birthday and convinces her to flee (*Mujer* 15). Furthermore, Agamben claims that potentiality is more than the ability to do one thing or another: "The greatness—and also the abyss—of human potentiality is that it is first of all potential not to act, *potential for darkness*" ("On Potentiality" 181; italics in original). Potentiality is both the potential to act and the potential to not act; it is the ability to do something and the ability to refuse to do something, at the same time. As such, the space of potentiality is a threshold in which decisions can still be made. If this space were to foreclose the possibility of choosing evil over good or vice versa, then there would be no possible choice, no actual state of potentiality. Potentiality, then, is this opening of a threshold in a space already occupied by innumerable normative demands, both political and moral; in this threshold, decisions can be made, for better or for worse, to agree or to disagree with those demands. Going unnoticed opens such a threshold in which dissent becomes possible for those seemingly unimportant people, those bare lives whose ideas and voices remain unattended and who have no chance or no desire to participate in a state that has ignored and abandoned them. The

Chapter Six

politics of going unnoticed restores potentiality by opening a space in which anyone can register their dissent, can assume their right to do, to not do, and to resist or refuse to do an action.

Perhaps for the first time in her life, Linke acquires potentiality at the moment she decides to cut off her own head, and she takes advantage of this when she leaves the cabin and returns to the world. Of course, her unnoticed actions are never offered as a moral imperative to be followed by others; there is no discernible end goal explained in the text, no *a priori* manifesto to be fulfilled upon her successful decapitation. In the description of the act itself, Linke symbolically divests herself of her clothes as she attempts to sever all ties to her past by cutting off her own head. Though she struggles to achieve this act, she is both physically capable of this gruesome gesture and of refusing to do it; she puts up no resistance even when the dagger seems to acquire its own agency:

> La mano que quiere alcanzarla [la daga] no puede. Derriba el vaso con agua de la mesa y queda allí como una flor congelada. Es entonces cuando la daga va a demostrar que ella sí sabe hacerlo, y se desplaza atraída por las puntas de unos dedos. Claro que hacia una mano que está adherida a un brazo, que pertenece a su vez a un cuerpo con cabeza, con cuello. Una cabeza, algo tan importante sobre eso tan vulnerable que es un cuello … El filo penetró sin esfuerzo, a pesar del brazo muerto, de la mano sin dedos. Tropezó con innumerables cosas que se llamarían quizás arterias, venas, cartílagos, huesos articulados, sangre viscosa y caliente, con todo menos el dolor que entonces ya no existía. (*Mujer* 18)

The dagger is said to demonstrate that "ella" does know how to cut off Linke's head. The narrator achieves a grammatical ambiguity with regard to the antecedent of this pronoun, one of many stylistic traits by which Somers creates enigmas throughout her work. In this instance, "ella" can both mean "she" in reference to Linke and "it" in reference to the dagger, a grammatically feminine noun, impeding any attempt to decipher exactly who or what is being referenced. With the double reading, the dagger shows Linke how to cut off her own head and that it is capable of cutting off her head for her. Somers's grammatical ambiguity impedes the distinction between the woman and the dagger, between subject and object, between a living person and an inanimate thing. All the while, the narrative alternates between Linke's somewhat disembodied point of view and a third-person description of the events by the narrator or, perhaps, by the now animate dagger. In my analysis, these three perspectives are practically and purposefully indistinguishable; one phrase may be read in multiple ways like an errant palindrome that blurs distinctions between forms of life at the everyday level. This dagger-woman or woman-dagger acquires a potentiality of her own for the first time as she attempts to nullify the partitions that have structured her entire life.

After she decides to restore her head to her body, she chooses to leave the solitude of her cabin, which served only as a temporary threshold, and sets out into the world completely nude. She hesitates for just a moment while reaching for the door: "Hasta que la mano, retardándose algo más de lo común sobre las cosas, consiguió abrir la puerta luego de un crispamiento largo sobre el pomo" (21). Following this sentence is a large blank space, offering a visual opening within the narrative itself as she returns to the world. On the other side of the white space, Linke immediately struggles to orient herself: "Rebeca Linke sufrió un repentino vértigo. Quiso dominarlo aferrándose a algo. No había nada próximo" (22). The definitiveness of that last phrase, uncharacteristically short and concise within Somers's ambling syntax and endless sentences, shatters the fantasy of freedom. She experiences the open as pure, vertiginous abandonment. Nevertheless, she decides to persist: "Nunca había andado descalza sino en la alfombra o en la arena. Pero decidió soportar sin protestas los espinos" (22). She traverses the prairie, observes her body and the lines in her hand under the moonlight; for the briefest moment, nothing is there to support her, but there is also nothing that seems to stand in her way as she continues unnoticed along her errant path.

The politics of going unnoticed will not be an easy task, nor will it be without risks to those who step out of their disciplined space as in the case of Linke. Stepping into the open prairie is also stepping out of her unnoticed threshold; at the edge of the prairie she notices something else: "La vigilaban miles de ojos ocultos, la trituraban miles de dientes" (23). Not only does the prairie not provide any support, but also it is occupied by others who immediately notice, keep watch over, and threaten this nude woman who has stepped out of the place designated for her. The danger is evident: "le pareció, de pronto, que el bosque la había identificado, que la estaba espiando [y] lo cierto fue que la envolvió de repente en un silencio brutal, esa mudez de conspiración en muchedumbre" (23). This threat foreshadows the violence of the second half of the novel, but for the moment, she walks into the forest and wanders around until she comes into contact with other people.

First Encounter: Nataniel's Chains

Of the many encounters that take place in this novel between Linke and the townspeople, three are of interest for my analysis; they range from barely making contact, to provoking an angry mob with her nude body, and in the final encounter, to establishing a fleeting moment of dialogue with one other person who attempts to understand her dissent. First, Linke stumbles into a shack in the forest, where she disturbs a sleeping man, Nataniel, who is in bed with his wife. In a dream state, he starts to speak to her, unable to figure out exactly who she is. She tells him to touch her: "Ven, toca, estoy desnuda. Tomé mi libertad y salí. He dejado los códigos atrás, las zarzas me arañaron por eso" (27). At the moment he almost awakens, he forces himself upon his sleeping wife. Seeing this, Linke fears that this new phase of her life will come to an end: "Volvería a ocurrir lo de siempre, los bienes compartidos con miedo, el mundo del engaño y del robo, otra vez las inmundas ropas cubriéndola" (28). She runs out of the shack, knocking things over, and leaves Nataniel behind. In this first encounter, she barely peeks her head out of her unnoticed threshold, quick to run away before he realizes what has happened, since she does not know what he might do to her. Later, she mocks him because of "los cerrojos en que viviría aun sin creerse prisionero" (33). Though she finds another person still chained in the darkness, as in the Platonic allegory, she does not actually free him; rather, fearful that he will drag her back inside and shackle her to the wall, she prefers to run back into the forest at night.

Second Encounter: The People's Terror

The second encounter takes place with the townspeople as a whole, and it will prove her fears of losing her newly acquired potentiality to be well-founded. In *The Open*, Agamben defines the anthropological machine as the mechanism by which, in both ancient and modern times, the notion of man has been produced "through the opposition man/animal, human/inhuman" that presupposes the existence of man: "the machine necessarily functions by means of an exclusion (which is also always already a capturing) and an inclusion (which is also always already an exclusion)" (37). The space of exception at the center of this articulation is "perfectly empty," and what results when a human being is placed in that empty center is "a life that is separated and excluded from itself—only a *bare life*" (38; italics in original). In my analysis, from the moment Linke becomes the woman-dagger or dagger-woman, "ella" not only recovers her potentiality but importantly occupies and exposes the emptiness and contingency of the division that marks the boundary between man and animal, human and inhuman.

Engaging in the politics of going unnoticed is to attempt to deactivate or render inoperative these pervasive, divisive machines without first securing a visible position within the governing institutions and everyday practices that power them. Though the divisions they create allow a body to partake in the political process, they also form the trap of biopolitics; they divide humans into competing, disciplined categories that facilitate the total surveillance and control of those very bodies who at the same time are expected to accept these divisions as perfectly natural and carry out the roles assigned to them. The threshold in which one goes unnoticed pries open the space between the dichotomies created by the biopolitical machine, rendering some of the partitions it creates inoperative, in order to restore the potential for dissent and disagreement to that person. In *The Use of Bodies*, Agamben warns that those who inhabit "the central emptiness" separating man and animal, or between any of the other biopolitical dichotomies, must know that to do so is "to risk ourselves in this emptiness" (92). Linke is such a bare life, a nude woman, who has occupied this empty space between man and animal, human and inhuman, man and woman, and risked her own life in order to deactivate this dividing machine, albeit temporarily.

At the first sight of dawn, the narrator explains that Linke had not planned anything beyond her decapitation: "Su desnudez, su libre determinación, habían comenzado con la noche y sin mañana previsible" (*Mujer* 34). Now her nude body and her

Chapter Six

newfound potentiality are about to be fully revealed under the morning light to the world around her. Along her errant path, she comes to the outskirts of a small town that she describes as a "zona de peligro": "Esa área sin relieve y la luz creciente la estaban convirtiendo [a Linke] en un blanco perfecto" (37). She runs into two men, twins, who are shocked at their discovery: "¡una mujer desnuda en medio del campo!" (38). They run back to the sleepy town and interrupt everyone's daily routine:

> Fue en aquella sucesión vulgar de circunstancias, donde nunca ocurriera nada fuera de ordeñar las vacas y transportar los tarros al tren lechero, sembrar, casarse y tener hijos que harían después las mismas cosas, incluso ir el domingo a la iglesia, morir, continuar pasándose el apellido, donde prendió la noticia de los gemelos. (42)

This life ordered only by habit, by the tacit and unreflective acceptance of the biopolitical organization of these people's lives, is described with utmost disdain. Linke's disruptive actions, the recovery of her potential, is immediately rejected by everyone in this town. As Núria Calafell Sala explains, their rejection results from the fact "que ni saben leer el mensaje de Rebeca Linke ni pueden llegar a comprenderlo" ("Sabotaje" n.p.). Linke's nude body presents itself as an enigma that cannot and will not be deciphered by these people. Faced with this problem, the twins decry what they do not understand as an "escandaloso amoralismo," and they form an "ejército bárbaro" to hunt her down, justified only because it acquired "el matiz popular" (*Mujer* 43). Nataniel will be one of the few who refuses to join the angry mob despite his lack of comprehension. In the light of day, this nude woman will be subjected to the violence of a popular will that intends only to maintain the status quo despite the poor quality of life it requires of all of them. As a bare life, Linke has been banned and abandoned by the law; therefore, she may be sacrificed for walking down this errant path and stepping out of the place assigned to her.

Before they become an angry mob, the townspeople turn to their local priest for guidance. He offers his paternalistic recommendation: "vuelve a tus hijos, tu campo, tus quehaceres humildes" (58). Soon after, he explains to one woman that "la vida en escala pequeña [...] me han dicho algunas mujeres aquí mismo, es suficiente para conquistar la paz que se ha extraviado" (59). The priest's primary goal is to prevent Linke's dissent from spreading to those around her, because this would awaken them from the slumber of their small lives and could incite a larger revolt. The priest's actions may be understood as representative of the institutional desire to achieve the total management of bare life, which is one way of defining totalitarianism, whether it take place within a democracy, a dictatorship, or a revolutionary state. According to Agamben, twentieth-century totalitarianism—more than carrying out the last great tasks of nineteenth-century nation-states, "nationalism and imperialism"—has taken on the task of managing bare life itself in the generalized state of exception when all other historical duties appear to have been lost: "Do we not see around and among us men and peoples who no longer have any essence or identity [...] and who grope everywhere, and at the cost of gross falsifications, for an inheritance and a task, *an inheritance as task*?" (*Open* 76; italics in original). When faced with the loss of an inheritance, an essence, an identity, a history, a purpose in life, individuals and peoples can be enticed by the promise of authoritarian, totalizing control; even as such control further divides them from one another and restricts their potentiality, these defined roles and places purport to restore meaningful, historical tasks to the people. This is what Somers's priest offers the angry townspeople too late.

The impetus toward the total biopolitical management of a community is not strictly enforced from above. The townspeople in the novel form, borrowing a term from Beasley-Murray, what may be considered a multitude, but one that brings "death rather than life, setting off a chain reaction" that cannot be attributed to the state (257). As Somers's narrator explains, they choose to punish Linke for exposing their lost inheritance and their total lack of potentiality under a regime that divides and controls them:

> En cuanto a la mujer, aquel desnudo les había recordado con demasiada insistencia lo que ellos se cubrían. La criatura desvestida tras el desasosiego que arrojara en sus lechos, les acababa de traer el terror de sus almas en descubierto, el soñarse pesadillescamente con sus rencores al viento, con sus pequeñas miserias sin cortinado espeso. (*Mujer* 108)

Desiring to return to the habit of their routines, despite it not being a particularly easy or satisfying life, Linke's nude body reveals everything this community had been ignoring, its miserable living conditions and the resentment and pain that accompanies such a life: "Cómo no condenar, entonces, aquella desnudez que obligaba a las suyas" (78). Linke has recovered her potentiality, and her nude body only forces them to recognize everything that they lack. In their desperate haste to cover everything once more, but also in their rage against their own misery, they turn into a destructive mob that sets fire to the priest's home—who now regrets his appraisal of the nude woman—before hunting down Linke "con sus picas, sus horquillas, sus palas" (107). Not unlike what Trigo describes as the reaction caused by the Cuban Revolution in the Uruguayan imaginary, the townspeople's violence is a reaction to having the lid taken off their demons. In order to return things to the way they were, this community decides to eliminate the nude woman in Uruguay who irreparably revealed what they had all been hiding and can serve as their scapegoat. With such a violent act, the mob seeks to close the opening created by Linke. They chase her, she flees toward the river, and the final image of the novel is that of her bruised, nude body floating face down through the river in the forest.

The state of exception forecloses the communal space to any actor who seeks to open it through dissent, and this closure is all too often reinforced by everyday actions. The threat, which is also the appeal, of this sort of totalitarianism has not waned after the return to democracy in the Southern Cone nor after the death of Fidel in Cuba; the Pink Tide has begun to subside in Latin America, and everywhere in the West today authoritarian politics is winning even at the supposedly democratic polls. The biopolitical machine is churning faster every day, and increasing numbers of people negatively affected by it have become its ardent supporters. This choice to defend these biopolitical divisions, this demand from below that everyone else give up their potentiality and accept the structures and laws that violently order their lives from above, has become the biggest obstacle to creating equality and justice within a radically democratic framework today.

Third Encounter: Juan's Dissent

The remaining question, therefore, is what does the politics of going unnoticed achieve if Casey has to flee the authoritarian institutions that rise in Cuba, if Konsideransky's cave-tower can only be read ironically, and if Linke dies in the end? Before Linke's death, the narrator explains the following about her: "Odiaba desde siempre las moralejas, rechazaba las conclusiones finales y los mitos que las generan en un mundo que de pronto se abre en volcán, en aluvión de lodo, en silencio de sombra que anda en busca del cuerpo desintegrado" (Somers, *La mujer desnuda* 119). The politics of going unnoticed proposes a different reaction and a different type of decision-making. In reaction to a space that is suddenly thrust open, like the townspeople's world when confronted by the nude woman, Linke rejects the narratives that attempt to justify the violent actions that would return the spewing ash and flowing mud to its former place or too quickly talk over the silence of that disembodied shadow. Linke knows the failure of this politics is not a historical necessity, nor are the biopolitical divisions naturalized by these townspeople. She accepts the risk of occupying that central emptiness in order that a radically other politics might become possible.

This is when the third important encounter takes place. Her politics does have a significant impact on one man in particular: Juan. Going unnoticed cannot restore the conditions of possibility for a radically democratic politics of dissent in the open if it were to only guarantee potentiality for the one who goes unnoticed; this would be to follow the model of Pasternak or to accept Konsideransky's *yomismo* literally. As the townspeople seek the guidance of the priest and then eventually turn on Linke, she and Juan engage in a different sort of relationship. They have a long, meandering conversation in which he at first attempts to domesticate her, to end the suffering he assumes to be the result "de su soledad, de su abandono" (98). However, he listens to her reaction: "No, Juan, yo no sufro" (98). She explains that she does not desire to go back to her previous life, to be subjected once more to a man who makes decisions for her.

After their romantic encounter, Juan is attacked by the mob, and the entire town is about to catch fire as the flames spread. With the flickering firelight threatening them from one side and the murderous townspeople from the other, in his dying moments Juan may not completely understand Linke's intentions or actions; he never truly solves the enigma of her nude body. However, her presence has caused a sudden change for him, finally allowing her to be as she now is, as she has chosen to be. He says to her: "Tú, yo, nosotros ... La voz había surgido de la nada. Quedaba suspendida en el aire con la misma ingravidez de una pluma, una hoja" (114). In a dialogue that foreshadows the ethical encounters I analyze in the final chapters, despite the untraversable distance between them, this "nosotros" that barely forms from their attempted dialogue hangs softly in the air. Juan insists that Linke run away and leave his dying body behind; he wants the last thing he sees to be the backs of her legs as she tries to escape the mob. Juan attempts to engage her on her own terms, and his only demand is for her "caminar, irse" (118). As she leaves, she reflects on her situation: "No habría futuro para el amor, pensó, apenas si un breve presente, tan precario como intenso" (118). Their encounter lasted no longer than the flash of a present that exposed her to him. By engaging her in dialogue, he also steps out of his habits and routines; in the end, he only insists that she continue along her errant path, that she not abandon this politics. Juan is the only person in this narrative that encourages her to keep walking along her errant path, to continue the politics of going unnoticed, and to produce future openings in other unexplored territories.

This is not a huge success given that both Linke and Juan die, but she did achieve a first, rough start for the arduous task of restoring her potentiality and opening a space for dissent and disagreement where it had been previously blocked. This politics, difficult as it is to carry out alone, becomes incredibly fraught with tensions and literal threats as those who go unnoticed step out of their threshold and become perceived by a broader community. What I have mapped in this chapter have only been the rough starts toward a politics that becomes possible by going unnoticed. The failures of those who go unnoticed to revolutionize an entire society, to ensure radically democratic institutions, should not erase the real impact that they leave in their wake. Linke's nude body had a profound, transformative effect on at least one other person. It may only be a small change in a complex society governed by massive institutions, but it is a change that affects another human being. She has created a slightly better situation for one person, even if this small, temporary intervention did not incite a structural revolution.

Of the political gestures I have analyzed to this point, Linke exemplifies the importance of stepping out from thresholds in which one's actions go unnoticed. The politics of going unnoticed can be successful only insofar as it deactivates the divisive machines that erect partitions between individuals and throughout communities. Once a barrier has been rendered inoperative, those who go unnoticed will need to step out of their thresholds and be perceived by others. Casey's exile and Linke's death warn of the real dangers of engaging in a politics of dissent and disagreement. However, in the following chapters, I analyze the aesthetics and ethics of this politics that opens an errant path for engaging with other individuals and for constructing new forms of community between them. The aesthetics of writing in plain sight attempts to render inoperative narratives founded on essentialist fictions about the need to purify the body politic from the radical other, whereas the ethics of being perceived then engages that other in an open, unending dialogue that recasts the enemy as an adversary to be included in the political community. Deactivating these divisive machines may be an endless, arduous task, but the aesthetics and ethics that I derive from the politics of going unnoticed provide a series of tools for breaking open these partitions wherever they may be built.

PART THREE

The Aesthetics of Writing in Plain Sight

> Y yo pienso, no puedo dejar de pensar, en cuántas
> cosas tuvimos a la vista pero nunca vimos realmente.
> Porque no sabíamos en qué dirección y ángulo mirar.
> Porque nunca miramos dentro de ciertas sombras.
> Jorge Enrique Lage, "Epílogo" (44–45)

To go unnoticed is not to be invisible. The protagonists who go unnoticed do so in plain sight of all those around them. For some, going unnoticed is simply the unfortunate result of being perceived as unimportant, whereas for others it provides an opportunity to carry out prohibited or discouraged tasks. In the following chapters, I analyze the narrative forms used by Calvert Casey, Juan Filloy, and Armonía Somers to represent their unnoticed protagonists without revealing every aspect of their lives under the harsh lights of the public sphere. Though not an aesthetic movement in the traditional use of the term, the texts under consideration here coalesce around a practice that I call "writing in plain sight." Writing in plain sight is a tactic that allows one to attend to what has always been apparent on the surface of hegemonic politics, to all those things, as Jorge Enrique Lage writes, that "tuvimos a la vista pero nunca vimos realmente" (44).

By writing in plain sight, these authors pry open and transform the visible but unnoticed narratives that underwrite hegemonic politics. This process takes place through Filloy's intervention into the gaucho genre, Somers's appropriation of family romance and cookbooks, and Casey's exploration of Havana's sewers and nightlife. Despite the differences in content, their works overlap at key points. Casey and Filloy write primarily within national traditions. Filloy and Somers are quite explicit in their rewritings of nineteenth-century texts. Somers and Casey share an intimate exploration of the human body, its illnesses, and its waste. By looking at the visible but unnoticed surface of discourse, each author divests politicized traditions of their burdensome symbolic weight and reconfigures essentialist myths that only serve the interests of the ruling elite.

My own work here as critic should not be mistaken as engaging the type of method envisioned, for example, by Fredric Jameson in *The Political Unconscious*. For Jameson, the task of the critic is not only to historicize but also to reveal an underlying and repressed ideology at work in a text through the tension generated between what is present and what is absent. He defines this method as one in which "the 'false' and the ideological can be unmasked and made visible" (53). My intention is not to challenge this method *tout court*, but rather to insist that other critical tools are necessary, because on the one hand, as Beasley-Murray reminds, "it is not as though the workings of power are hidden" (205). They often lie in plain sight, albeit ignored, on the surface. On the other, as Verónica Garibotto argues in her analysis of the reappearance of nineteenth-century texts and tropes in contemporary literature, "La reemergencia del pasado lejano excede la voluntad alegórica" (5). These rewritings engage an allegorical mode of writing, but they are always in excess of that mode of allegory in which the past is only a veil for the present.

Attending to those who go unnoticed and to what they write and rewrite in plain sight is not a heroic activity. It is not an attempt to scour the depths of something like the Sator Square or to solve the enigma of Linke's nude body and ultimately reveal their true, underlying, or repressed meaning. In this sense, my method more closely relates to the various practices Stephen Best and Sharon Marcus unite under the banner of surface reading: "we take surface to mean what is evident, perceptible, apprehensible in texts; what is neither hidden nor hiding [...]. A surface is what insists on being looked *at* rather than what we must train ourselves to see *through*" (9; italics in original). My readings begin by seeking that threshold of perception from which I can analyze and reconfigure what is written in plain sight on the surface of these texts in historical and political contexts. As a result, I establish dialogues between texts and subjects that traditionally have been kept apart by disciplinary, national, or generic bounds.

This chapter unfolds as a series of movements toward the open. Each section begins with a palindrome that I have chosen from Filloy's *Karcino*. The errant paths of these three palindromes connect Filloy to Somers and Casey by charting the movements from direct toward subtler rewritings of nineteenth- and early twentieth-century aesthetic and political traditions. Along the way, the gauchos will be stripped of their heroic attire, the body politic will be exposed to infectious disease, and the people will revel in the filthy and the impure. Overall, the narratives that found essentialist myths to subdue and control individuals for the political interests of a ruling elite will be rewritten by looking at the habitual workings of power that exist in plain sight.

Chapter Seven

¡AY, EPOPEYA!; or Filloy's Gauchos at the Origins

Epopeya is the Spanish word for both a heroic act and epic poetry. With this interjection, Filloy's palindrome registers an exhaustion or frustration with heroism, in general, and the literary traditions responsible for creating monuments to it. In the case of Argentina, the gauchos and the gaucho genre occupy one of the spaces dedicated to the celebration of national heroes through literature. I have chosen Filloy's interjection "¡AY, EPOPEYA!" as my starting point for interpreting his interventions into the gaucho genre's archives (*Karcino* 73). Here I analyze three short stories about gauchos from *Los Ochoa* (1972), the first of four books that comprise his "Saga de los 8A" or Ochoa Family Saga. The Saga continues with *La potra* (1973), *SexAmor* (1996), and *Decio 8A* (1997), and these narratives span the nineteenth and twentieth centuries in and around Río Cuarto, a city in Córdoba Province, near where many of the fictional plots take place.[1]

Filloy's narratives relate the lives of different gauchos whose untold stories become intertwined with the densely populated archives in which the so-called desert landscape of Córdoba Province has been imagined and documented. Rather than mythologize the so-called Interior as a repository of the national essence, Filloy's writing can be described, to use the category developed by Laura Demaría, as "escritura *en* provincia": "una escritura 'situada,' marcada por el lugar de enunciación desde el que se narra la provincia pero que no refiere a un ser identitario sino a un archivo de historias en constante movimiento" (*Buenos Aires* 420–21). As Filloy interrogates and rewrites this national tradition, I argue that his protagonists are divested of the symbolic weight imposed upon them in order to write in plain sight the stories of their at times violent, at others banal, misadventures throughout the Argentine provinces. Avoiding essentialist constructs and regionalisms, I analyze the type of narrative that can be written about the gauchos by starting from this exhaustion of the *epopeya*, by writing when no fixed origin at the center, no solid ground below, and no moral absolutes above will be permitted to orient the gaucho genre. Instead, Filloy's Saga constructs original narratives that displace a number of the genre's essentialist conventions, while proposing an open-ended relationship between the figure of the gaucho and the history of the nation through an exploration and transformation of nineteenth-century archives.

The *Gaucho Jodón*

"As de espadas" is the second story in Filloy's *Los Ochoa*, and it is the first of two stories about the second gaucho of the family, Primo Ochoa. At a party to celebrate the Centennial of Argentine Independence on July 9, 1916, Primo joins three other men in a game of *truco*, a card game played by almost every gaucho in the genre that easily lends itself to national allegories. This narrative begins by recalling that possibility: "En la mesa de truco se tocan los cuatros puntos cardinales del país" (21). However, the game is guided by "un demonio jodón y sagaz" and requires players "matizar los caprichos del azar" (21). Deceit and chance are its only underlying principles. Once Primo realizes he and his partner are going to lose the game, he plucks a tick from a dog and sneaks it among his opponent's snacks. About to win, Cuquejo bites into the tick, and its blood bursts into his mouth. In a rage, he tries to stab Primo but trips on a chair. Primo hits him on the head with a carbonated water bottle, and Cuquejo falls, cracks his neck on another chair, and dies. This narrative ends with Primo, the gaucho, in jail before eventually being pardoned for his crime. At Filloy's Centennial truco match, a new national hero does not arise.

Situated within the archives of the gaucho genre, it may appear that Primo is simply another in a long line of *gauchos malos*. In Hilario Ascasubi's *Santos Vega* (1851), for example, these bad gauchos are defined in sharp contrast to their counterpart, the good gauchos. Ascasubi's narrator tells the story of two twins, Luis and Jacinto, the bad and the good gaucho, respectively. Consistent throughout this entire text is the binary that divides these two brothers from the moment they first appear:

> Ansí, desde charabón, / el mellizo más flauchín / descubrió un alma tan ruin, / y perversa de tal modo, / que con buena crianza y todo / salió un saltiador al fin. // Este se llamaba Luis, / y el otro hermano Jacinto, / criatura de un istinto / humilde como perdiz. (338)

Jacinto's story is brief, since it is relatively free of drama, whereas Luis reappears over and again to commit violent crimes. The bad gaucho never transforms into a good gaucho; the only solace is the happy ending achieved upon Luis's death. In this sense, Ascasubi prescribes the forced disappearance of the bad gaucho, of the thieving, unrestrained gaucho type, that impedes Argentina's modernization.[2]

Filloy's gauchos do not fit within this moral binary; rather, they pry open this opposition and deactivate its ability to partition individuals into rigidly opposing moral categories. Primo, put bluntly, is an obnoxious drunk. He plays tricks on everyone in his youth, and as an old man in another story, "Carbunclo," he gets thrown in jail for urinating on the veterinarian's lawn and insulting his wife after proudly shouting: "¡Miren, carajo, apriendan! ¡Esto se llama mear!" (*Ochoa* 36). In response, Filloy's narrator invents a new category for Primo called the *gaucho jodón*: "Don Primo, ya raspando la sesentena, mantenía fresca por doquiera su modalidad de gaucho jodón. De gaucho jodón, pero no malo" (38). *Jodón* can be translated as "damned irritating" or "tricky, sneaky." The *gaucho jodón* is neither good nor bad; moral absolutes prove too extreme to register Primo's disturbing irreverence, what in many cases are banal insults, jokes, or tricks unworthy of eternal condemnation. For this reason, his story cannot be elevated through nationalism as the ideal, patriotic citizen.[3] This *gaucho jodón* is an irritating trickster and nothing more.

Filloy's invention of the *gaucho jodón* represents a drastic departure from many of the classics of the genre and their critical reception around the turn of the twentieth century. Rama demonstrates that gauchesque poetry was not written by gauchos but rather by and for the lettered elite in pursuit of their own political and economic interests that often came into conflict with the gauchos: "El poeta no sirve a su público sino a las elites que él integra o que lo dirigen y financien" (*Los gauchipolíticos rioplatenses* 52). Furthermore, Josefina Ludmer analyzes how the figure of the gaucho is constructed and manipulated by this elite:

"The gaucho genre implemented this conjunction: it constituted a literary political language, politicized popular culture, and left its founding mark on Argentine culture" (69). Masking their place of enunciation under the guise of popular, oral culture, the genre's canonical authors and critics use the voice of the gaucho to speak to the masses of the nation. They transform the very subjects who were disdained as outlaws and vagabonds during the nineteenth century into an essentialist symbol around the Centennial to root the modern nation within an imagined, rural tradition. Though Filloy is yet another lettered elite appropriating the gaucho genre, his intervention actively strips it of the empty, nationalist gestures of his predecessors in order to leave the gauchos in plain sight of all those who might celebrate these absent, irritating figures as heroic role models.

Dismantling the Original Gaucho

Leopoldo Lugones is one such critic who desperately works to create a national hero out of this literary tradition for his own political purposes. At the Teatro Odeón in Buenos Aires in 1913, he presented his treatise on the gaucho genre, casting it as Argentina's epic poetry. He later expanded and published this work as *El payador* in 1916 to coincide with the Centennial. "It was a timely invention," Sarlo explains, "for immigrants from Italy, as well as Germany and Central Europe, were arriving by the thousands in Buenos Aires, and the intellectuals were worrying about the future of their culture" (*Jorge Luis Borges* 37). Situated in this context, Sarlo demonstrates that Lugones's appeal to the gauchos and the genre stems from an ideological desire to delimit and control official Argentine culture in the face of rapid immigration to Buenos Aires. From the capital, Lugones turns toward the provinces and claims to find the supposed repository of the national essence, a place considered by him to be uncontaminated by foreign influences.

Lugones understands the epic hero as righteously spreading Western civilization along his journey, and he seeks to prove that Argentina has such a hero—the now absent gaucho. He constructs a direct link between this national tradition and the origins of Western civilization, which for him is located in the songs of medieval troubadours and epic poetry. After an impressive etymological exercise that traces the ancient roots of the word *payador* in Greek, Latin, and other Romance languages, Lugones declares in the prologue to *El payador* that the gaucho genre is the essential tradition of the Argentine nation: "Título este libro con el nombre de los antiguos cantores errantes que recorrían nuestras campañas trovando romances y endechas, porque fueron ellos los personajes más significativos en la formación de nuestra raza" (xvii). His etymologies intend to prove that all roads lead from the eighteenth- and nineteenth-century gaucho's *payada*—a musical, rhetorical competition—to the dance and poetic composition of the medieval troubadours. Though he describes these singing gauchos as errant subjects, he locks their movements into a fixed, retrograde itinerary to monumentalize them as the Argentine equivalent of the precursors to European epic poetry. For Lugones, if the gauchos are Argentine troubadours, then the *Martín Fierro* (1872)—in his view, the best of the gaucho genre—is the Argentine epic poem. According to his positivist logic, after only one century of independence Argentina is poised to become one of the great Western nations, because Argentine literary traditions follow the same line of historical progress seen in Europe.

El payador is a complex text in which Lugones scours the Western archives—from the *Odyssey* and the *Iliad* to the *Divine Comedy* and the *Cantar de Mio Cid*—to prove the value of a local tradition by situating the gaucho genre alongside already consecrated texts. This strategy can be described, to use Derrida's term, as "archive fever": "a compulsive, repetitive, and nostalgic desire for the archive, an irrepressible desire to return to the origin, a homesickness, a nostalgia for the return to the most archaic place of absolute commencement" (*Archive Fever* 91). On the one hand, Lugones raises an immobile monument to the gaucho as the originary, yet absent, figure whose essential moral qualities are said to persist in the modern Argentine man in contrast to the uprooted foreign immigrants. On the other, Lugones grasps for some unreachable link that might prove Argentina's merit within Western civilization at the start of the twentieth century.

I like to imagine that Filloy exclaimed "¡Ay, epopeya!" after reading Lugones's fiction of the original gaucho in *El payador*. In order to restore the complexity of the gaucho genre after Lugones reified it into self-serving monuments, both the genre at large and the figure of the gaucho will have to be interrogated and transformed. In their prologue to *Poesía gauchesca*, Jorge Luis Borges and Adolfo Bioy Casares dismantle Lugones's entire argument by demonstrating that the *Martín Fierro* is not even an epic poem:

> Ello es erróneo. Ni la compleja historia argentina cabe en las guerras de frontera de mediados de siglo, ni el protagonista [...] puede ser emblemático de un país. Lo cierto es que la epopeya argentina no ha sido escrita; está acaso esbozada en la heterogénea obra de Ascasubi. La novela, en su doble carácter de testimonio de una época y de plena declaración de un destino, está ilustremente dada en el *Martín Fierro*. (xxi–xxii)

By displacing the poetic genealogy to Ascasubi and enshrining Hernández as the forefather of the Argentine novel, Borges and Bioy Casares attempt to make Lugones's painstaking etymologies and essentialist references to the archive irrelevant to any discussion of Argentine aesthetics and politics.[4]

Of course, these two authors are not impartial historians of the genre. Demaría argues that their prologue, selections, and notes throughout the anthology present an implicit political ideology: "Con la desmitificación de Hernández responden a la apología del nacionalismo; con la revalorización de Ascasubi y su uso de la gauchesca como arma política atacan al peronismo" ("Borges y Bioy Casares" 27). They contest the historical revisionism that constructed Rosas as a national hero while they decry Peronist politics as dictatorial. Nevertheless, central to their essay is the imperative to destroy and discard Lugones's errors in analyzing the genre as well as his essentialist definitions of Argentine culture that close it to future interventions. In "El escritor argentino y la tradición," Borges makes many of the same arguments as in the prologue with Bioy Casares; however, for Argentine culture to become worthy of the laurels Lugones would bestow upon it, Borges argues that it must be capable of exceeding the particular customs and traditions of local culture: "Quiero señalar otra contradicción: los nacionalistas simulan venerar las capacidades de la mente argentina pero quieren limitar el ejercicio poético de esa mente a algunos pobres temas locales, como si los argentinos sólo pudiéramos hablar de orillas y estancias y no del universo" (554). Rather, the only trait worthy of applying to his entire nation is "la versatilidad argentina," the ability to adapt, change, and be skilled at various endeavors (555).

Proto and the Ochoas

Whereas Borges and Bioy Casares uncover the underlying ideologies motivating writers like Lugones to appropriate the genre, Filloy's narratives write in plain sight the lives of otherwise unnoticed gauchos, as in the case of Primo, none of whom can be elevated as universal heroes. Of course, the concept of the hero is far from a universal. An individual's status as hero only exists within the closed confines of a group identity celebrating their triumph, often through violence and conquest, over another. Only a small change in perspective is necessary to lay bare the violent acts committed by individuals in their will to power and the absolute banality of such narcissists that get celebrated as epic heroes. For this reason, Ernesto Laclau calls for a new type of hero, one who can confront the tragedies of political violence "and admit the contingency of her own beliefs, instead of seeking refuge in religious or rationalistic myth" (*Emancipation(s)* 123). If there should be more heroic narratives—and I am not certain there should be—then Laclau argues for the need to represent those heroes as the particular, complex, and even contradictory human beings they are without ignoring the often violent context in which their heroic deeds took place. Filloy's narratives represent the gauchos along the lines described by Laclau, but in the process the word "hero" will prove to be an unlikely description of the gauchos at the origins of the Ochoa Family Saga.

Born just after Argentine independence, Proto Ochoa is the family's earliest recorded member. His story is also the first of the collection, titled "El juído (El patriarca)," but his status as the patriarch is secondary, literally placed in parenthesis, to that as "el juído." The verb "juir" is used throughout the genre as the gaucho's pronunciation of "huir," meaning "to flee, to run away, to escape (from)," and "el juído" can be translated as "the fugitive." In Canto II of *La ida*, the first half of the classic *Martín Fierro*, Fierro emphasizes this verb, "juir," as he describes the life of the gaucho: "Estaba el gaucho en su pago / con toda sigurida; / pero aura... ¡barbaridá!, / la cosa anda tan fruncida, / que gasta el pobre la

Chapter Seven

vida / en juir de la autoridá. [...] // Ansí empezaron mis males, / lo mesmo que los de tantos" (Hernández 120–21). Whereas Lugones would solidly ground Fierro as the national hero in an immobile monument, Filloy's narrative restores the gaucho's errancy as expressed in the classic through the verb *juir*.

Proto, this other founding father, is an outlaw on the run after assaulting and disfiguring an officer: "Güeno, lo golpié del lao zurdo rebanándole l'oreja" ("El juído" 12). To avoid punishment, he deserts his post in the army, flees to the unincorporated nineteenth-century countryside, and takes refuge among the Ranquel. Establishing an affinity with the most well-known gaucho, Proto slightly adapts the *Martín Fierro*, further underscoring his own errancy: "Lo mesmo le pasó a Martín Fierro: *Anduvo siempre juyendo / Siempre pobre y perseguido / No tuvo cueva ni nido / Como si juera un maldito; / Porque el ser gaucho, carajo / El ser gaucho es un delito*" (10; italics in original).[5] The classic text is written in the present tense, allowing a critic like Lugones to generalize Fierro's story as representative of all gauchos; Proto's translation into the past tense restores the particularity of Fierro's experience, though he retains the same conclusions: to be a gaucho is a crime. From this beginning, the patriarch of the Ochoa family, one particular gaucho among thousands, appears in perpetual motion.[6] His only connection to the nascent nation-state is as a fugitive and outlaw.

Before introducing this errant figure, the prologue to *Los Ochoa* grounds the entire Saga on quicksand from the first sentence: "Esta nativa 'Saga de los 8A' no es un engendro literario, sino una concreción de hechos y episodios de seres humanos, emergidos en la superficie de diferentes actualidades en una región de 'tierra adentro,' entre médanos y guadales de la 'pampa seca'" (5). On the one hand, the scare quotes around "tierra adentro" and "pampa seca" showcase the irony with which these terms are employed; the clichéd description of the Pampa as a dry, lifeless, no man's land is discarded. On the other, the narrator retains the words *médanos* and *guadales* to describe the province as being composed of dunes and sandy bogs. In this regard, Filloy's narrative is consistent with other nineteenth-century descriptions of the Pampa. In *Una excursión a los indios ranqueles* (1890), Lucio V. Mansilla along the path from Calcumuleu to Leubucó describes the difficulty of riding through "los médanos de movediza arena" (119). Though a challenge to be overcome by the expanding state in Mansilla's narrative, Filloy's Saga appropriates this shifting terrain as the only possible grounds for a national narrative in the provinces. Trying to remain immobile or erect permanent monuments on such terrain would be futile, but the Ochoas know how to traverse the surface of this landscape that constantly shifts under their feet. In Filloy's stories, the only originary figures are those who resist reification as common folks in a slow-paced region imagined as the reservoir of a simpler past. The human beings who learn to make do in the changing realities of these provincial lands cannot be so easily co-opted by the nation-state for allegorical or institutional purposes.

Filloy's prologue ends by making serious play with the linear logic of genealogy. The narrator lists the names of the Ochoas whose year of birth could be found in the public record:

1821, Proto Orosimba 8A	1915, Mil 8A
1842, Primo 8A	1921, Decena 8A, melliza
1843, Segunda 8A	1921, Docena 8A, melliza
1863, Novena 8A, La Nona	1930, Once 8A
1877, Quintín, 8A	1935, Sexto 8A
1894, Octavo 8A, gemelo	1942, Décimo 8A
1894, Noveno 8A, gemelo	1963, Crisanto Funes 8A
1900, Tércer 8A	tataranieto de La Nona.

(*Ochoa* 8)

The Ochoa Family is organized chronologically as a genealogy, not a branching family tree, that spans from Independence to the 1960s. They all write their last name "8A" as a shorthand, because the family name is a homophone for "eight a" in Spanish. Also, they use another shorthand when their first names are ordinal numbers; for example, Octavo Ochoa, a homophone for Eighth Eight A, writes his name as "8°8A" (90).

In observing this chronology of numerically named Ochoas, the strict ordering of a genealogy, traditionally conceived as a direct path from the present back to the pure origin, errs away from linear logic. The first Ochoa in the list is Proto Orosimba, the fugitive, whose name is also a suffix meaning "origin" or "beginning." He is followed by Primo, Proto's son and the second gaucho in the family. A possibly shortened form of "primero, first," since he writes his name "1°8A," "primo" also means "cousin," suggesting at the same time a second origin for the Saga and a displacement of direct lineage. Proto and Primo are followed by the third person in the list, the first woman, Segunda, whose name is a homophone for the feminine inflexion of "segundo, second." Tércer, whose name shifts the stress and shortens the word "tercero, third" appears as the eighth person in the list, after Novena (feminine "ninth"), Quintín (diminutive "fifth"), and the twins, Octavo (masculine "eighth") and Noveno (masculine "ninth"). These names perpetually displace any and all numerical order, and other family members not listed here appear throughout the Saga. This list ends with Crisanto Funes, whose name does not carry on the number game but takes a radical detour from this logic altogether. Crisanto is described as the great-great-grandson of La Nona, a common name for a grandmother among Argentine families of Italian heritage. This inclusion is perhaps anachronistic and out of place, since the great waves of Italian immigrants arrived in Buenos Aires roughly half a century after La Nona's birth; however, her presence within the Ochoa family directly challenges Lugones's desperate attempt to isolate Argentina's national essence from those same immigrants by writing them into its origins.

The competing numerical logics between the dates and the ordinal numbers create a tension that moves back and forth along this genealogy. The dates order it along a linear path; the homophonic first names do not simply reverse this order, but rather they scatter it, *al vesre* and *al verse*, beyond recognition without abandoning the genealogical structure or removing the Ochoa family from Argentine territory. In "Nietzsche, Genealogy, History" (1971), published only the year before Filloy's *Los Ochoa* appeared in print, Foucault analyzes Nietzsche's use of genealogy as a method for calling into question the intrinsic worth of moral values by demonstrating how they were created and modified over time: "[Nietzsche] finds that there is 'something altogether different' behind things: not a timeless and essential secret, but the secret that they have no essence or that their essence was fabricated in a piecemeal fashion from alien forms" (142). A genealogical exploration for Nietzsche, Foucault, and by extension, Filloy, "disturbs what was previously considered immobile; it fragments what was thought unified; it shows the heterogeneity of what was imagined consistent with itself" (147). In this sense, the genealogy placed at the beginning of Filloy's Ochoa Family Saga turns against the chronology of historical progress and opens a path through the Argentine archives where perfectly ordered obstacles had previously blocked the way. The gaucho stories of Proto and Primo continually disrupt and reconstruct these archives with incredible detail.

While in Ranquel territory, Proto's path crosses with Mansilla, and Filloy's story expands *Una excursión* much in the way that Borges reopened the *Martín Fierro* in his fictions. Jens Andermann analyzes two main currents of Mansilla's poetics, arguing that Mansilla focuses on "clasificación, taxonomía, topografía" and, at the same time, on "una crítica política y cultural de la mera expansión del poder central, que es acusado de ignorar la verdad del país" (108). Mansilla journeys across the provinces and bears witness to the supposed realities of the "Interior"; he expects his experience to grant him the authority to make policy recommendations, though they would be ignored. In *Una excursión*, the story of Rufino Pereira, a gaucho who tells Mansilla he deserted the army after being falsely accused of crimes, becomes paradigmatic. When Mansilla asks Pereira where he is from, who his parents are, and why he was enlisted in the army, Pereira's only answer is "No sé" (228). His origins are perhaps the most imprecise of any gaucho in the entire genre, making him the perfect blank slate, a name that can stand for any other gaucho. Mansilla later narrates how he transformed this supposed criminal into an ideal soldier by appealing to his sense of honor, loyalty, and duty. In this particular instance, Mansilla quickly elevates Pereira's story to that of a universal form: "Nuestros campos están llenos de Rufinos Pereiras. La raza de este ser desheredado que se llama *gaucho*, digan lo que quieran, es excelente, y como blanda cera, puede ser modelada para el bien" (231; italics in original). And Mansilla claims to have the magic touch, capable of transforming these Rufinos Pereiras, all the *gauchos malos*, not into *gauchos buenos*, but rather into loyal soldiers of the state. Though operating from different ideological positions, both Mansilla and Lugones generalize from the story of one particular gaucho in order to construct essentialist images of heroic individuals for the nation-state from these provincial bodies.

In "El juído (El patriarca)," Filloy's Proto becomes another one of these "Rufinos Pereiras," but the change in perspective dismantles Mansilla's universalist logic. Filloy's narrative does not trace the journey from Buenos Aires to the provinces; it begins from within that shifting terrain of Córdoba Province I described

Chapter Seven

above, and Proto is already in Leubucó well before Mansilla arrives. "Vení. ¡Vení rápido!" shouts someone in Leubucó, "¡Está por llegar el Coronel Lucio V. Mansilla!" (*Ochoa* 16). Perhaps hearing about Pereira's luck in having his crimes absolved, Proto decides to try his hand when he learns that the sergeant whose ear he cut off was killed for becoming insolent with one of his superiors:

> Lo trabajé al curita pa'qu'el coronel Mansilla me perdonase. Total, muerto el perro se acabó la rabia ... Pero en el ejército nu'es así. El coronel alegó que lo mío er'una insubordinación muy grave; y la muerte del alférez una cosa justa "en defensa de la jerarquía militar." ¡Mire la palabra qui'usan pa'joder a quien rebana un'oreja y no a quien quita una vida! (18)

Proto and the one-eared officer—he holds the rank of *alférez*, the lowest commissioned rank—committed similar offenses: they were both punished for insubordination. Proto fled to avoid punishment, but the *alférez* was killed in order to defend the military's hierarchy. Proto's clever critique points out that all he did was cut off someone's ear, not kill anyone, yet he is still seen as having committed a greater crime than that superior officer in the military who killed the one-eared *alférez*. Though Proto will be forgiven for his crimes and goes on to serve under Mansilla for many years in Filloy's narrative, thus confirming Mansilla's generalized claims about reforming the *gauchos malos* in this particular case, Filloy allows the errant Proto to maintain a margin of difference. Just before the Conquest of the Desert that would exterminate the indigenous, Proto critiques the violent logic that values hierarchy—power derived from maintaining rigid order—over human life. Proto may not be a heroic individual, but he signals the hypocritical workings of power that lay in plain sight of even an uneducated criminal.

A Gaucho by Any Other Name

What still remains is the question of what type of national narratives can be written without heroes, consecrated grounds, and mythical origins. In my analysis, Filloy provides an example of this type of narrative in "Carbunclo." This story is the sequel to Primo's misadventures as the *gaucho jodón*. Now in his sixties and in jail for urinating on the veterinarian's lawn, as I described above, Primo's cell mates vaguely recall some epic story from his youth—the story of Cuquejo and the tick from "As de espadas." They beg him to retell the story, even though he warns it was "una trigedia" (49). Primo is perfectly positioned to tell any version or perversion of the story, to borrow Borges's phrase.[7] He could have invented the past as a glorious era full of epic heroes to guide his fellow countrymen through present insecurities toward the only future he personally deems acceptable. He could have masked a particular ideology under this nationalist narrative, but what he relates is completely consistent with the events narrated in "As de espadas." His cellmates are disgusted by the story and shocked that he is "tan repugnante," and they no longer recognize him or his deeds as heroic (52). When narrating his own history, Primo sidesteps the *epopeya* and writes his status as the *gaucho jodón*, neither righteous nor evil, right on the surface.

Primo sees no point in hiding unpleasant historical details. Transforming Shakespeare's maxim, Primo leaves the following lesson: "Llámele jazmín a la mierda y apestará lo mesmo" (53). As I read it in this context, Primo decries the ultimate futility of erasing the violent origins of the nation and replacing them with regionalist myths and essentialist constructs. Whereas Borges thoroughly dismantles Lugones's rigid arguments and demonstrates the future potential for reviving the gaucho genre as the fiction that it is, as a narrative of the past that can always be rewritten, Filloy's gaucho stories return to the national archives to restore the complexity, and even at times the banality, of the gauchos and the provincial lands they continually traverse. These subjects and spaces certainly comprise an important place in Argentina's past, but elevating them as the timeless source of a national essence only distracts from the machinations of sovereign power. Ultimately, Filloy's narratives revive the gauchos and the genre from Lugones's immobile monuments to demonstrate that such texts are simply a convention for ordering one's perception of the past and that different, even more ethical, national narratives are possible without erasing that past or calling it by another, more pleasant, name. By writing this national past in plain sight, Filloy opens the way toward a politics not premised on the violent will to power that too often invents divisive categories as moral imperatives in the service of power and greed.

Chapter Eight

¡SOMETAMOS O MATEMOS!; or Somers's Mandrake Syndrome

"¡SOMETAMOS O MATEMOS!" can be translated as "Let's subdue or let's kill!" (*Karcino* 79). This palindrome is as gruesome as it is succinct. By invoking this phrase, an individual can attempt to rally a unified, ordered group behind a violent mandate—the choice to either subjugate or exterminate an already excluded, yet unnamed other. However, the only decision allowed to the included individuals, this "we," is one of means and degree, not substance; each person is required to decide only if the excluded individuals should be made impotent or should be killed. Cleverly, the speaker provides no alternatives here, in effect subjugating both those called "we" and those called "them" to his hegemonic will. The simplicity is bone-chilling. Three words spread over the entirety of the political landscape to chain all bodies into place. Employing a totalizing logic, all ambiguity is dispelled; no longer is there room for choice, movement, questions, or disagreement without risk of death. Everything is known. Everyone is visible. Nothing foreign remains.

Of course, I have been arguing that palindromes are not so simple, and in practice, even the most violent regimes can only project total clarity as their ideal horizon. Still, transparent, brief language maintains a hold over political discourse, claiming to cleanse the body politic of any disorder or ambiguity, while actually eradicating the potential for disagreement and democracy. In this context, I propose reading Armonía Somers's fiction not as an antidote, but rather as a necessary complication of such discourse. Though her fiction does not readily appear to be invested in politics, at least not in the narrow sense of the committed writer, she provides another option to the totalizing impulse of this palindrome and the type of political discourse it implies.

Chapter Eight

I find Somers to be an enigmatic writer, that is, a writer who situates enigmas at the center of her narratives. In *Un retrato para Dickens* (1969) and *Sólo los elefantes encuentran mandrágora* (written between 1972 and 1975, but not published until 1986), Somers engages in dialogue with international narratives that preceded the historical avant-gardes, including British and Spanish family romance and an Argentine cookbook. Her novels slow the drive toward total visibility once they become infected with what I call, borrowing a phrase from *Sólo los elefantes*, "el Síndrome de la mandrágora" (324). Similar to the illness affecting the protagonist of *Sólo los elefantes*, in my analysis the Mandrake Syndrome disturbs and unsettles all-too-tidy transcendental fictions by moving down into the everyday where confusion and ambiguity cannot be overcome. What is at stake here is a conception of the body politic—to the extent that it can be metaphorized as a body—as one that must always remain infected with enigmas that are never to be prevented, sutured, treated, or cured from outside or above. By writing these enigmas in plain sight, while never revealing their solution, I argue that her fiction generates a movement toward a radical democratic politics. Whereas Filloy rewrites the national gaucho tradition at the origins of his family saga, in this chapter, I focus on how Somers engages with texts from England, Argentina, and Spain in her retrospective fictions. I begin with *Un retrato para Dickens* (always quoting from the 1969 edition), because this novel establishes the need to construct an enigmatic fiction whose political consequences will infect the entirety of *Sólo los elefantes*.

The Unsolvable

Un retrato breaks with the unity of the nineteenth-century realist family romance that Somers cites by rewriting Charles Dickens's *Oliver Twist* (serialized 1837–39). Comparing the two novels, Dalmagro concludes that the legibility and verosimilitude of Dickens's novel "se contaminan con un discurso ambiguo, en que las piezas están desarticuladas, fragmentadas" ("Revés" 176).[1] In Dickens's novel, Oliver, an orphan boy, is ultimately reunited with his family and his inheritance; Mr. Brownlow "gratified the only remaining wish of Oliver's warm and earnest heart, and thus linked together a little society, whose condition approached as nearly to one of perfect happiness as can ever be known in this changing world" (*Oliver Twist* 413). In contrast, Somers's anonymous orphan girl sits abandoned in a police station, grasping desperately for a sense of humanity. According to Víctor Escudero, what she learns at this early age is only "la incertidumbre de lo real" ("Sujetos descompuestos" 1–14). She tells her story in a series of flashbacks. Interpolated into the narrative structure are seemingly disparate texts: rewritings of biblical scenes from the Book of Job, selections of an Argentine cookbook, including recipes, and a retelling of the plot as seen from the perspective of Asmodeo, the family parrot, who is also the demon reincarnated from the biblical story. By the end, the girl and the parrot explain that she was raped and afterward threw herself into the sea before being rescued and brought into the police station. In *Un retrato*, there is no linear progression nor restoration to the family or the nation, only a broken girl exposed to a violent world.

In addition to fragmenting both the form and content of Dickens's novel, Somers establishes a distinction between, on the one hand, the many strange and fantastic but ultimately deciphered mysteries and, on the other, the unsolvable enigmas that endure throughout the novel. Ana María Rodríguez Villamil attempts to overcome the criticism leveraged against Somers that her literature is dense and illegible. She purports to bring clarity to Somers's narratives through a structuralist analysis of the fantastic elements—employing a primarily Todorovian framework—of *La mujer desnuda* and other short stories. In the conclusion, the critic briefly mentions the fantastic elements of *Un retrato* that she says contaminate the novel's more realist moments:

> La fusión de lo real y lo imaginario se da, entonces, al final de la novela. Si bien la contaminación se da también a lo largo de los capítulos supuestamente realistas, por la inclusión del loro Asmodeo. La ambigüedad creada por la contaminación de ambas esferas [...] se produce aquí al final. (190)

In her analysis, the final chapter allows for a culmination, in which two of the seemingly unconnected narratives of the novel come together; in retrospect, Asmodeo the demon and parrot can be read as the thread that sutures these fragmented plots.

For Rodríguez Villamil, this contamination produces the ambiguity that allows her to classify the novel as fantastic, an ambiguity that brings clarity by restoring the fragmented narrative arc. Indeed, she insists that Somers's narratives employ different formulas that "buscan la vía iluminativa es decir, la de la revelación, ya sea por la belleza o la fuerza de una imagen, ya por un sentido oculto que finalmente salta a la vista, ya por la irrupción de lo insólito" (192). I agree that certain mysteries are resolved by the end of many of Somers's narratives; they drive the plot by creating suspense and often confirm the presence of the fantastic. Yet, I still feel utterly confused every time I finish reading almost any of her texts, because a number of enigmas always remain unanswered. As in gothic fiction, Ana María López Abadía explains, *Un retrato* "acaba con la idea del 'gran despertar,'" which is to say that no messianic figure will appear "solucionando milagrosamente la situación" (n.p.). Rather than seek a form of clarity for Somers's aesthetics, I prefer to analyze the effects of these enigmas that permanently block introspection, impede access to knowledge, and contaminate political discourse with inscrutable elements that cannot and will not be solved.

In *Un retrato*, one of the intertexts introduced under the Documents section are copies from an Argentine recipe book, *El Pastelero y Confitero Nacional* (1914) by Francisco Figueroa, found by the orphan girl. She tries to decipher the strange world that surrounds her from her juvenile perspective, what she calls "mi limitado margen de conceptos" (*Retrato* 41). What perplexes her is that there are seventy-seven recipes for *bizcochuelo*, a type of sponge cake. She poses a riddle to Guillermo: "Lo que quisiera saber es qué gusto tiene una cosa, una cosa que se puede hacer de setenta y siete maneras, y que se llama siempre bizcochuelo" (43). The adult man laughs away her question and assumes she is simply hungry, but she yells at him for dismissing her. She thinks to herself: "Nos mirábamos alguna vez como extranjeros que se encuentran en un cruce de trenes y sus idiomas sin traducción los hacen partir con el alma cerrada" (43). Guillermo lets her ask another question that he attempts to answer, but this riddle about the *bizcochuelo* remains like those untranslated languages.

This missed encounter is framed beforehand with a prologue from Figueroa's recipe book and afterward with three different *bizcochuelo* recipes. Reveling in self-worth, Figueroa titles the prologue "La verdad esclarece e ilumina" (*Un retrato* 30). The Argentine—not Uruguayan—author of these recipes proclaims the greatness and purity of "nuestra Cocina Nacional" with no irony at all (30). His prologue—a text that has been copied and reprinted in Somers's novel—explains how his recipes, these national treasures, had been stolen, copied, and reprinted without his permission in other volumes of Argentine recipe books.

Overall, Figueroa's prologue is constructed as a monument that flaunts the unique face of his National Cuisine for public consumption; the food is to be digested, the book, bought and read, the monument, viewed and praised. However, the orphan girl is not so easily convinced of this unity, and not because she is Uruguayan or is so naïve that she thinks there is only one recipe for any given dish. She confronts the luminous political narrative masquerading as a simple recipe book by posing an enigma. In the case of the *Bizcochuelo*, which serves as a synecdoche of the Nation, she asks how there can be seventy-seven versions of a proper noun, how a heterogenous collection can ignore its own plurality and assume a unique, total, and singular identity. Only the orphan girl manages to attend to the uneven surface on which Figueroa constructs his universalizing vision. She calls attention to the visible but unnoticed fact that Figueroa's perspective is as particular and limited as her own, the difference being that his is oriented by the same hegemonic impulse that governs Lugones's elitist manipulation of the gaucho genre.

While reading the surface of this document, copious typos that do not exist in the rest of Somers's novel become apparent: missing accents and punctuation marks, misspelled words, and excessive capitalization.[2] A footnote certifies that this document is a "copia fiel" of the expanded second edition of the recipe book, a second edition that still has many mistakes despite being elevated as the National Recipe Book (33). In adopting the little girl's limited perspective and paying attention to her naïve questions, the imperfect surface that supplements a previous edition that possibly had an even greater number of errors announces a fracture in the supposedly deeper message about the unity of the nation. The prologue's author intends to erase this multiplicity and these fractures with his single text on National Cuisine—exemplified by the *bizcochuelo*—and with a single subject—us—but he makes too many mistakes in his foundational gesture that tries to speak for so many others. In the face of the orphan girl's interrogation, his only hope might be to appeal to his fellow countrymen with the rallying cry, "¡Sometamos o matemos!"

Chapter Eight

Enigmas and the Mandrake Syndrome

Instead of either criticizing Somers as an illegible writer or attempting to bring greater clarity to her works, I propose another way to interpret the role of enigmas that remain unsolvable in plain sight on the surface of her narratives. In *Stanzas*, Agamben reflects on the classical figures of Oedipus and the Sphinx in order to distinguish two models for approaching an enigma. In mythology, those travelers who failed to answer the Sphinx's enigma were killed, never to learn the answer; Oedipus was the first and only to correctly answer her riddle, after which she killed herself. Considering these myths as alternative theories of signification, Agamben argues:

> Every interpretation of signifying as the relation of manifestation or expression (or, inversely, of coding and eclipse) between a signifier and a signified (and both the psychoanalytic theory of the symbol and the semiotic theory of language belong to this type) places itself necessarily under the sign of Oedipus; under the sign of the Sphinx must be placed every theory of the symbol that, refusing the model of Oedipus, focuses its attention above all on the barrier between signifier and signified that constitutes the original problem of signification. (138–39)

The Oedipal interpretations are those that claim to find and reveal the meaning hidden within an enigma; they employ a hermeneutical strategy to reveal truth by the light of knowledge. In contrast, interpretations under the sign of the Sphinx, or surface readings, mark the opening within language, the gap that blocks the truth from the representation that is made of it. Furthermore, in his analysis of Aristotle and Heraclitus, Agamben explains that the enigmatic provides "a glimpse into the abyss opened between signifier and signified," somewhere between "the *legein* (saying) and […] the *kryptein* (hiding)" (139). Enigmas, under the sign of the Sphinx, do not shroud any meaning under their surface. Rather, they expose, in a brief glimpse, the infinite distance that only imperfect and improper discourse can attempt to traverse without ever reaching the truth itself. Somers's orphan girl refers to many of her questions as "mensajes sin clave" (*Retrato* 28). There is discourse here, but no master key to decipher it. In this sense, Somers's enigmas can be read like a palindrome or the Sator Square; they may appear to hide a specific truth, but there is not necessarily a secret meaning tucked away in some fold that is awaiting the arrival of the most astute analyst, the cleverest hermeneutical exercise, or someone's lucky guess in order to be revealed, illuminated, or otherwise brought into the light.

While the enigmas in *Un retrato* install a level of uncertainty in parts of the narrative, they spread across the entirety of Somers's disorienting *Sólo los elefantes encuentran mandrágora*. For its autobiographical elements and extension across time and space, its attempt to narrate everything, Nicasio Perrera San Martín situates this novel as one of the many "grandes novelas totales," and the first written by a woman in Latin America ("Armonía Somers" 27). However, in my analysis, I contend that this novel resists that totality and even challenges the possibility of forming such a totality. To the extent that there is a plot, it might be summarized as a series of journal entries written by Sembrando Flores while she is being treated for a mysterious disease in a hospital bed. Her thoughts range from more realistic memories to abstract concatenations of objects, animals, people, and colors. Flores is eventually cured only to be killed in a car accident. In a footnote, the fictional editor, Victoria von Scherrer, further notes that she organized these handwritten journals, deciphering poorly written words "de modo que no se notaran las carencias" (*Sólo* 254). In the epilogue, von Scherrer explains that the text is not comprised solely of Flores's journals; in fact, it contains sections that von Scherrer wrote based on her own notes and memories of conversations she had with Flores (329–31). The fictional editor never reveals which parts of the final manuscript are hers and which are from Flores's journals; she simply points to the fact that they exist somewhere on the surface of the text.

However, this type of plot summary feels disingenuous or, at least, incomplete. My experience reading the novel more closely resembles the sensation of being pulled by a strong current through a chaotic dreamscape with no place to plant my feet or rest my eyes. It is this overwhelming confusion that I want to foreground as I analyze the political intervention of the novel. In another context, Richard has advocated for this sort of oblique language:

> También creo necesario defender el secreto de estas opacidades y refracciones contra la tiranía lingüística de lo simple, de lo directo y de lo transparente, hoy ejercida por las comunicaciones

> sociales que han dejado a la lengua sin giros fabuladores, sin el recoveco poético-narrativo de las duplicidades y ambigüedades del sentido. La razón práctica, el lenguaje directo y el saber útil son ahora socios mayoritarios en esta campaña de la transparencia. (*Residuos* 14)

Somers's fiction, in my analysis, works against this campaign of transparency. Without always clarifying the contexts in which the following quotes are enunciated or explaining the relationships between the different characters, I read a selection of disjointed ideas related to her enigmas from various points in the narrative. These enigmas contaminate and infect the totalizing discourse of transparency with the Mandrake Syndrome. This phrase appears in the novel as a way of naming the difficulty of knowing another person: "Fue la primera y la última vez que la vi, doctor Nessi, era tan bella y tan atroz que no puedo describirla si como amiga o enemiga. Llame a esto el Síndrome de la mandrágora en sus apuntes científicos, verá cómo se universaliza el término" (*Sólo* 324). This confusion between friends and enemies, between what is lovely and terrible, inside and outside, self and other, is what must contaminate otherwise transparent language if the potential for political dissensus is to be sustained. The Mandrake Syndrome is one way to name this confusion.

In *Sólo los elefantes*, Somers incorporates texts from a variety of genres and disciplines, including a nineteenth-century Spanish novel, *El manuscrito de una madre* (1872) by Enrique Pérez Escrich, and the medical-scientific discourse of Flores's doctors. When they enter into contact with Flores's journals, both of these become infected with the enigmas that they otherwise seek to cure, fraying their edges into loose threads and punching holes in key expository moments. Dianna C. Niebylski has studied how Somers's novel flows as if composed of "random acts of 'leakage' from one discourse to another" (111). Drawing from the image of lymph that pours excessively from Flores's body, she establishes this image of a narrative that flows across and drips through the holes of what she labelled the "disembodied epistemologies of the twentieth century (medicine, politics, existential philosophy, psychoanalysis)" (96). Building from Niebylski's analysis, I contend that Somers's enigmas are the empty holes that hide nothing, thus allowing such leakages to take place and undermining the authority of these disembodied disciplines to make totalizing claims.

Throughout *Sólo los elefantes*, fragments of Pérez Escrich's *El manuscrito* are incorporated into the narrative; sometimes they are copied directly and other times the characters modify them or mix in their reactions to the plot. In both novels, a dying woman writes a form of memoir in a journal, but these two manuscripts could not be more dissimilar. In *El manuscrito*, Ángela dies without revealing the identity of her son's father to him; she proclaims shortly before she dies: "Ese secreto no asomará á mis lábios, conmigo bajará á la tumba" (Vol. 1, 16). While dramatic, she is not being truthful. She entrusts a small chest to her doctor that contains a manuscript in which she explains who is the father and why she has kept his identity a secret. Pérez Escrich's novel is centered on this guarded manuscript and whether or not the truth it contains will be revealed to her son, Daniel, before he marries Clotilde, his half-sister. After countless plot twists, including duels, a recovery from being shot in the head, and kidnappings, in volume two Ángela's doctor tries to convince the Marquesa, Clotilde's mother, to reveal the truth in order to prevent her daughter from committing incest. The Marquesa is hesitant, but the doctor exclaims: "¡Qué importa querer ocultar lo que el tiempo tarde ó temprano ha de arrojarnos al rostro!" (Vol. 2, 350). Such certainty that eventually all will be revealed is the foundation on which Pérez Escrich's violent novel is constructed.

Despite a very abrupt ending, Daniel and Clotilde read the mother's manuscript only hours before they had planned to elope, and all outstanding plot lines are resolved. No *cabos sueltos* remain in the novel, because, as the narrator ensures the reader, "es preciso atarlos todos y hacer con ellos una madeja que lleve agradablemente entretenida la curiosidad hasta el final de la obra" (Vol. 2, 176). All secrets are revealed, all loose ends are tied up, and the tragedy of incest is prevented.

However, this transparent narrative also charts the itineraries of two violent, vengeful men who destroy the lives of all those around them. The General, Daniel's father, focuses only on protecting his honor and tries to have the doctor killed various times rather than reveal his infidelities; the Count offers Daniel his protection and makes him his heir as a ruse to get Daniel to commit incest in order to get revenge on the General. Other stories of mistreated

Chapter Eight

and abused women, one of whom was decapitated after her death and now her skull rests on the Count's mantle, fill these one thousand five hundred pages. The General and the Count attempt to subdue and kill everyone who threatens their glorious triumph over the other. Though everything comes to light in this novel and prevents one final tragedy from taking place, this supposedly happy ending pales in comparison to the greed, aggression, misogyny, and petty violence that entertains the reader at every point along the way.

Flores's journals in *Sólo los elefantes* take a different approach to loose threads and revelations of the past. Halfway through chapter seventeen, the narrator—it is not always discernible whether Flores, von Scherrer, or a third person narrator is speaking—says: "Pero era necesario retomar los cabos sueltos antes de la posible entrega de la memoria junto con lo que irían a leer en sus vísceras, como otros lo hacen en las borras del café, el día del descuartizamiento" (*Sólo* 217). Flores appears to have the same desire as Ángela to reveal everything, but her memory and, more importantly, her sick, medicated body prevent her from telling a coherent, straightforward story. The medications cause dreamlike, hallucinatory states, and she drifts in and out of childhood memories as doctors and nurses prick her body with needles. Loose threads in her narrative constantly fray and split. Even right after this quote, there is a section break that cuts the narrative short. More loose threads are started in this novel than those that will be neatly resolved by the end.

One example has to do with how Flores, as a little girl, learned about mandrake. She begins reading about it in a book called *Ciencias Ocultas*. In the novel, there is a block quote that begins explaining what the mandrake is, but the quote is cut short by an ellipsis. The narrator explains this abrupt ending: "Y es claro que enseguida quitó la página que hablaba de eso, ya que si todo el mundo se ponía a leer tales cosas éstas perdían misterio, y sin misterio no quedaba nada, lo restante era un esqueleto al viento" (*Sólo* 125). Unlike Ángela who found a way to have her secrets revealed posthumously, Flores destroyed the only page on which the mandrake's secrets were written. This missing page never returns, nor does she rewrite it at any point in the novel. As Zanetti explains, this lack of revelation becomes "uno de los modos de socavar un mundo invadido por la torpe confianza en lo ya definido, por los slógans y el lugar común" (*La dorada garra* 422–23). Somers's enigmas constantly undermine this stubborn trust when the last pages on which everything would have been revealed are ripped out of her narratives, never to be recovered.

In addition to dabbling in the occult sciences, Flores's journals also record the medical-scientific discourse used by her doctors as they probe her body to determine the cause of her illness and treat its symptoms. After an early round of unspecified tests, the doctor tells Flores that they came back negative; he only knows that the problem is not in her kidneys. Nevertheless, he names her illness "Quilotórax" with the qualification that this is based on what he knows so far (*Sólo* 35). This clarifies little for Flores: "La palabra quedó flotando en el aire de la habitación como un objeto volador no identificado" (35). The explanation of what is happening to her is encapsulated in an untranslatable alien language that she hears but cannot understand. Her confusion is amplified as the medical staff frequently speak among themselves in a technical language that only serves to mask their ignorance with the inaccessible discourse of scientific authority.

As two guards that "parecían dos esfinges" stand watch outside her hospital room, another doctor takes over the investigation (36). The journals record his analysis as follows: "Ya conozco la historia. Pero si según mi teoría esto pudiera ser consecuencia de (…), ya que han sido descartadas todas las posibilidades para conjeturar un (…)" (36). Somers sprinkles many of her narratives with ellipses, and in *Sólo los elefantes* they punch holes in medical discourse, erasing what might have been technical vocabulary Flores did not understand, words in the manuscript that the fictional editor could not decipher, or perhaps theories that were later proved incorrect. Of course, this is only speculation on my part. No footnotes or explanations in the epilogue exist, nor are these phrases reconstituted later. What has been lost in the abyss of those ellipses cannot be recovered from inside or outside of the text.

The gaps marked by ellipses could be dismissed as symbols of the questions that always exist at the early stages of any investigation, whether it be scientific, humanistic, or interdisciplinary. By the end, the doctors do cure Flores of her illness and send her home. Yet, an ellipsis blocks even one of the doctor's explanations of an injection and a violet-colored pill that will cure her. He says the pill is "cloruro de metil rosa anilina, o cristal, violeta, es igual a (…). Y dibujó en un papel los armónicos hexágonos con que habla la fabulosa química" (*Sólo* 306). Methyl chloride, aniline rose, and crystal violet are all actually existing organic compounds, but the rest of the doctor's explanation is cut short. Instead, he is said to have drawn its molecular structure to show it to Flores, and on the following page, an image of a compound appears, presumably the same one. Curiously, it is not made clear which of the three compounds this diagram supposedly represents, nor does this technical image clarify or reveal higher-order knowledge about the cause or cure of Flores's illness. By the end of the novel, even the cure that takes place is left unexplained as ellipses and illustrations attempt to cover over the enigmas that plague the medical-scientific discourse in this novel.

Immunity and Contamination

What might seem strange is that the narrator in *Sólo los elefantes* does not engage in a more straightforward critique of political discourse similar to that undertaken by the orphan girl in *Un retrato*. Rather, medicine and science become the fields most thoroughly infected with the Mandrake Syndrome. How, then, can Somers's literature that critiques medicine be understood as a political intervention?

To answer this question, I will turn to the political logic of immunity that cuts across a number of seemingly disparate disciplines. For my purposes, literature, medicine, and politics intersect when the paradigm of immunity is applied to the metaphor of the body politic. As Roberto Esposito demonstrates, the logic of immunity that guides biopolitics has been at play throughout the history of Western political thought.[3] Tracing the etymology of "immunity" to the Latin *immunitas*, Esposito explains that *munus* refers to an obligation or duty, whereas someone said to be *immunis* is "disencumbered, exonerated, exempted" (*Immunitas* 5). To be immune is a privileged state in which one does not owe anything to anyone, is not bound by the law, and therefore, immunity takes on an anti-social status that breaks with *communitas*, or "the social circuit of reciprocal gift-giving" (6; italics in original). In addition to this legal status, the biomedical significance of immunity refers to a preventive method of fending off future diseases by inoculating the body with nonlethal levels of a virus to create antibodies that can target that same virus; thus, "[immunization] reproduces in a controlled form exactly what it is meant to protect us from" (8). The logic of immunity does not map a distinction between inside and outside. Paradoxically, it incorporates the other—the virus—into the self—the body—in order to destroy the other; an internal extermination becomes the means of protecting life.

For biopolitics, the immune paradigm gains particular importance as the social community is represented through the metaphorical figure of the body politic.[4] An analogy is established between the body that is prevented against illness and the community that must be protected against social ills, degeneracy, or abnormality. On the one hand, Esposito argues, "to be the object of political 'care,' life had to be separated off and closed up inside progressively desocialized spaces that were meant to immunize it against anything arising from community" (*Immunitas* 140). In this sense, the technologies of discipline remain intact, ordering every individual body into a visible, known place. On the other, by appealing to a desire to protect the overall species or political community, the technologies of biopower may be deployed to distinguish between those bare lives who will be made to live and those others on the inside who may be left to die, or more accurately, killed. What claims to be a concern for the health and longevity of human life also justifies its intention to exterminate given individuals or groups.

It is no coincidence that one of the quotes incorporated into *Sólo los elefantes* from Pérez Escrich's *El manuscrito* involves the following decontextualized warning about taking action against the violent General: "Nos hallamos en un tiempo que el gobierno, para librarse de los que él cree enemigos del orden, emplea el sistema preventivo" (*Sólo* 146). While Somers's novel may be referring indirectly to Bordaberry's dictatorship that generalized state violence against Uruguayan citizens in the name of exterminating the Tupamaros, the lack of specificity allows me to read this critique as one that touches on while also exceeding the national context.

In this sense, the Mandrake Syndrome serves as an alternative to the immune paradigm as it exists within and beyond Uruguay. Neither the Mandrake Syndrome nor any other critique would be effective as a purported negation of the immune paradigm, because immunization is already a negation of an internalized negative, the elimination of difference. As Esposito says, to further negate and destroy "would mean to repeat the same procedure" (*Immunitas* 16). Furthermore, immunization is not simply the evil opposed to a good community; immunity and community are bound together in contemporary biopolitics, and neither of these concepts will disappear anytime soon. Instead, Esposito attempts to rewrite those militarized metaphors that too easily justify the destruction of all foreign bodies. In fact, this destructive logic relies on a simplified notion of how the immune system works. As Donna J. Haraway explains, "The immune system is everywhere and nowhere. Its specificities are indefinite if not infinite, and they arise randomly; yet, these extraordinary variations are the critical means of maintaining individual bodily coherence" (218). The immune system does not preserve life by recognizing a difference between self and other. Turning to the example of pregnancy, Esposito demonstrates that the mother's immune system aggressively attacks the fetus; the only way to avoid a miscarriage is for the father's antibodies to be sufficiently foreign so that the mother's immune system ignores the fetus and attacks the father's antibodies. It is the incorporation of the difference of the father, and not the sameness of the fetus within the mother, that generates and protects the new life. "From this perspective," argues Esposito, "nothing remains of the incompatibility between self and other. The other is the form the self takes where inside intersects with outside, the proper with the common, immunity with community" (*Immunitas* 171). This more complex representation in which each individual body cannot be simply disciplined, suppressed, or killed opens the logic of immunity toward a generative impetus, one that has the potential to create new life and to expand the community. Read in this context, the Mandrake Syndrome is not an illness to be prevented or cured, nor do Somers's enigmas immunize against foreign bodies. In Somers's fiction, enigmas continuously contaminate any and all discourse that seeks total clarity and purity, that attempts to eliminate difference and dispel ambiguity.

As the novel's title has always announced, only elephants will ever find the mandrake, and moreover, as the narrator says, "los elefantes encuentran mandrágora en el camino del paraíso" (*Sólo* 310). Dalmagro offers a detailed analysis of the mandrake as a symbol of desire, utopia, the fantastic, the uncanny, the esoteric, magic, and even the sacred in Catholicism. She asserts that "Encontrar la mandrágora es encontrar la posibilidad de contar una historia que permita reconstruir el sentido de la vida, aunque, como en el caso de *Sólo los elefantes* ... ese sentido sea inasible" (*Desde los umbrales* 332). This is to say that the mandrake, the possibility of a complete and transparent narrative, can only be found during the march toward the afterlife. If such a thing as the afterlife even exists, the narrator says, the problem will not be solved: "Tantas versiones, pues, y una sola cosa verdadera, aquel puente roto entre una y otra orilla. Y el río de la muerte demasiado ancho y oscuro para cruzarlo a nado y volver luego con noticias" (*Sólo* 236–37). Even as Flores relates her own life in the form of a chaotic dreamscape while still alive, or as von Scherrer reconstructs her journals and their conversations, she does not find the mandrake. That broken bridge between life and death, between signifier and signified, is never mended. And Flores celebrates this imperfection and confusion: "vivan las misteriosas parejas de los signos que nadie descifrará, que mueran de una vez todos los topos del mundo tratando de descubrirles un sentido lógico" (311). Somers's novel narrates the impossibility of fully illuminating the past and the present, of revealing all bodies under the lights of the public sphere, and it celebrates the effects of the Mandrake Syndrome as its enigmas spread across the entirety of such totalizing, political discourse.

At one point in the narrative, Flores listens to Erika as she criticizes another person: "Es completamente idónea, dijo la pelirroja Erika con una voz que creía secreta, no sabe nada de nada ... Idónea significa otra cosa, le susurró Flores al oído" (193). Flores thinks Erika meant to say "idiota, idiot" instead of "idónea, ideal," but Erika is convinced that she used the correct word. I would like to end this section by taking Erika's language at face value, to read it literally for what it says on the surface, wherein not knowing everything is ideal. This is the effect of the Mandrake Syndrome: to let a lack of total knowledge and clarity, a partial knowledge and vision full of enigmas that generate new ideas, new questions, and new life, to let all of this generative imperfection become an ideal state of existence at both the individual and communal levels. As a critic, I may not be able to follow the heroic model of Oedipus as he solved the enigmas of the Sphinx; Somers's fiction,

Chapter Eight

especially *Sólo los elefantes*, still remains quite incomprehensible to me. But what do I know, as von Scherrer says at the very end is this: "No sé, no sé nada de nada, soy completamente 'idónea,' como decía Erika Fraudenberg" (331).

Chapter Nine

Supuso su puS; or, Casey's Wasted Narratives

"Supuso su puS" does not lend itself to a simple translation, but it does open a space in which Casey's politics and aesthetics may unfold (*Karcino* 79). The verb *suponer* means "to suppose, to consider something to be true or existent" and also "to have a certain value or importance." It is also used in the expression *suponer un problema*, which translates as "to pose a problem." In this palindrome, what is being considered as of value and also posed as a site of interrogation here is someone's pus, their excessive secretions that are wiped off and thrown away or flushed down the drain. Pus is considered to be disgusting and revolting. It erupts from the body and can prove symptomatic of illness or disease. It repulses and repels one's gaze. Yet, this palindrome calls for an interrogation of bodily secretions, like the lymph constantly flowing from Sembrando Flores's ill body, of that which would otherwise be ignored, actively avoided, or quickly disposed and forgotten.

Bodily waste and wasted bodies appear frequently throughout Casey's essays and rewritings of prerevolutionary Cuban literature. In "Hacia una comprensión total del XIX," for example, Casey criticizes a certain branch of Cuban aesthetics, in particular the Romantics, for hiding so many of the nation's problems: "El romanticismo tuvo entre sus defectos hacernos creer en un mundo sin moscas y sin peste" (127). As he understands it, they represented the colonial island without flies and pestilence, without anything that would sully its image; instead, they constructed an artificially clean, tropical paradise. In this chapter, I demonstrate how Casey recovers the "flies and pestilence" of the past and represents the present by drawing from a long-standing, though infrequently celebrated, Cuban tradition of reveling in filthy places packed with writhing, drunken bodies who come together despite the rigid social barriers meant to keep them apart. Both his fiction and aesthetic values were laid to waste in the Sixties; his project would not be adopted or approved by the Cuban Revolution that he sought to defend. Nevertheless, Casey's texts—what I call his "wasted narratives"—evaluate the political and aesthetic potential of the frequent appeal to metaphors of waste, filth, and scum that he locates in the Cuban archives before and during the Revolution.

The story of Cuban aesthetics and politics in the Sixties is often told as one of increasing censorship. The debates surrounding the documentary *P.M.*, the internment in the UMAPs of so-called dissidents, many of whom were only presumed to be gay, and the swift reversal of judgment regarding Heberto Padilla and his national prize-winning poems are frequently situated along a chronology by which the Cuban Revolution devolved into an authoritarian regime. These moments help explain why the fervent, global enthusiasm for the Revolution's potential withered into disenchantment, and my own study certainly takes place within this history.

In my analysis, Casey develops a fascinating, perhaps even more revolutionary, aesthetics than the one that came to pass in Cuba. I hesitate to elevate his piecemeal writings into a formal canon for the Cuban Revolution—as Lugones attempted with the gaucho genre for Argentina—because Casey never wrote a systematic monograph comparable, for example, to the monumental, conservative poetics defended by Cintio Vitier in *Lo cubano en la poesía* (1970). In contrast, between his arrival in Havana in 1958 and going into exile in 1965 for fear of being sentenced to the UMAPs as a gay counter-revolutionary, Casey wrote a series of loosely connected essays for *Lunes de Revolución* (1960–61) and republished some with Ediciones R in *Memorias de una isla* (1964). In these essays, he speaks publicly as a national critic on Cuban literature, art, dance, theater, and music. Together with his short fiction from the Sixties, I analyze a selection of his writings as a sort of Benjaminian constellation of texts, objects, and practices that form a singular aesthetic project in support of a revolutionary politics.[1]

Casey's fiction unfolds as his protagonists explore Havana's sewers in "Meditación junto a Caballería" (1964) and the forgotten histories of the capital city in "Mi tía Leocadia, el amor, y el paleolítico inferior" (1962). Notably, this exploration of literal and figurative waste is not an isolated, aberrant moment in the history of Cuban literature and film, but one that he locates in certain works of prerevolutionary Cuban authors, especially Ramón Meza's *Mi tío el empleado* (1887) and Miguel de Carrión's *Las impuras* (1919). Instead of further canonizing that mythical Romantic image for the Cuban nation in the early years of the Revolution, Casey proposes an aesthetics without the lofty, normative values that would exclude sullied objects, disreputable places, and people getting totally wasted. In addition, I argue that the aesthetics he proposes indirectly defends the controversial film, *P.M.*, despite his silence on the topic in public, which allowed him to go unnoticed in these debates and remain in Cuba for years after *Lunes de Revolución* was shut down in 1961. Finally, within this constellation, Casey's posthumously published "Piazza Margana" (1969)—his own "P.M." in my estimation—in which the narrator imagines taking refuge among his male lover's intestines, no longer appears to be as out of place within his collected works.[2]

Nineteenth-Century Trash

In "Meditación junto a Caballería," published in *Casa de las Américas* in 1964, Casey's narrator stands along Caballería Wharf. This wharf is one of the oldest in Havana, where shipments of tobacco were inspected under colonial administration (Blatchford, "Reports" 51). The narrator watches a worker open a manhole cover and descend into the city's sewer. Though aqueducts had been constructed as early as the sixteenth century to provide water to Havana's residents, it was not until the colonial administration of Governor Miguel Tacón from 1834–38 that public works were significantly expanded in a beautification project meant to bolster support for Spanish rule. Elegant markets, boulevards, and monuments were built, as well as discreet sewer lines necessary to hide all refuse (Scarpaci, Segre, and Coyula 38). In 1913, the municipal government built the modern sewage system referenced in Casey's story. It consists of two discharge pipes, one emptying into the Almendares River and the other into Havana Bay, relying on the currents of the Florida Straits to carry waste out to sea (Scarpaci 80). Looking across the bay, Casey's narrator wonders: "¿Qué dantesca visión surgiría ante nuestros ojos si algún día decidieran

Chapter Nine

cerrar la boca al agua fresca del Océano y desecar la bahía con una succionadora gigantesca?" ("Meditación" 50). His question is not simply rhetorical, since he will imagine himself exploring the pipes that run beneath "el negro silencio adonde jamás llega la luz" (50). The infernal vision that rises during his subterranean exploration of literal waste serves as an entry point into the Cuban narratives that Casey defends for the Revolution.

The narrator imagines diving into the sewers that typically remain out of sight of the city's inhabitants who nonetheless depend on this structure to remove what they no longer value. He turns against the current of fetid sludge and takes stock of the refuse that flows beneath the streets and into the bay:

> Bajo los focos pálidos colocados a grandes tramos pasan lentamente los restos de la vida, sellos, envolturas, cristales, sangre, ámpulas, uñas, apuntes, cabellos, anillos, [...] puñales, óvulos, ojos de vidrio, navajas, secreciones, amenazas, [...] notas suicidas, encajes, espermatozoides, rectificaciones, botones, manifiestos, [...] plumas, antídotos, papeles de bombón. (51)

In this massive list only partially quoted here, he accounts for toiletries, food, bodily secretions, written texts, fabrics, accessories, flowers, cleaning supplies, animals, chemicals, birds, toys, and other bits of discarded junk—all remnants of life, he reminds the reader.

Typically, the waste flowing through sewer lines would be described as worthless filth, a normative value that can be applied to objects, but also to people and behaviors. William Cohen explores a theoretical history of filth and explains: "All of these versions of filth have one thing in common: from the point of view of the one making the judgment, they serve to establish distinction—'*That* is not me'" (x; italics in original).[3] "Filth" becomes the label of disgust for the other. Yet, in Casey's fiction, the refuse is not located over there, but here, on the surface of the text, among the remnants of life explored by the protagonist. By refusing the hasty generalization by which everything in the sewers becomes filth, the narrator stumbles upon this series of discarded objects. As they flow together, they invoke an incredible array of human emotions and beg to be formed into narratives that tell, for example, how a dagger came to be thrown into the sewer, or why a suicide note was written and then discarded. How many thousands of otherwise wasted stories could rise from this list by simply removing the label "filth"?

Seemingly unimportant, this literal trash and death flowing through the sewers is recycled and given a place within Casey's aesthetics: "Son los restos de la creación y la destrucción, el himno póstumo, extraño y deletéreo del amor y la vida que jamás llega a resonar más allá de algún glu-glu subterráneo y discreto que musitan los ácidos al liberarse" ("Meditación" 51). The affective remains of human connections in all their contradictory and unattractive forms flow through the sewers as a quiet symphony. They do not become objects of beauty as in a perverse reversal of values; however, the fact that someone has decided to cast these things aside will not serve as just cause for their exclusion from Casey's conception of a revolutionary Cuban narrative.

Since this sludge never truly disappears, Casey takes it upon himself to wade through it in his short stories and study in his essays a selection of Cuban authors whose narratives at least hint at the "flies and pestilence" of the nation's past. In Casey's texts, what was flushed into the sewers returns in unexpected ways and feeds cycles of life and death: "El Océano acoge la corriente incesante que se diluye en la marejada y alimenta a los peces que la ciudad volverá a devorar, nostálgica quizás de un pasado inmediato" (51). Waste feeds the fish that will be eaten by the city's inhabitants and turned back into waste by those same citizens who reflect imperfectly on the past when they exclude that subterranean gurgling from their nostalgic recollections. Though Casey's characterization of nineteenth-century Cuban literature at times verges on flippant generalizations about the inappropriate application of Romanticism to Cuban narrative, he argues for the need to represent the unsightly, noxious, and lewd elements of human life that flow beneath the streets of every palace and every shack in the capital city and across the island in order to avoid nostalgic and idealized visions of a simpler past, a better people, and a mythological origin of the nation and the Revolution.

In Havana in 1964, Casey also published *Memorias de una isla*, a collection of his writings that includes an ambitious essay, "Hacia una comprensión total del XIX." Casey calls for a study of the everyday experiences of Cuba's nineteenth century

Chapter Nine

in order to arrive at a broader understanding of both the past and the present. Although he does not carry out this project in his brief text, he points toward such a totalizing vision: "Si políticamente no significamos nada para el mundo y tuvimos que esperar a que avanzara mucho el XX para comunicar algo de importancia a la humanidad, alguien tendrá que hacer algún día el gran análisis político del siglo XIX cubano" (122). He later describes this potential somebody as "algún Joyce por nacer o en proceso embrionario" (122). Casey's hesitation is not that of an insecure scholar. Beneath his waffling lies a sarcasm directed toward Ernesto "Che" Guevara's disdain for those so-called guilty, effeminate, or otherwise defective intellectuals—Casey's "we." Guevara frequently casts aside those intellectuals who were born before the Revolution as if they were the lingering refuse of a bygone era.[4] He says that Cuba must wait for the truly revolutionary intellectuals to come, those who will be born, raised, and educated fully within the revolutionary topography.[5] The youngest of these, Casey wryly suggests, could be gestating now. Nonetheless, this gay intellectual, born to parents of Batista's Cuba and raised in imperialist Baltimore, wants to get started on this enormous task: "Mientras aparezcan uno y otro, hagamos nuestra pequeña tentativa para acercarnos a una comprensión más cabal de lo ocurrido" (122). Casey refuses to sit around in an ivory tower and waste time.

Casey's aesthetic project is guided by two interrelated principles, one regarding the content and the other the form of Cuban narrative predating the Revolution. On the one hand, Casey calls for a historical analysis of "la masa desconocida": "de la que nadie habla o habla sólo de paso, de la gente que nunca salió en las crónicas de *La Habana Elegante* [...], la que la Condesa de Merlín nunca trató aunque fue servida por ella" ("Hacia" 122–23). So much is known of the upper classes, Casey explains, "pero desconocemos prácticamente el lado sórdido de la vida colonial [y de] la gente de segunda o de ninguna categoría, los olvidados de la Condesa, los que Heredia no pudo ni mencionar, porque la vocación romántica se lo prohibía" (124). If the Cuban Revolution was a revolution for the unknown masses to break the chains of dictatorship and neocolonialism, then surely the plight of those masses—how they came to Cuba, what roles they served in colonial and Republican society, how their labor yielded economic prosperity for others while they were relegated to the margins of high society, history, art, and literature—must be understood. What more pressing question than that of the discarded history of Cuba's defects: its colonization, its long-lasting slave economy, its misogyny, and its homophobia? Casey proposes that such a critical understanding and revision of national history and art, one without myths and heroes, serve as a guide for building a truly revolutionary society by assuming this contemptible past and working to eradicate its residual effects.

On the other hand, Casey asks a question that still plagues Cuban and, more broadly, Latin American literary and cultural history: "¿Cómo reconstruir costumbres sin caer en el costumbrismo?" ("Hacia" 119). Similar to the critiques leveraged at the elite appropriation of the gauchos in Argentina, Casey's concern is that this recuperation of the Cuban masses would be represented in a way that idealizes their history as one of simple, hardworking provincials living among bucolic, tropical landscapes, what he refers to as "la visión edénica" (125). In this context, Casey blames the Cuban Romantics for propagating this image; a quote with which I began this essay continues as follows:

> El romanticismo tuvo entre sus defectos hacernos creer en un mundo sin moscas y sin peste; el gran impulso liberador e individualista del héroe romántico le hizo ver el cielo siempre purísimo o envuelto en sombras cárdenas, y la visión que nos quedó del XIX es esencialmente romántica. Terca y torpemente, Villaverde ve castillos de Walter Scott en los montes de Pinar del Río. (127)

The Cuban Romantics, as Casey depicts them, could trudge through the swamps of Cuba and still describe them as a tropical paradise set for epic struggles and sublime realizations in order to assert Cuba's cultural parity with the most glorious of European landscapes. Furthermore, these writers were enmeshed in the spirit of capitalism; the Romantic hero, a symbol of individual prosperity who rises above the crowd, stands in direct opposition to the revolutionary shift toward the collective. For these reasons, Casey argues that the Romantics are the greatest culprits in perpetuating the capitalist myths that fuel nostalgia for a glorious, national past that never really existed. Whether his broad analysis of the Cuban Romantics is fair or not, he raises a valid question: What

Chapter Nine

would be more dangerous for the success of the Revolution than a widespread nostalgia among its citizens for the island's colonial and neocolonial past?

Casey proposes, in part, that the nineteenth century be understood "sin el falso brillo a que nos habituaron, y a que nos habituamos con no poca complacencia" (130). Unwilling to wait for those gestating intellectuals to mature, he positions himself as one who will dive headfirst into the squalor. Víctor Fowler-Calzada analyzes Casey's condemnation of what could be called the colonial Cuban canon: "Heredia, Miahle, Landaluce, Villaverde, Meza, La Condesa de Merlín, the two Betancourts, La Avellaneda, Hazard, Valdivia and Fornaris," plus the European writers, Flaubert, Dickens, and Charlotte Brontë (190). These writers created that false shine and concealed their own complicity, intentionally or not, with the colonial order. Fowler argues that the mid-twentieth-century literary magazine *Ciclón* serves as a potential remedy to the problem Casey analyzes. I agree with Fowler's interpretation, but it will not be necessary to leave Casey's writings to find moments in which this image of a shiny, happy Cuban past is replaced. Moreover, Casey says that those nineteenth-century writers lied in creating the Romantic image of the past, but their incompatibility with Casey's present aesthetic and political project does not mean they should be cast aside and forgotten: "Sus mentiras y sus verdades, en otras palabras, su espléndido o su mediocre esfuerzo impotente, son la gran clave para entender el pasado y la costumbre, y esa cosa más huidiza aún que se llama el estilo" ("Hacia" 121–22). Those so-called liars, the likely enemies of the Revolution, are necessary; similar to Pasternak, they can be brought into the fold, because there is something that persists in their texts worth recovering but only after recognizing that they are not impartial observers of the past.

Elsewhere in Casey's essays he attempts to recover a handful of Cuban writers, or at the very least, some parts of individual texts, and he builds from these moments in short stories of his own. In "Meza literato y los Croquis Habaneros," Casey evaluates Ramón Meza's *Mi tío el empleado* (1887) as both the author's best work and a high point in nineteenth-century Cuban narrative, because the author "supera las limitaciones del costumbrismo" (27). Casey locates a representation of the past without *costumbrismo* in Meza's writings, but he recognizes that Meza still harbors sympathies toward the racism of the early Republic following the abolition of slavery. *Mi tío el empleado* follows Vicente, a penniless, incompetent Spaniard who arrives in Havana, gradually rises through the local bureaucracy, and earns a title of nobility due only to nepotism. In addition to the critique of colonial values, the opening scenes of this novel are of particular importance for the line of inquiry sustained throughout Casey's writings. The narrator, Vicente's nephew, describes their first impressions of the capital as they disembark:

> Por algunos puntos del muelle nos era casi imposible transitar: y mucho más, llevando á cuestas el mundo. Carretillas, barriles, palancas, grandes vigas de madera, cabrestantes, tablones enormes, hombres cargados con sacos, todo se movía á un tiempo, en todas direcciones; aquello era una actividad febril, un torbellino que nos causaba vértigos, un espectáculo nuevo, desconocido y que parecía el más cruel derrumbe de todas las acariciadas imaginaciones de mi tío. ¡El, que creyó encontrar bosques de palmeras, de árboles con frutas tan bellas que semejasen globulillos de cristal de mil colores! ¡El, que creyó encontrar indios con taparrabos de plumas pintorreadas, carcax lleno de flechas untadas con venenoso jugo, terciado á la espalda, y narices y orejas taladradas por macizas argollas de oro que podrían arrancarse tan sólo con darles un fuerte tirón! (Meza, Vol. 1, 18–19)

In contrast to Vicente's Romantic vision of Cuba, this "balumba" of "hombres cubiertos de sudor, gritando, corriendo y dándonos empellones" provides the only setting for the protagonists as they find lodging and explore their new home (Meza, Vol. 1, 17). Where the uncle expected vast, tropical landscapes, he and his nephew found only the crowded, chaotic frenzy of the wharf. Where he expected picturesque natives, they found only sweaty, aggressive laborers.[6] Though Casey may have to dive into the sewers to find this side of Cuban reality in the Sixties, Meza's protagonists, fresh off the boat from Spain, see nothing but the dingy, urban underbelly of colonial commerce and fall into complete disillusionment along the wharf. For representing these urban masses and the city without the quaint hues of *costumbrismo*, Meza's novel earns Casey's praise: "Después de esto, las chirimoyas despiden un olor menos fragrante" ("Hacia" 128).

Chapter Nine

In "Mi tía Leocadia, el amor, y el paleolítico inferior" (1962), Casey indirectly rewrites certain scenes from Meza's novel, but he shifts the focus from the uncle to the aunt. Whereas Meza's narrator organizes the plot in chronological order as he tells the story of his uncle's despicable and undeserved social ascent, Casey's narrator recalls bits of his aunt's life and local changes in the urban landscape through brief flashbacks. Meza's narrative thoroughly critiques the boy's club that protects the uncle despite his incompetency; in contrast, Casey's narrative recounts fragmented scenes of the aunt as she cooks for neighborhood organizations and participates in grass-roots political campaigns. Unlike Vicente, Leocadia cannot benefit from sexist, back-room negotiations, and her political goals are oriented toward the collective good. Meza thoroughly documents and critiques exclusionary practices, and Casey proposes potential solutions on a smaller scale.

Furthermore, these flashbacks take place while the narrator sits in a Woolworth's five-and-dime shop:

> La otra tarde entré en ese inmenso almacén de cosas útiles y de cosas inútiles que llamamos en Cuba "Ten-Cén" […] y que en La Habana es más lujoso que en ninguna otra parte gracias al éxito fabuloso que alcanzó, porque cuando lo trasladaron a la esquina de Galiano se convirtió en una especie de círculo social para todas las clases. ("Mi tía" 37)

This is not an accidental setting for this story. In Greensboro, North Carolina, the sit-in protesting segregation in the United States on February 1, 1960, also took place in a Woolworth's. The company's name is already associated at the time with the Civil Rights Movement, and in Casey's story, it serves as a place in Havana where people of all genders and classes from different social and racial backgrounds mingle among both useful and useless items.

As nervous and uncomfortable as Vicente in the first volume of *Mi tío el empleado*, Casey's narrator describes the frenzied crowd that surrounds him:

> El público bullía sin cesar, chocando los que entraban por la puerta de San Miguel con los que venían del interior de la gran tienda. El local estaba superiluminado. Un hombre subido en una escalera de mano cambiaba, entre la muchedumbre

> que lo rodeaba, un anuncio que decía "super-cake gigante de frambuesa" por otro que decía "hot-dogs a 15." ("Mi tía" 40–41)

In Casey's story, there is a change in the lighting in this commercial space. Meza's narrator mentions greasy-floored shops in the wharf that were "iluminados allá en el fondo por una débil claridad azulosa" (*Mi tío* Vol. 1, 21). Whereas Meza's Havana exists within a bluish-gray haze, and its crowds and chaos are available in plain sight, Casey's Havana sits under fluorescent lights that should bring clarity to everything around them. However, those lights only illuminate the daily bargain, what is right here, right now, and prepared for consumption: giant cakes and cheap hot dogs.

For Casey's narrator, it becomes necessary to block out the modern world's harsh lighting in order to recall even the smallest detail about local history. "Mi tía Leocadia" is structured around a constant tension between the bright, noisy present and dim images of the past set in this exact spot. The narrator reconstructs some of these moments from memories and others from his knowledge of history, while also imagining fictional scenes set in a poor suburb, a royal estate, or a tropical forest devoid of human life, since no record of the remote past exists. At times he mentions specific dates, but he also speaks generally of:

> todos los millones de seres humanos que vivían en ese momento y hacían el amor y desfloraban vírgenes y sollozaban y apuñalaban a un hermano y se masturbaban y comían y compraban miel y pensaban lo que yo estoy pensando ahora y se iban a guerras y se secaban las llagas, y de cuyas vidas no queda nada, nada, nada, ni el menor recuerdo. ("Mi tía" 39)

Here he points toward the everyday stories made possible by shading his eyes from the over-illuminated present so that he may pay attention to the remnants of human life, to the waste flushed into the sewers, to the millions of people cast aside in the past and the present after being labeled "human garbage." However, no heroes rise from the mist. No epic struggles against evil take form. No totalizing narrative of the past becomes possible. These millions of people loved and hated, had sex and ate food, and perhaps they also anticipated the narrator's same thoughts. He is no modern exception standing above this ancient crowd. Though every trace of their lives is completely lost, just as his will be lost decades or centuries from now, he wonders how many of them might have died, been buried, and turned into the dust that was later excavated and used to make the concrete that now forms the walls of the Ten-Cén where he sits ("Mi tía" 39). His fiction cannot fully recover those lost voices, but not for any fault or lack of his own; all that anyone can do now is allow their imagination to open the empty spaces in which those stories could have taken place.

Every time his narrative starts to gain traction, however, the noisy, over-illuminated present breaks his concentration and leaves him trembling as all eyes focus on him. He explains one such interruption: "Una mujer delgada y nerviosa se sentó a mi lado y empujándome el codo con un movimiento brusco me hizo derramar parte del café con leche sobre el mostrador. Los colegiales y los empleados del mostrador estallaron en risas que difícilmente podían contener" ("Mi tía" 45). Whether attempting to narrate those millions of unknown people lost to history or the memories of his aunt who used to live in the building that is now the Ten-Cén, his task is made all but impossible in this overcrowded, over-illuminated present in which everyone is shouting and moving about in a frenzy. The narrator struggles to focus on his memories and tell the story of his aunt. In the end, the distractions and taunts from the crowd are too great. He writes that his aunt died, he drinks his coffee, and he goes home. For Casey, these are the conditions and limitations within which a revolutionary Cuban narrative of both the present and the past must be written in plain sight.

Getting Wasted

In addition to Meza, Casey dedicates considerable effort to recuperating the less respected Miguel de Carrión's *Las impuras* (1919) in the essay "Carrión o la desnudez" (1964). To begin, Casey explains that he does not consider Carrión to be among the best writers. Nevertheless, he praises Carrión for divesting Cuban narrative of Romanticism and showing complete indifference toward false national values: "Donde otros ven el brillo, la riqueza o la promesa de enormes riquezas, [Carrión] ve la sordidez, la pobreza, el parasitismo, el crimen, la corrupción política, la inseguridad agobiante de la vida económica cubana" (Casey, "Carrión" 43). Carrión has taken a cue from Zola's Naturalism in choosing how to depict early Republican society. Though Casey desires good writers, he is not willing to waste the work of a minor author who portrayed the historical content that Casey considers to be of vital importance to understand the nation's past and to construct a revolutionary present.

In general, content matters more than form in Casey's defense of Carrión. In particular, he considers one scene to stand above all others: the rumba scene at the house on Calle Factoría that reimagines the dance parties of Cirilo Villaverde's *Cecilia Valdés* (1882). The dance scenes from both novels share many characteristics, but they are set almost one hundred years apart. In *Invención de la Habana*, Emma Álvarez-Tabío Albo maps the changing cityscape of the Cuban capital over this period. Around the 1830s—the setting of *Cecilia Valdés*—Havana was a walled city protected more from expansion and uncontrolled growth than military attacks, "estableciendo con precisión los territorios frecuentados por cada clase social, que sólo se mezclaban en las zonas residuales o marginales de la ciudad" (*Invención* 94–95). Álvarez-Tabío Albo stated that these strict spatial and social divisions only began to dissolve by the last third of the century; greater social mobility was accompanied by waves of demolishing, redesigning, and constructing new, less divided spaces. By the early twentieth century—the setting of *Las impuras*—Álvarez-Tabío Albo explains that "la ciudad parece haber caído en manos de los marginales, los únicos capaces de poseerla y disfrutarla" (127). During the early Republic, the urban landscape was more fluid, but the individuals traversing it became more withdrawn (127).

The *cuna*, a social event in early nineteenth-century Havana, provides the setting in which Villaverde's protagonists can meet and mingle despite belonging to different classes, races, and genders. In *Cecilia Valdés*, the crowd at the *cuna* is described as "un hervidero de cabezas humanas" and a "tan extraña como heterogénea multitud" that danced "con furor" (36). Yet, these young, swaying bodies observe a certain propriety: "Por sobre el ruido de la orquesta con sus estrepitosos timbales, podía oírse, en perfecto tiempo con la música, el monótono y continuo chis, chas de los pies" (44). In this party, the protagonists dance the

Chapter Nine

Cuban *danza*, which played an important social role: allowing young men and women to mingle. It is during this *danza* that Leonardo Gamboa, the white son of a wealthy slaver, falls in love with Cecilia Valdés, a mixed-race young lady who passes as white and turns out to be his half-sister; they are kept apart by those few protagonists who know they are siblings, but the *cuna* allows them to meet.[7]

When compared to the second dance party in *Cecilia Valdés*, the *cuna* no longer appears as a utopian space. At the second party, the characters also represent a cross-section of Cuban society with "gente de todos colores, sexos y condiciones" (249). Unlike the *cuna* that was open to anyone, here invitations are required, and Cecilia is treated as the belle of the ball. She dances with both black and mixed-race men, but the narrator explains that "había marcada diferencia entre los negros y los mulatos. Con éstos, por ejemplo, bailó dos contradanzas, con los primeros sólo minués ceremoniosos" (250). Cecilia may dance with black men, but only for the stuffy, hierarchical minuet whose forms correspond to eighteenth-century aristocracy; during the minuets at this exclusive social event, no real social barriers are crossed.[8] She also appears to cross social barriers during the more democratic and informal *contradanzas* that she dances with mixed-race men, but only to those who incorrectly assume she is white; in reality, she is dancing with men of mixed race like herself.

Regardless, Cecilia later adds that the only dance that mattered to her was the individual, intimate *danza* she enjoyed with Leonardo in the first party. In retrospect, Cecilia undermines both the potential openness of the *cuna* in preferring that isolated *danza* with Leonardo and the potential openness of the *contradanzas* during the more exclusive party when she describes its faults as consisting of "la música ruidosa y chillona, las mujeres desgarbadas y feas, los hombres petulantes y necios" (371). To Cecilia, the second party was a wasted evening among filthy individuals. Overall, in *Cecilia Valdés*, these dance scenes only allow for superficial contact across social barriers, and in the few moments this appears to occur, the protagonist looks upon them with disgust.

Though Villaverde crafted a nuanced representation of the despicable social values of Cuba around the 1830s, in "Carrión o la desnudez" Casey argues that *Cecilia Valdés* leaves much to be desired: "Pero la 'cuna' de Villaverde, con toda su gracia y frescura maravillosas, palidece ante esta rumba de Carrión, bullanguera y sombría, cruel y sin esperanzas" (62). In comparing these novels, it is the lesser writer, Carrión, who successfully imagines a space in which colonial divisions and capitalist individualism are almost entirely eroded, and he achieves this effect in *Las impuras* without coloring the rumba with nostalgic hues for the post-colonial nation.

In the chapter of *Las impuras* titled "Orgía," the rumba scene takes place at Felicia's house on a poorly lit street in the city. On this balmy evening, upwards of fifty people from all walks of life attend the event: "Aquella muchedumbre de hombres y mujeres hablaba poco, entregándose furiosamente al goce del baile, que no era a veces sino un lúbrico frote de cuerpos, lenta y cadenciosamente arreglado al compás de la música" (Carrión 352–53). The writing lacks finesse, but then again, so does this scene of writhing, drunken bodies who have cast aside all social protocols as they rub against one another. The dancing grows ever wilder:

> A medida que el tiempo transcurría, la orgía iba haciéndose más animada y más brutal. Las caras, apopléticas, empezaban a reflejar la vaguedad de la inconsciencia, mientras los cuerpos se movían casi automáticamente y se proferían enormidades y desvergüenzas sin el menor reparo. Un ruido compuesto de mil ruidos, un clamor continuo en que se mezclaban las notas del piano, los chillidos de las mujeres, las voces roncas de los borrachos y el frote de los pies de los bailadores sobre el áspero pavimento, llenaba la casa entera, desde la sala hasta la cocina. (355)

These faces and bodies, no longer individuals separated by race, class, gender, or sex, appear on the brink of a stroke as they act from unconscious desires instead of according to social protocols. Unlike the defined musical styles of *Cecilia Valdés*, the room is overtaken by a cacophony in which instruments become indistinguishable from the uproar of the drunken crowd.

This wild writhing of humans who have come together in pure joy to abandon, temporarily, social order and propriety earns Casey's approval:

> La rumba de la calle Factoría es la escena culminante y magistral de la obra. ... Allí están todos, vivos y "verracos," los que pagan y los que se hacen pagar, mantenidos y explotadas [sic], buenos

> y malos, falsos y auténticos, girando a los danzones de un pianista espectral. ("Carrión" 61)

Here there are no moral judgments and no others cast out from the party, nor are there heroes or role models to be found among the crowd. All of these distinctions and values have been suspended within this frenzied mass for a brief period that struggles to sustain itself as the plot barrels headfirst toward its Naturalist denouement.

Casey's aesthetics are intended to shore up the Revolution by drawing attention to the social, economic, and cultural history of the masses with all its contradictions and limitations. He seeks to represent those masses without resorting to *costumbrismo* or the ideals of the Romantic imagination, even when this means that the subjects being represented do not appear as model or moral citizens. He does not defend relativism or an insipid form of postmodernism in which anything goes; rather, he makes room for those who, according to lingering, prerevolutionary social protocols, risk being cast aside like the remnants of life he finds in the city's sewers. These undervalued people are in many cases the very masses who bore the burden of ensuring the island's prerevolutionary economic success and its military victories against Batista's regime. Casey removes those long-standing and persistent value judgments as he seeks out the stories of wasted lives in Havana's sewers and among the drunken crowds of Cuba's past.

With and Through the Filth

In my analysis, Casey's project could lead to a renewed defense of *P.M.*, the documentary directed by Orlando Jiménez Leal and Sabá Cabrera that was officially censored in Cuba in 1961.[9] In doing so, Casey's aesthetics and politics diverge from the Revolution he intends to support, especially as Castro aligns his government with the Soviet Union and subjects all cultural production to censorship. Though Casey did not draw this connection in any of his essays, nor would he have been permitted to do so after 1961 in Cuba, I find it productive to situate the rumba scene in *Las impuras* as a literary antecedent of both *P.M.* and Casey's posthumously published short story, "Piazza Margana."

The debate sparked by *P.M.* can appear today to be completely disproportionate to the banality of the film itself. Running for only fourteen minutes, it documents Havana's nightlife in a series of vignettes. There is no dialogue or plot, only images of the city as seen from boats and cars and of people of all races drinking, dancing with one another, and listening to or playing music. There is neither perceivable violence nor the graphic display of sexualized bodies. What is documented in *P.M.* is the joy and delight that can be experienced when people come together and dance to live music. In "Pasado Meridiano," Néstor Almendros claims that in this film there is "un gran amor por el ser humano, por el hombre humilde, por el hombre anónimo y hay amor hasta para el pobre borracho desorientado" (n.p.). Precisely this inclusion of even the disoriented drunkard is what allows me to situate *P.M.* alongside those Cuban texts praised by Casey.

The choice to represent the masses of the Cuban Revolution as joyful human beings could have been interpreted in 1961 as a positive portrayal of the success of the Revolution. In an interview, Jiménez Leal summarizes the debate surrounding the film: "La Revolución quería mostrar en ese momento su más brilloso realismo socialista: la exaltación del obrero con fusil en alto, banderas ondeando, himnos patrióticos" (Zapata and Jiménez Leal n.p.). Though *P.M.* does not show Cubans who quickly organize themselves to defend and build this new society, these Cubans still know how to delight in the society they are building; they are not emotionless drones carrying out a dictator's orders.

Of course, all of this is speculation about events that would not come to pass. In "Palabras a los intelectuales," Castro explicitly states that matters related to artistic expression are subordinate to the survival of the Revolution: "Porque lo primero es eso: lo primero es la Revolución misma y después, entonces, preocuparnos por las demás cuestiones" (n.p.). From his perspective in June of 1961, the Revolution is under threat, and until this perpetual state of emergency passes, those remaining artistic forms not evidently aligned with the Revolution have the potential to damage it. As Richard theorizes, remains and vestiges are "lo que el sistema de racionalización del conocimiento no sabe bien cómo integrar a sus marcos de análisis por considerar que carecen de firmeza y consistencia" (*Residuos* 78). In order to construct a totalizing vision of the revolutionary event, Castro decrees that everything except seemingly smooth, transparent language be discarded until the Revolution is secure. Cuba must appear as an actually existing utopian space populated with highly organized and trained citizens who are prepared to defend their homeland against imperial forces. In this manner, Castro demands a Socialist Realism without "flies or pestilence," one that illuminates only positive, even propagandistic, images of the Revolution similar to the Romantic vision of Cuba, with its epic landscapes and mythical heroes. These are the very aesthetic values that Casey criticizes for their misleading simplicity and for the danger they pose to the Revolution itself.

In contrast, Casey dives into the sewers and combs through the sludge seeking out the remains of what had been cast aside. Similar to Somers's attempt to puncture totalizing discourse with enigmas, Casey attempts to sully that shiny, coherent narrative of a perfect Cuba with the refuse, waste, and filth he finds underground. But the goal is never to damage the Revolution. Casey's aesthetics proposes a partial restoration of those wasted elements to the surface of public discourse. A truly totalizing vision of the past would be impossible, since it can only be built from the broken pieces, decomposing remains, and slippery memories of what had been cast out, killed, or ignored in the past. Given these limitations, Casey's aesthetics and politics call for narratives that write in plain sight the cycle of life and death, the contradictions and criss-crossings of meanings and significations, and the filthy, messy images of Cuban reality that betray the State's logic. He does so in order to eradicate the residues of prerevolutionary social hierarchies and capitalist values that threaten the prosperity of the Revolution. Well aware of the stakes even from exile, Casey would not defend *P.M.* after it was censored and the organizations for which he worked—*Revolución*, *Lunes de Revolución*, and the television program on which *P.M.* aired, *Lunes de Televisión*—were officially closed later in 1961. Yet, his aesthetic values, in particular his praise for the rumba scene in *Las impuras*, mobilize the same arguments as those used to defend the value of *P.M.* within the Revolution, and his revolutionary history of Cuban aesthetics would not be complete without recovering this wasted film.

Within this constellation that ranges from *Cecilia Valdés* to *P.M.*, Casey's "Piazza Margana," can now be read as a text that is not as out of place within his collected works as it might first appear. This short story was written in English, in contrast to almost all of his other works, and during his exile in Rome. Casey had been writing a novel, titled *Gianni, Gianni*, but upon his suicide in 1969, "Piazza Margana" was the only portion of the manuscript he chose not to destroy. He entrusted it to Rafael Martínez Nadal, asking him to publish the story in England when he thought it appropriate.[10] In my analysis, "Piazza Margana" brings together all of the ideas discussed above regarding both the content and the form of a revolutionary aesthetic project that was intended to support the Cuban Revolution that wasted these efforts.

In Casey's only story to represent openly gay characters, the narrator watches as his boyfriend cuts himself while shaving. First, he imagines devouring every piece of his lover's body in a cannibalistic demonstration of his love. This brief scene then shifts toward the narrator's imagined journey into his lover's body:

> As I write ... I know that I will be with you, travel with you, sleep with you, dream with you, urinate and generally defecate with you, make love *with and through* you, hate with you, think, cry, grow senile, warm, cold and warm again, feel, look, jerk off, kiss, kill, pet, fart, fade, flush, turn into ashes, lie, humiliate myself and others, strip, stab, wilt, wait, wail, laugh, steal, quiver, waver, ejaculate, linger, backscuttle, pray, fall, doublecross, triplecross, ogle, browse, goose, suck, brag, bleed, blow with and through you. (188, italics in original)

During his journey, the self and the other remain at an untraversable distance from one another, because the narrator, though inexplicably shrunken to the size of a cell in his lover's body, never fuses with his lover's body or mind, nor does he romanticize sexual practices as the pinnacle of democratic communion with the other.[11] As Rojas argues, this penetration of the other's body does not take place "como posesión, sino como abandono y persistencia" (43). The narrator's journey takes place *with* and *through* his lover's body, but never *as* nor *in the place of* the other. It is his love for the other man that will grant him access into his body, to commune and communicate with him from within him, through him, as he shares in this series of human endeavors without moral judgment.

Chapter Nine

The narrator's ability to express his love does not rely on an idealized vision of his lover or of the human body. Instead, comparable to the narrator in "Meditación junto a Caballería," he imagines diving headfirst into this man's bloodstream, flowing past the electric charges in his brain, and eventually descending into his intestinal tract where he is "endlessly attracted, embraced, and rejected by the myriad shapes, the tentacular beings of the uncharted forest, the tiny monstrous flowers, the endless process of creation and destruction" ("Piazza" 192). In both the city's sewers and the lover's intestines, the cycles of life and death, creation and destruction, delicacy and monstrosity, food and feces, coexist in a complicated jumble that Casey chooses to represent in its complexity.

What type of narrative, then, can be written within this delicate, imperfect, limited space full of wasted ideas, objects, and bodies? His journey culminates as follows:

> I could write endlessly about my passage through the semilunar folds, the opalescent light where the strangest creatures, half-animal, half-vegetable, open and close, degenerate and regenerate, disembowel in mass suicides only to swap fragments and reunite, seconds later. That part of my trip takes years, so strong is the fascination of the sickly glare, which takes on a subtly different shade under each fold. I let myself be embraced by the billion creatures swarming through me, crowding in the thick juice through which I swim in silence. I choose one at random, perhaps the most attractive, perhaps the most horrid one, and let myself be engulfed and swallowed like a corpuscle being devoured by a white cell. What infinite quietude, what peace then … How come I never thought of this? This is happiness. There is no other word. (192)

Though in "Meditación junto a Caballería" Casey concentrates on the destructive and decaying elements that flow through the sewers, in "Piazza Margana" his aesthetics is not one that chooses between binaries, between light and dark, creation and destruction, treasure and trash, self and other, propriety and impropriety. Under an opalescent light, the narrator's body sways back and forth between states of being, not quite animal or vegetable, not fully opened or closed, wherein what is created cannot be separated from what is destroyed. He desires to revel in the swarm of creatures he encounters. Here he describes the gut flora; recent studies have confirmed that they number, not in the billions as he says, but around one hundred trillion bacterial cells that form a symbiotic relationship with their host, a beneficial and necessary relationship but one that is not without harm to either side.[12]

In this final image, the narrator accepts his banal role within this incomprehensibly massive crowd in which the distinction between attractive and horrid loses its relevance. What he imagines to take place is cohabitation, imperfect and seemingly impossible as it is, within this corpuscle, within the swarm of gut flora, with and through the intestinal tract of his lover's body. Here, now, for an unspecifiable amount of time, he feels happy. Not exceptional, not heroic, not romanticized; just reveling in the filth. This is one example of the types of wasted narratives Casey proposes as best capable of telling the history of Cuban culture and representing the Cuban people as they worked toward the construction and consolidation of the revolution he had imagined to be possible—even though that was not the revolution that came to pass, and even though Casey's aesthetics never found a place within the national imaginary.

PART FOUR

The Ethics of Being Perceived

> The fact that must constitute the point of departure for any discourse on ethics is that there is no essence, no historical or spiritual vocation, no biological destiny that humans must enact or realize.
>
> Giorgio Agamben, *The Coming Community*

Between the seemingly individualistic process of going unnoticed and the gestures toward new forms of community analyzed throughout the previous chapters an untraversable gap appears to have opened. Going unnoticed is only ever a temporary state when someone turns away from totalizing institutions, slips out of their gaze, and opens lines of flight along which one's perception of the political and aesthetic organization of the world are irreversibly reoriented. These practices do not produce new heroic individuals who rise above the crowd to see and govern with total clarity, nor do they uncover an essential foundation for the political community. The politics of going unnoticed has no *a priori* goals; rather, it effects a disordering or a disruption on smaller scales. If those who went unnoticed had decided to remain in the shadows or to hide instead of write in plain sight, then the politics of going unnoticed would slip into solipsism, self-preservation at any cost, or a renewed bid for hegemony—in other words, into Filloy's *yomismo*. Yet, Calvert Casey, Juan Filloy, and Armonía Somers imagine characters who establish dialogues with others from their seemingly unimportant positions. In this final part, I analyze the new dialogues that become possible as a result of these disruptions. By going unnoticed and writing in plain sight, different people and groups allow themselves to be perceived from within new thresholds that have been pried open between the high walls and rhetorical devices used to divide and isolate them from one another in the service of hegemonic politics and inequality. These practices are what I call "the ethics of being perceived."

I have a particular definition of the word "ethics" in mind that distinguishes it from "morals." These terms are frequently used as synonyms, and their connotations vary drastically from one context and author to another. Today, morality and moral values are associated with religious, national, or other forms of identity-based appeals for appropriate behavior, whereas ethics relates to the business world as it establishes a variety of codes of conduct for its employees. For my purposes, this common-sense distinction names more or less equivalent practices by which one group tells its members and others how they ought to behave. In philosophy, rulebooks for behavior are studied and developed under the umbrella term, "normative ethics," which encompasses three main subfields: 1) virtue ethics,[1] which emphasizes virtue or moral character as the foundation for good actions; 2) consequentialism,[2] which analyzes the outcomes of actions; and 3) deontology,[3] which determines duties and obligations. Despite their specific perspectives, each of these three branches of normative ethics is concerned with establishing the boundaries by which virtuous or moral actions are defined. This outline, although hasty, can serve as a guiding map for a variety of ethical theories that do not interest me at present; as a shorthand, I prefer to label all such theories and rulebooks that map the distinction between good and evil, virtue and vice, proper and improper, under the term "morals."

An ethics of the politics of going unnoticed plays out in the threshold spaces pried open between normative binaries wherein such distinctions lose their clarity and, therefore, their expediency for a hegemonic politics that seeks to divide human beings from one another in the service of economic and social inequality. This does not mean that any action can now be considered acceptable within any community. Rather, this ethics takes place within a constellation of texts that historicize the particularity of seemingly universal moral categories. In *The Genealogy of Morals*, Friedrich Nietzsche critiques moral values by calling into question their "intrinsic worth" and claim to universality through genealogical and etymological analyses (155). Nietzsche concludes that "the origin of the opposites *good* and *bad* is to be found in the pathos of nobility and distance, representing the dominant temper of a higher, ruling class in relation to a lower, dependent one" (160). He contends that the concept of "the good" was not something attributed to oneself from above or outside but rather an internally applied term by which a ruling class legitimized its claim to power. While he ultimately reduces the question of moral values to class distinctions, Nietzsche's analysis lays the groundwork for interpreting "the good" and "the bad" not as universal categories, as thinkers from Plato to Kant have argued, but rather as historically contingent values that structure a society through the belief that one's own community *is* good, while those who are said to be in opposition to, different from, or simply residing outside this group's imagined limits *are* bad or evil. Building from his analysis, today the essentialized morality that claims to know what is good (e.g., "us," the proper) and what is bad (e.g., "them," the improper) can be interpreted from within a broader context that contests exclusions based on gender, sexuality, race, and any other mode of ideological identity, as they intersect with and reinforce class distinctions.

Once the supposedly universal categories of, for example, good and evil are determined to be historically contingent, it becomes possible to refuse to participate in a politics that simply marks the other, whoever they, you, or I may be, as immoral in order to justify power relations. In "What is Enlightenment?" Foucault expands on Nietzsche's analysis and proposes a way of thinking that does not center on deciding whether one is "'for' or 'against' the Enlightenment": "one must refuse everything that might present itself in the form of a simplistic and authoritarian alternative" (313). What interests me is this refusal of the false dilemma. Instead of adopting an attitude of rejection—of casting aside what is labelled "inhuman" or "filth"—he proposes adopting a "limit-attitude" that can move beyond the "outside-inside alternative" or beyond any other simplistic and authoritarian binary, whether they be political, ethical, or both (315). This refusal to name, divide, and cast aside as if from a universally true, but actually solipsistic, moral standpoint serves as a necessary starting point for the ethics of being perceived.

"Politics" in the present study has not served as a synonym for "will to power" or for "hegemony." I have defined politics as a gesture that produces an opening for dissent and disagreement within a democratic framework. Similarly, "ethics" is not the equivalent of any "morality" or "moral code," nor anything that resembles a "normative ethics" built on empty signifiers or totalizing, seemingly transparent language. The ethics of being perceived is not an attempt to reconfigure the world into new distinctions between good and bad actions, between the proper and the improper, between the norm and the exception, or between us and them. Moral values are not autonomous, intrinsic to individuals, or universal; in fact, they are among the most powerful tools employed from above and below to secure the hegemonic status of any individual who exercises his will to power. Furthermore, I do not prescribe a path of action that must be followed in all circumstances; none of the protagonists studied in this chapter rise as universal heroes. Rather, the ethics of being perceived names the unending, arduous task of restoring the conditions of possibility for an inclusive, political space wherein dissent and disagreement among individuals and communities can come to take place through dialogues in which no other is cast as the enemy to be obliterated but rather as an adversary to be debated.

Chapter Ten

Exposure through Dialogues

Somers's novel, *De miedo en miedo (Los manuscritos del río)* (1965), opens with the phrase, "Estábamos bailando" (7). This "we" announces a common identity between the male narrator and an anonymous woman, suggesting an *a priori* origin of this plural subject already in the middle of a shared activity. However, the brief story of this "we" is really a flashback to the time the narrator lied about his identity in order to trick a guest into dancing with him at the hotel where he worked as a bellhop. He speaks for himself but only narrates the woman's direct dialogue once, when she asks him, "¿Y tú, qué estudias?" (7). She has been consumed by this "we." She does not speak of or for herself or for both of them at any moment; her voice is only used as a device to elicit more information about the narrator. Meanwhile, he explains how he dodged her questions to keep her close and continue dancing: "Seguimos desplazándonos durante el resto de la noche, con mi sexo primeramente a quemarropa, y luego casi a cuerpo traviesa, único dato seguro sobre mí que podría ofrecerle por el momento" (7). Threatened by his weaponized sex, the woman literally becomes a warm object on which he grinds his body, and the "we" he uses to bind her to him poorly masks the lies that found their experience as common. In this flashback, the woman was appropriated both physically and rhetorically by a man who hid his true identity in order to trick her into doing as he pleased. No ethical encounter takes place in this opening scene.

Being-With

Going unnoticed cannot be a permanent position inhabited forever by an individual. Jean-Luc Nancy describes how the notion of being an individual commonly implies that one is "closed off from all community" and detached "from a formless ground," but he insists that in actuality "there is no singular being without another singular being" (*Inoperative Community* 27–28). No such thing as an individual exists; there is no life outside or detached from another life but only "the network, the interweaving, and the sharing of singularities" (27). In this sense, he argues that the only possible ontology, which will no longer be understood as ontology, is the always shared co-existence of singular plural beings: "Existence *is with*; otherwise, nothing exists" (*Being Singular Plural* 4; italics in original). This existence is no longer Heidegger's Being but a being-with, a sharing of the world between singular plural beings that cannot become detached from one another.

Of course, this does not mean each of us communicates clearly and transparently with one another. Rather, each of us can only attempt to communicate with others through language, which he defines as "the exposing of plural singularity" (Nancy, *Being Singular Plural* 84). Language is the imperfect, incomplete, and transitory medium by which a (singular plural) I becomes exposed in dialogues to (singular plural) others; these fleeting dialogues allow only for the perception of brief glimpses into one another's existence. Furthermore, language is incorporeal. It does not exist in the world as if the world were a receptacle or body that contained it, but rather it is the outside of the world that opens thresholds in which these singular pluralities can expose themselves to one another:

> It [Language] is the whole of the outside of the world; it is not the eruption of an Other, which would clear away or sublimate the world, which would transcribe it into something else; instead, it is the exposition of the world-of-bodies as such, that is, as originarily singular plural. The incorporeal exposes bodies according to their being-with-one-another; they are neither isolated nor mixed together. (84)

For Nancy, there is no such thing as an individual who waits alone for the language of an other to erupt in their life and either transform or annihilate them. Instead, each singular plural being, which is always a being-with, is limited to exposing their plural singularity to others through language. What is exposed is neither an essence nor a fixed identity but the necessary co-existence between these plural singularities and the ways in which they establish relationships among themselves.

In my analysis, those who go unnoticed inhabit thresholds that temporarily allow them to avoid perception along their lines of flight. However, thresholds are not self-sustaining caves or isolated chambers that can protect a singular or bare life; they open between and within spaces and leave those inhabiting them exposed on multiple sides to other bare lives, to others who are exposed to them as well. This exposure is not the same as granting visibility to that person or to the identity they are said to represent; in this sense, "to expose" is not a synonym for the verb "to reveal," because the latter implies the possibility of a clear and total comprehension of the self and the other. Rather, these exposures take place through language in the instant of a flash, in the same instant that can create a photograph as easily at it can destroy an entire roll of film. Only through such exposures of language can an ethical dialogue take place, and only through ethical dialogues can the infinite task of creating community even begin.

That I do not exist alone in the world is the most challenging lesson at stake in the contemporary world. To this point, going unnoticed has opened a series of political and aesthetic tools for deactivating the binary divisions of biopolitics that isolate bare lives into clearly defined, brightly lit spaces. Somers's fiction in particular allows me to take a next step toward the ethics of being perceived that becomes possible as all of these singular plural bodies begin to dialogue with one another as the non-essentialized, radically heterogeneous, and constantly disagreeing pluralities that each of us together has always been.

And

The flashback at the beginning of *De miedo en miedo* provides a contrast to the dialogues that Somers's narrator, now older and married, establishes with another woman who comes into the bookshop where he works. "Busco cierto libro raro," she says, initiating their first dialogue (*De miedo* 11). Both the man and the woman begin their encounter as a singular I approaching another. The first time the narrator uses a first-person plural verb, it is introduced not with "nosotros" or an assumed "we" as in the flashback, but rather with "ella y yo" (12). The narrator briefly links them together, not as one plural entity whose union predates the narrative, but rather as two people exposed to

Chapter Ten

one another. To borrow a phrase from Nancy, this type of "and" marks "the appearance of the *between* as such: you *and* I (between us)—a formula in which the *and* does not imply juxtaposition, but exposition" (*Inoperative Community* 29; italics in original). This exposure of the common space between them only takes place for an instant. Once she pays, the "and" connecting them disappears: "Ella salió con su libro. Yo fui por mi chaqueta [...] y me lancé tras el rastro" (*De miedo* 13). However, the narrator now recognizes his place within the common space that simultaneously links and separates them, and he chooses to follow her and to engage with her across and throughout that space.

In the bookshop, possibly set in Paris, the owner sits on the upper floor, "un lugar estratégico," from which he watches over every aspect of the business, including the narrator's interactions with customers (*De miedo* 12).[1] In order to talk to her, the narrator must follow her into the street to ask her about the handkerchief she keeps sealed in an envelope in her purse that he glimpsed as she paid. Now outside and away from the all-seeing eye of the owner, he explains his interest in what he perceives to be their shared fear of germs, microbes, and contamination, but he also tells her about his wife and son; he is not trying to conquer her as he had done with other women in his youth. Their conversation is a bit awkward, but eventually she smiles, "iniciando [...] una especie de frente común, mientras la muchedumbre [les] enviaba gratuitamente sus vapores de cuerpo" (13). These two hypochondriacs make an exception for one another and strike up a random conversation in the middle of the street at midday surrounded by so many other unknown bodies. Each shares their different approaches for avoiding the most used parts of coffee cups at cafes and the parts of doors with the most fingerprints. Despite their precautions, they agree they still feel sick all the time. Their constant fear of germs that drives their desire to go unnoticed leads them to being perceived by one another for a brief moment before they go their separate ways.

Given the size of the city, the narrator recognizes how difficult it would be to find her: "En una ciudad llena de cuevas de la que cada cual sacará su cabeza a la mañana, ella se me acababa de perder como la pequeña piedra de un anillo, en esa forma tan insidiosa de dejarnos con el aro vacío" (*De miedo* 17). After their exchange, he is left only with the absence that takes the shape of her former presence. Since he does not know very many details about her, he decides it is best to forget her: "Pero uno no se echa en busca de pequeños fragmentos incapaces de recomponer el todo" (17–18). His obsessive-compulsive instincts leave him resigned to ignore those seemingly unimportant details that he does remember—her voice, her smile, her handkerchief—since a more complete and totalizing encounter, something more like the perfect palindrome, could not be formed from them.

Somers's narrator may have approached this second woman in a very different manner than the one from his youth, but he mistakenly rejects the idea that—as Casey's narrator in "Notas de un simulador" states—seemingly unimportant details offer splendid clues. Resigned to never see the woman again, that evening at home he begins writing fragmented journal entries to record his most intimate, untoward thoughts, the type that cross everyone's minds but are rarely spoken for fear of how others might react. In his first entry, for example, he is frustrated by his screaming infant son, and he asks in writing "¿será preciso suprimir al niño?" (*De miedo* 19). He does not regret the thought: "Me quedé fascinado sobre la concreción de aquella voluntad exterminadora" (19). However, he is well aware of the moral outrage that would result from anyone who might find his manuscripts full of reflections on murder, suicide, and death—acts which he will never commit. He considers eating his texts, flushing them down the toilet, or asking his wife to burn them, but he decides to throw them in the river every night once he is finished writing. In the process, he comes to appreciate a sort of piecemeal acquisition of an imperfect knowledge:

> Es decir que yo, que he tenido siempre tanto miedo de morir por inmersión, comencé a guardar más de mí en aquel fondo lleno de ahogados azules que por encima. [...] La vida había sido un acontecer lineal, como una novela fuera de moda dividida en capítulos. Pero el río, siempre hambriento de mí, quería mis pedazos, fueran o no consecutivos. (19–20)

He begins to understand the ravenous desire to approach and listen to the words of another person even when those are only bits and fragments of ideas randomly tossed around. He expresses an emergent appreciation of the narrative modes made possible by the avant-gardes in their attempt to smash institutions and conventions, those same texts that by the Sixties were being published within cultural markets. Simultaneously, he undergoes an opening toward the type of incomplete, errant dialogues that he comes to have with the woman he met at the bookshop in which their lines of communication always exceed what is said out loud.

On a random day, the woman returns to the bookshop, and throughout the novel, they continue to meet in other places and talk about their lives, an activity the narrator describes as "componiendo nuestro mundo compartido" (*De miedo* 21). This common space has to be built from their mutual confessions, by exposing their most intimate thoughts, those unimportant, but destructive ideas that continually haunt them. Nevertheless, there is always some distance between them. The narrator describes a pause in one of their early encounters: "Nos quedamos unos minutos más como suspendidos de un hilo, incapaz [yo] de resistir si alguno de los dos no disminuía la tensión de algún modo" (23). A subtle, almost imperceptible shift between subjects—characteristic of Somers's syntax—manifests itself here; the sentence begins in the first-person plural by which the narrator describes what he and the woman are experiencing together, but it quickly jumps mid-sentence to his limited, interior experience through the singular adjective, "incapaz." Only he is incapable of maintaining this dialogue. He refuses to speak for the woman on this topic, thereby recognizing the distance that still exists between him and her.

Exposing Infinity

Dialogues, either those written in the narrator's river manuscripts or spoken with the woman, become a possible tool for bridging the gap toward new forms of community. Of course, this one man has been very slow to arrive at a moment in his life when he is prepared to expose his thoughts and engage in dialogue with another person, and only this random stranger is willing to attempt to dialogue with him. The narrator does attempt to have this type of conversation with his wife: "Quiero que hablemos ahora mismo —le supliqué— de esas cosas sin importancia que nos han sucedido alguna vez, pero que siguen provocando destrucción como la bomba de Hiroshima" (*De miedo* 37). She mumbles something in return and ignores him. Caught in the details of their everyday life, they never speak of anything so intimate and dangerous. *De miedo en miedo* will not end with a utopia of shared dialogues among happy citizens. This novel remains within a tiny threshold between two strangers who meet in public and go unnoticed by everyone else as they embark on the arduous task of establishing a dialogue just among themselves by exposing their fears to one another.

For example, he begins to tell the anonymous woman how he feels when she is not around, explaining that he imagines her nearby and writes stories about her: "me compongo mis novelas con tu sombra" (*De miedo* 66). He had never told anyone about his manuscripts, and realizing what he had inadvertently blurted out to her, he says, "Sentía que alguien había proyectado una luz fugaz sobre mi cabeza como a un ladrón escondido en las sombras" (66). This brief flash of light exposes a tiny bit of him to her momentarily. Since this exposure was unplanned and unannounced, she was not prepared to focus her attention on it; rather, she only managed to glimpse, ever so slightly, something he had been keeping hidden. This fleeting exposure through fragmented dialogues that can never completely reveal one person to another will serve as my entry point into the ethics of being perceived named in these final chapters.[2]

They continue their dialogues over the following years as they meet in public, write letters that end with ellipses, and cut off their conversations abruptly, leaving so many other stories forever untold. One day, as they walk from their meeting place back to the bookshop, the woman recommends the following to start their dialogue anew: "Tú eliges algo que te haya quedado inexpresado, sin poderlo comunicar a nadie. Y lo vamos desplazando como si estuviésemos solos" (67). They do not plan to fully state or comprehend exactly what the other wants to express. Rather, they attempt to pass their ideas back and forth across the gap separating them, shifting and slipping around on the surface of their stories in no particular order, while trying to avoid groups of boy scouts and other strangers in the streets who keep crossing their path.

Their confusing, fragmented, non-linear conversations exceed what is actually said. In this sense, their dialogues are similar to a form of communication that Emmanuel Levinas calls "saying." As opposed to "the said" that states an essence as if it were a fact or a piece of easily transmittable information, saying is the condition of possibility for the unending communication of the other's alterity: "Saying is communication, to be sure, but as a condition for all communication, as exposure" (*Otherwise than Being* 48). Insofar as it unblocks communication and exposes the other's alterity, saying requires a temporalization other than succession and regression, other than "a linear regressive movement, a retrospective back along the temporal series toward a very remote past" (10). The said pretends to be definitive; it falsely claims to have revealed visible and known others to the self by reducing the other to the self. In contrast, saying more closely describes the dialogues between the man and the woman in Somers's novel, wherein one self engages with another self in unending dialogues through which tiny bits of their experiences and ideas flash briefly, even incomprehensibly, before one another's eyes.

Exposure, being perceived by another person, creates enough anxiety on its own. Though Somers's narrator seeks out these dialogues with the woman, the lack of answers to his existential queries at times exacerbate his fears: "Me había acogotado una ansiedad mortal de aclaración, de desciframiento" (*De miedo* 36).[3] But similar to ArteletrA, the Sator Square, and all of Somers's enigmas, there is no true meaning to be deciphered or unveiled; there will always remain an excess to what is capable of being said across this distance through language. Refusing to calm him by pretending she now understands, the woman describes those parts of him that she can only approach distantly as his "infinity": "No sé de lo que estás hablando, pero se trataba también de tu infinito" (70). Even if over time he were to expose every single aspect of himself to her, still she would have to be capable of perceiving and comprehending an infinite amount of information. Instead of working toward a total representation of the other, they opt for gradually exposing ever smaller fragments of their experiences, which they still find overwhelming to comprehend.

Parallel to the concepts of saying and the said, Levinas theorizes the discursive interactions between a self and an other using the terms infinity and totality. In sum, he argues that there are two approaches to establishing this interaction, both of which require language. The totalizing approach is the one that "reduces the other to the same" (*Totality and Infinity* 42). To totalize is to swallow up the other by annihilating anything that stands out as different from the self. The narrator's approach to the woman at the hotel in the flashback could be understood as totalizing in this regard. In contrast, "infinity" is the word Levinas uses to evoke the untraversable distance that always separates a self from an other and to demonstrate that every other is irreducible to any self. Despite this distance, he insists that language can serve as a medium across infinity, but only in certain circumstances: "Mediation (characteristic of Western philosophy) is meaningful only if it is not limited to reducing distances. For how could intermediaries reduce the intervals between terms infinitely distant?" (44). An infinite distance can never be traversed, and for Levinas the ethical relationship takes place during the face-to-face interaction wherein each self recognizes the impossibility of fully reaching the other and, importantly, refuses to reduce the other to the self's experience and knowledge. Language, in the form of dialogue, can limit its function to that of an imperfect medium—an exposure or a saying, but not a revelation or the said—that allows for a self and an other to approach one another face to face.

This type of exposure in which a self can be perceived by another opens the potential for an ethics of going unnoticed. In the case of Somers's narrator and the woman, they expose their faces to one another in an asymmetrical relationship and remain separated by an infinite distance. Nevertheless, once the narrator accepts this infinite, untraversable gap separating himself from the woman, he notices that they both experience an insatiable desire to continue their dialogues instead of going back to their everyday routines: "Mi costumbre de mostrarle las entrañas y su desesperación por revolverlas y encontrar símbolos, nos empezó a fanatizar, a impedir el curso hacia adelante de la vida" (*De miedo* 34). Yet, it is precisely their eagerness to pay attention to these fragments of conversations that allows them to continue exposing their faces to one another, thus opening and reopening the potential for dialogue.

Both Levinas and Somers approach a similar ethics; however, an important difference should be noted. Levinas frequently writes from the perspective of the same—referencing, for example, the other's "irreducibility to the I" (*Totality and Infinity* 43). Alternately, Somers's fiction exceeds the interpretation that would identify the man speaking in the first person as the same and the woman as the Other. The man's interiority is inaccessible to the woman. This is not due to his totalizing will to power, but to his "infinity," to his and every person's irreducibility to a singular essence. Although he speaks in the first person and is the narrator, she is not consumed by him as was the woman in the flashback; rather, this woman points out his irreparable alterity to her, his "infinity." In my analysis, the woman exceeds any attempt to read this structure as if the interlocutor, an anonymous woman, is a way of conjugating the Other as Woman, that is, as Man's radical alterity. Nor is it simply an inversion of binary values wherein the Other becomes Man as Woman's radical alterity. Rather, each of them experiences the infinite distance from knowing him or herself and from knowing the other person.

When read alongside *La mujer desnuda*, the anonymous man in *De miedo en miedo* becomes a sort of "nude man" whose journey allows him to err from prescribed paths and moral duties toward a radical divesting of himself in the face of this woman and all the readers of the parts of his fragmented narrative—the novel itself, the river manuscripts—that are thrown into the river. For example, the narrator says: "Sentí [...] que nos habíamos puesto al desnudo interiormente como bajo un relámpago" (*De miedo* 74). Similar to the anemic Rebeca Linke after cutting off her own head, he later feels as if he has lost all of his blood: "Sentí durante algunos segundos que había quedado anémico, debilitado por mi hemorragia definitoria" (90). Without the fantastic elements of *La mujer desnuda*, the narrator here experiences the same bloodletting and nude exposure to the world as Linke. Both the nude woman and the nude man share parts of themselves in brief flashes to those around them; both can be constituted as someone's other, and both will find it impossible to fully know themselves.

In this way, Somers's protagonists refuse to be elevated to the status of universal representatives of their respective genders. The politics of going unnoticed, and the ramifications it has for an ethics here, does not allow for the type of visibilization of the exposed subject or of the identity group; the subjects who go unnoticed attempt to open up a dialogue with others—or with the others within themselves—by refusing to assimilate the other to the self and by constantly exceeding any line of communication that might try to identify the self with any other. Yet, this is not to say that this ethics does not have implications for feminist, queer, and other forms of subaltern critique, for it opens the possibility of forming a community between people despite their differences.

Nancy argues that there is a common "that precedes all solitude and all exception, all sexual differences or people, a common without which no isolation or separation would take place" (*Disavowed Community* 71). This common "only takes place in an instant," which he defines as "the infinitesimal suspension of time where gazes—voices, silence—are exchanged and bodies touch. In this suspension, something appears—one might say, a world" (71–72). By being perceived, through exposure, those who go unnoticed open the potential for these impossible-to-fulfill dialogues to take place among all sorts of people and, by extension, the potential for sustained dissent and disagreement that can allow for the temporary creation of a common world to come.

In my analysis, this exposure takes place along the path opened by the errant palindrome. Against the current of a chronologically structured text, the flight of the errant palindrome passes back and forth over that which was going unnoticed. This flight opens the conditions of possibility for saying with unattended fragments that which always remains irreducible to what is said and always exceeds any attempt at totalization or essentialization. The exposure of these previously unnoticed people does not take place under the harsh, all-pervading lights of the public sphere, but instead flashes unexpectedly from among the swirling lights and shadows of the Sixties. The narrator and the woman expose something of themselves in their dialogues before deciding to end their brief, errant encounters and go their separate ways. At the woman's insistence, they turn their faces away from one another, thus closing the lines of communication temporarily opened between them. This arduous, infinite task of engaging in dialogue cannot be sustained by only two people indefinitely. Every self and every other will have to decide whether or not to carry out this process by which the open transforms into a world that only exists within the space and time, the instant, of these dialogues. Whereas Somers remains at the everyday level where these dialogues take place, Filloy offers a glimpse of what this community might look like on a larger scale.

Chapter Eleven

From Monodialogues to Pandemonium

In a rare moment in Filloy's *Vil & Vil: La gata parida* (1975), the General becomes giddy with nostalgia for a game he used to play: *la gata parida*. He claims that children from the provinces like himself *inventan sus juegos*, unlike their less virile counterparts who grow up in the capital, which is ironically the national seat of power he now conspires to take through a military coup (41). Here he explains how to play *la gata parida*:

> En un banco [...] nos sentábamos tantos muchachos como cabíamos. Los que no cabían estaban alertas, esperando turno para sentarse. Porque el juego consiste en hacer caer a los de la punta, a fuerza de empujar con el cuerpo, los hombros y las caderas. Lo principal es mantenerse sentado en el banco, resistiendo los empellones para no ser desplazado y caer. Es un juego de machos que excita el amor propio. Porque cuando cae alguno, los que esperan, o el mismo caído, ocupan ese lugar libre en la otra punta del banco y prosigue la pechada hasta voltear al del extremo. De izquierda o derecha, lo mismo da. Lo importante es ubicarse y conservar enérgicamente el puesto. ¡Es de lo más divertido! (42)

The game, which literally translates as "the birthed cat," is a struggle for hegemony via brute force similar to "king of the hill." The verb *parir*, or "to give birth," also means "to come up with, to create (an idea)." Its usage in the phrase *la puta que te parió* and other vulgar phrases is evoked in the name as well. Furthermore, the game links masculinity with violence and the ability to stand one's ground, all the while encouraging a heightened individualism that respects only the self's will to power. Such thoughts bring tremendous pleasure to the General who makes use of these strategies to secure power at the center of the

Chapter Eleven

bench; once achieved, he will stand his ground by any means available to him, knocking down political opponents from the left and from the right without hesitation or concern for their wellbeing. There is no ideology worthy of his commitment other than self-preservation and self-love. In this sense, *la gata parida* is the children's game that teaches the politics of *yomismo*, the ideology committed only to its sole member's self-interest, closing any and all ethical gestures.

Vil & Vil was published originally by the Macció Hnos. Editores in Río Cuarto, Argentina. According to Mónica Ambort's interview, Filloy had already attempted to publish it in 1968, but did not find a publisher until 1975 (163). This was one year before the military coup that established the dictatorship that called itself the "Proceso de Reorganización Nacional"—a blatantly obvious euphemism that cloaks a violent regime in moralizing robes. After the coup in 1976, Filloy was arrested and interrogated about this novel's contents. He was eventually released after convincing the military officers that the ideas expressed in the novel were only those of his fictional characters, not his own, which he has since said was not true (163–65). In the novel's "Nota previa," the narrator claims this novel is "de anticipación":

> Cronológicamente, sin embargo, está situada en una época tan cercana a nuestra actualidad que parecen confundirse. Quien quiera confundirse que se confunda. [...] Por el curso que llevan las cosas en los países latinoamericanos, esta novela acontece a menudo y, forzosamente, variando detalles y circunstancias, acontecerá. (*Vil* 6)

The events to which he refers appear on the previous page under the title, "Historia reciente," in which he lists thirteen coups that took place in Latin America, ranging from the one that removed Juan Domingo Perón from power in 1955 to the one against Arnulfo Arias in Panamá in 1968 (5).

In retrospect, it might be tempting to read this novel as one that foretells the coming of the terrorist state in Argentina from 1976–83. Nevertheless, *Vil & Vil* is much more than a vague premonition about future events. In my reading, this novel takes account of the generalized state of exception operating throughout Argentina and Latin America in the era, and in the face of an impending, evident threat, it imagines a seemingly unimportant military conscript who manages to open a line of flight away from the General's power struggles. Whereas Somers restrains the scope of her novel within the tedious, everyday dialogues of just two strangers, Filloy represents this opening toward dialogue at the largest scales, this opening toward a community. He calls this grandiose and terrifying dialogue that takes place across space and time "pandemonium." In this pandemonium—full of vile beings who shout and disagree—the ethical implications of the politics of going unnoticed are briefly exposed (182).

Monodialogues among Antagonists

Told from the perspective of a conscript, *Vil & Vil* narrates the antagonism between the narrator and the General. The narrator interrupted his studies at law school to fulfill his mandatory military service and now works as secretary and chauffeur to the General. The narrator glimpses the General's strategies as he plots and executes a military coup against the government. Each of the ninety-eight chapters is divided into three sections. The first is always composed of a brief dialogue with the General. The second is told in the first person from the conscript's perspective, allowing him to provide context for the dialogues and advance the plot. Many of the third sections read like excerpts from the conscript's journal, although this is not confirmed in the text; over the course of the novel, these sections pry open the antagonism between the General and the conscript and, similar to the errant palindrome that erupts from its crystalline form in the third reading, these sections open toward a free-form space for experimental narrative structures wherein the pandemonium will arise.

The first section of chapter one establishes the antagonism between the General and the conscript:

>—A ver, ese melenudo piojoso, que se apure.
>—Grrmgrr ...
>—¡Cómo! ¿Qué dijiste? A ver, repetí lo que gruñiste, si sos macho.
>—Znnsmmx ...
>—¿Pensás sobrarme, entonces? Desgraciado de mierda, te voy a romper el culo a patadas. (7)

In their public interactions, the General exemplifies the universal ambitions of an individual point of view; he only interacts with others by ordering them to do as he pleases. In Levinasian terms, it can be said that the General's "universal thought is an 'I think'" (*Totality and Infinity* 36). He is the authoritarian figure whose will may not be challenged, and he is only interested in conversing with others insofar as they help him achieve his own goals.

These brief dialogues are better described as "monodiálogos," Filloy's neologism from the subtitle of *Yo, yo y yo (Monodiálogos paranoicos)* originally published in 1971. "Monodiálogo" combines "monólogo" and "diálogo," and I have translated it as "monodialogue." Unlike the monologue of a lone character who speaks out loud, the monodialogue always involves multiple speaking characters. For example, Maximiliano Konsideransky in "Yo y los intrusos" is interrupted during his solitary walks up and down his spiraling cave-tower; the entire short story takes place while the reporter and his mule are present, even though they exercise little to no influence over the stream of thought spoken out loud by the male speaker.

In the monodialogue, the dominant male speaker rambles on, often for long paragraphs, while his interlocutors—of varying numbers and identities—say little more than a few sentences. In other short stories in *Yo, yo y yo*, when someone requests to speak, if they are not blatantly ignored, they are often silenced:

>—Pido la palabra.
>—La tengo todavía. No me interrumpa. ("Yo y la madre patria" 32)

And if they assert themselves, they are often insulted:

>—Si usted se empeña, iré. Que decidan mis compañeros. A mí la fiesta me gusta. La frivolidad es la espuma de lo profundo. Lo afirma un pensador local.
>—Cretino. ¿Qué sabe ese cretino? A lo mejor es un tipo de esos que confunden trivialidad con superficialidad.
>—Yo también la confundo. Ergo …
>—Ergo, usted también es un cretino. Lo superficial es siempre algo muy serio. ("Yo y el mundo subterráneo" 109)

In other instances, the interlocutor's bewildered reactions are transcribed in the text as nothing more than ellipses, at times with exclamation points:

>—… ("Yo y los anónimos" 77)
>—¡…! ("Yo y el arquitecto" 16)

As a rule, the interlocutors are only allowed to participate within the monodialogue when they ask questions that allow the dominant speaker to expand upon his thoughts; only those who appease the dominant speaker are respected within the monodialogue's asymmetrical power relations. If the interlocuters do not concede to the dominant speaker's authority, they are demoralized as improper and inauthentic agents of a lesser or evil will. This degradation becomes the dominant speaker's justification for using violence against dissenting voices in order to triumph over them.

In this sense, monodialogues structure the first section of each chapter of *Vil & Vil*. The General is particularly aggressive and has little patience for his interlocutors. The monodialogue is his preferred rhetorical strategy for developing the moral framework wherein every other is defined *a priori* as an enemy who must be coerced into a consensus or otherwise eradicated. However, in contrast to the monodialogues in *Yo, yo y yo*, the subordinate conscript is the narrator of this novel; his is the privileged perspective, while the General's monodialogues are always the shortest of the three sections in each chapter. The conscript, who otherwise would be of so little historical importance within this plot to overthrow the government, always has two sections after the monodialogues in which he resists the General's attempts to flatten out his will and reduce it to his own.

Though he has a lot of contact with the General, the conscript is well aware of the limits of his position: "El diálogo es imposible en la escala militar. El diálogo implica paridad natural entre dos personas. [...] En la escala militar siempre hay un superior y un subalterno. El superior, por su propio status, no desciende ni condesciende a conversar amistosamente con inferiores" (*Vil & Vil* 24). The conscript would contest the General's monodialogic authority, but given his circumstances, he has to reign in his antagonism. Early on, he says, "Deseo que ni siquiera se sospeche de mí" (18). This attempt to not become the target of suspicion is part of the survival tactics that he has adopted, since he cannot desert his post nor does he know how to behave properly in the military. He describes these tactics as a "capacidad teatral" and recommends the following to his fellow conscripts: "lo principal que hay que hacer en el ejército es simular corrección. Cuanto más fiel la simulación del cumplimiento del deber, mejor" (27). Loyalty, an empty signifier *par excellence*, is not to be given to an

Chapter Eleven

officer. One must be loyal only to the performance of complicity and consensus. There is no doubt in the conscript's mind that "correctness" is simply the term the military's high command uses to signify unreflective obedience; as such, he does not actually aim *to be* correct or proper, but only *pretends* to be so. Appearances, not truth, are all that matter when the monodialogue constitutes power.

&

The narrator opposes the General from the very beginning; he was drafted into the armed forces while preparing for a civilian life. This opposition is firmly cemented when the conscript accidentally overhears that the General is planning a coup against the democratically elected government: "Sin querer, capté ese fragmento de conversación telefónica" (33). Filloy's conscript also knows what one of Casey's narrators suggests, that "fragmentos de la conversación [...] pueden darnos espléndidas claves" ("Notas" 51–52). By attending to these fragments and recording what he hears in his narrative, this otherwise unimportant conscript can begin to register his dissent that had been blocked by the monodialogue.

What he hears is the following: "Sí, claro. Preparamos la revolución porque la fuerza armada sin el poder no sirve para un corno. Le falta acción coercitiva. Carece de acción y dominio. No corta ni aprieta. Es como una tenaza a la cual le faltara uno de sus brazos" (*Vil* 33). Since the narrator cannot do much about this plan that he accidentally overhears, he is limited to registering his dissent through writing. He challenges the General's use of the term "revolución" to name his military coup by showing that it functions as an empty signifier by which the General rallies the other interest groups around his particular will to total power. The conscript writes: "Alterar la costumbre de la esclavitud, por meras mudanzas de amos y patrones, de carteles y monopolios, es cipayismo cien por ciento. Fuera de la francesa, la norteamericana, la rusa y la china, no ha habido otras revoluciones en el mundo" (220). The Mexican and the Cuban Revolutions are also curiously excluded from this list of true revoluciones, since the conscript has no sympathies with the PRI's institutionalization of their solitary will to power by the Sixties nor with Castro's increasingly authoritarian state. Instead, he argues that the General operates within the same neocolonial structures of dependence against which a true revolution would fight. At play in his critique is the implication that the General, despite his virility and claims to moral authority, would only at best become the puppet of foreign interests.

Regardless of whether the conscript is correct or not in his critique, I do not locate an ethics in his analysis. An ethics cannot take place by simply inverting the power relationship between two asymmetrically opposed poles, the General and the conscript, and showing the latter's fictional agency. This would only amount to turning the conscript's written text into an inverted monodialogue wherein the subaltern conscript acquires power to speak—a power that is rather limited, if not meaningless, in the face of a rising dictatorship. The conscript can write his rebuttal to the General, but the General still has the upper hand—the men with guns—within their world. For this reason, in my reading, the conscript's relationship with the General cannot be reduced to a story of the revolutionary hero versus the authoritarian villain. This would be to rely on the same form that the *barbudos* of the Cuban Revolution used to mythologize their opposition to Batista and U.S. foreign interests, thus claiming moral superiority and demanding subservience even as Castro turned toward the Soviet Union and ruled through authoritarianism.

Rather, I locate an ethics in the repetition of the adjective in the title, *Vil & Vil*. In *Paratexts*, Gérard Genette has studied how paratextual elements, including titles, constitute a "threshold" that "operate between text and off-text," framing a text for its readers and potentially influencing their reception of it (2). Filloy, as the author, pre-judges these two characters in moral terms by calling them both "vil." He morally condemns all of the characters and situations in his own novel. Both the General's and the conscript's claims to goodness, propriety, and authenticity are denied in the title that literally announces the repulsive qualities of both. Neither may claim moral superiority over the other. The General is a cruel, power-hungry man who does not hesitate to use force and violence to achieve his goals. Despite my own sympathies with the conscript's opposition to the General, he is not exactly the shining image of a philanthropic hero. Each is labeled with an equivalent descriptor, "vile," thus avoiding false universals like "good" and "evil," while also balancing out the asymmetrical power relationship that their military ranks create. Ultimately, the title displaces the question of who is right and who is wrong, and instead it announces the conjunction and collision of two mutually repulsive, antagonistic interests.

It may seem counterintuitive to cultivate an ethics from a text in which vile characters abound. Of course, I do not mean that such amoral individuals are the only ethical ones, nor does this mean I have ignored the asymmetrical power relation that exists between the General and the conscript. Such a proposition would be ridiculous, even reckless. What I propose is to reject and refuse the monodialogic strategy and the moral judgments of the title, while maintaining the ampersand that links the conscript and the General without forming a binary opposition between them. In *The Coming Community*, Agamben argues that moralizing value distinctions always block a community from forming. He elaborates a definition of the ethical opening: "Ethics begins only when the good is revealed to consist in nothing other than a grasping of evil and when the authentic and the proper have no other content than the inauthentic and the improper" (13). Agamben expands upon Nietzsche's analysis in which these terms are simply the particular, moralizing categories by which an identity-based group defines itself and casts aside its others. Ethics, for Agamben, takes place when and where a space opens up for both "the light" and "the darkness," for what is called "true" and what is called "false," for what is valued as "proper" and what is valued as "improper;" therefore, a space opens up for "us" and for "them." A place must be guaranteed for both, because "the darkness," "false," "improper," or "them" are not universals, but only particular labels like "filth" used by one group to cast another group as a threatening enemy and secure an internal consensus. The ethical opening must guarantee a radically inclusive space with no *a priori* moral value judgments or ideological ends so that no one, neither the conscript nor the General, can be banned or abandoned, jailed or executed. Only then can the General and the conscript enter into the type of arduous dialogues had by the man and the woman in Somers's *De miedo en miedo*. In order for it to be possible to engage one another across that infinite distance, to expose in brief, unexpected flashes, their thoughts and desires, each must approach the other as if the other is not the Other, as if the other is simply another person, another plural singular being who cannot be reduced to moral absolutes. These are the conditions of possibility for the ethics of being perceived. Without this, no ethical dialogues can ever take place and no equality can be established.

Pandemonium

Within the last third of the novel, the General triumphs and legitimizes his military coup over the radio by invoking the state of exception "en defensa de la salud de nuestra democracia" (*Vil* 258). However, the General is not committed to a democratic politics. He is only committed to the two main strategies—the monodialogue and *la gata parida*—by which he successfully realizes his will to total power over the military and all other national institutions. Facing the reality that he has no means of counteracting the General, the conscript desires to retreat as far away as possible from him; in the days just before the military coup, he even considers desertion, only to find himself confronted with the chaos of fear and a loss of moral certainty:

> Nunca había estado metido en un laberinto. Sabía lo que es la línea recta y lo que es la rectitud. Ya no. Me cruzan y entrecruzan mil senderos endemoniados. No soy dueño de mis designios. He perdido mi capacidad de optar. Pero esa luz de la deserción me está alumbrando. (*Vil* 237)

The conscript is not faced with a decision between the high road and the low road, a moral decision he claims to have been able to make successfully in the past; for the first time he finds himself confronted only with thousands of vile options in the midst of this cursed labyrinth. In this sense, there is no good choice to be made among the winding paths laid out in front of him, not even the one shining in the light. The only option he can hope for is to flee this labyrinth entirely, but as he says, he is not capable of choosing, because every choice is equally vile. He has lost, to use Agamben's terms, his potentiality; he has lost his ability to make a choice and to refuse to participate in the General's hegemonic game.[1] Further distancing himself from the role of the hero, he continues to serve the General and to carry on his romantic affair with the General's wife.

Chapter Eleven

Given the state in which the conscript finds himself trapped and his impossible desire to thwart the General's struggle for power, it is not surprising that his reaction is to dismiss all political action in a sweeping generalization about Latin America: "Todavía no existe vida democrática en las naciones latinoamericanas. La democracia recaba continuidad en el proceso de su perfeccionamiento. [...] Al desplazamiento por la fuerza, sigue una transición azarosa ... hasta otra nueva conjura o asonada lo desplaza" (*Vil* 228). The democratic process requires time and stability in which the potential for dissensus is continually guaranteed; here he decries the constant interruption of that process, the generalized state of exception, that never allows for the democratic process to take hold. Moreover, I want to consider the claim that politics in Latin America, or anywhere in fact, is nothing more than a grotesquely violent version of *la gata parida* wherever the state of exception and absolutist, authoritarian forms of hegemonic rule run rampant. The conscript makes an appeal for a more radical form of democracy to come into existence, and this imagined democracy would operate otherwise than in the form of the General's monodialogues and disturbing childhood games.

Within the experimental third section of his unnoticed text, the conscript opposes the General's violent strategies. His writing becomes the only possibility for producing a line of flight within that demonic labyrinth. As he searches for an alternative space in which an ethics can take place, he necessarily errs from the General's course of military action: "Mi desesperación es casi un pandemónium. Creo ya estar en él:" (*Vil* 182). He cements his opposition while introducing an ethical opening—the pandemonium, the hellscape populated by all sorts of demons and lesser gods—that will take place within the already occupied space of the wicked paths that cross back and forth over the conscript within the vile labyrinth of dictatorial morality.

The definition of this pandemonium follows the colon I quoted above; it is an eleven-page dialogue in which the voices of historical and fictional leaders from antiquity to the twentieth century shout, insult, joke, quibble, and demand to be heard. Among those names who speak in this pandemonium are: from Latin America, San Martín, Rosas, Liniers, Martín Fierro, Doctor Francia, Iturbide, Benito Juárez, Porfirio Díaz, Pancho Villa, Victoriano Huerta, Bolívar, Solano López, García Moreno, Sandino, Martí,

Guevara, Castro, Vicuña Mackenna, Neruda, Allende, Pinochet, Batlle y Ordóñez, Baltasar Brun, Getulio Vargas; from Spain, Torquemada, Fernando VII, Unamuno, Primo de Rivera, Millán Astray; and so many others, including Atila the Hun, Ghengis Khan, Julius Cesar, María de Medicis, Alexander the Great, Robespierre, Napoleon, Pepe Botella (Joseph Bonaparte), Ivan the Terrible, Woodrow Wilson, Stalin, Mussolini, Himmler, Clausewitz, Einstein, Mao, Trotsky, Ho Chi Minh, Sartre, Goethe, Freud, Bernard Shaw, T.S. Eliot (183–93).

Such a pandemonium is a historical impossibility, but it opens up along ARTELETRA's errant path in the experimental section of the conscript's writings. This fictional dialogue wanders about *al vesre* and *al verse*, rearranging the historical record so that these figures may face one another across the spatial and temporal distances that always separated them. Those who take part in this dialogue do so as demons or lesser gods; they are all just as vile as the General and the conscript who also speak in this pandemonium. When everyone is labeled as "vile," then the word loses its meaning; no one can be banned or abandoned or else everyone would have to suffer the same fate. This pandemonic dialogue ends with the following open-ended words of El Viejo Pancho (the nickname for the *gauchesca* poet José Alonso y Trelles) and Martín Fierro:

> El Viejo Pancho: —Todo puede suceder
> 'tando la tormenta armada.
> Martín Fierro: Yo he visto rejucilar
> y dispués no pasar nada ... (*Vil* 193)

No one voice can dominate this space; no one person can be removed from it either. Throughout, the friendships and enmities between these actors are not erased, but rather they are given the space in which their dissensus can play out. Similar to the discourses and ideologies that many of them generated, they are not restricted to dialoguing with the others from their own historical era or geographic region. Martí responds to Guevara; Marx, to Einstein; and Bolívar, to Primo de Rivera, for example. What tool is better than language, in Levinas's words, "to break the continuity of being or of history?" (*Otherwise than Being* 195). In the face of this powerful rupture through discourse, even the General who is typically so skilled at turning conversations into monodialogues and at standing his ground in *la gata parida* loses his hegemonic grip within this radically open, rhizomatic dialogue that ends with the equal possibility of both a future storm and a future tranquility in which every desire or nothing at all might come to pass.

The conscript's pandemonium imagines the ethical form that, in my reading, takes place in the space—characterized as the state of exception—where both the vile General and the vile conscript can face one another outside of the monodialogic structure and without a universal, paratextual judge determining who is good and who is evil. Pandemonium becomes a model for a radically democratic dialogue as it generates the conditions of possibility for dissent and disagreement among people who do not even believe they have anything in common. The struggle for power is not removed as in an unrealizable dream in which everyone holds hands and gets along, but it also ends without any particular individual rising above the rest to secure his hegemonic will to totality over the others. It is in this sense that going unnoticed—with its aesthetics and its ethics—imagines a path toward a radical democratic politics.

Chapter Twelve

Aiding the Adversary

Casey's short story, "La ejecución," begins with an epigraph from Franz Kafka's *The Trial* translated into Spanish: "¿Y el proceso comienza de nuevo? —preguntó K. casi incrédulo—. Evidentemente —respondió el pintor" ("Ejecución" 193). At the cited moment in Kafka's novel, the painter explains the intricate details and possibilities of the legal system that has ensnared K. In particular, what can begin all over again is the process of ostensible acquittal; if K. is acquitted in this scenario, he would be free temporarily, only to be arrested and put on trial again. The artist states that this is an unending process: "The second acquittal is followed by the third arrest, the third acquittal by the fourth arrest, and so on. That is implied in the very conception of ostensible acquittal" (*Trial* 160). This option appears to be the most likely scenario in which K. could be acquitted of the crimes of which he knows nothing, but it is also the option that never leads to a final and permanent verdict. In the end, K. is not granted an ostensible acquittal but is killed upon being found guilty of an unnamed, unproven crime.

Casey's short story rewrites Kafka's novel by returning to this infinite cycle of arrests and verdicts that can only come to an end—as the title announces—with an execution. In this story, Mayer is framed for committing fraud and a murder; he is arrested in his home one evening, taken to a police station to declare his guilt, thrown in jail, put on trial, and executed in the final paragraph. However, "La ejecución" is not a simple copy of *The Trial*, nor is it a farcical repetition of what was at first a tragedy. Casey's text is not a radical departure from or an ironic undermining of Kafka's novel in the way that Filloy and Somers rewrite Plato. Rather, I read Casey's Mayer as someone who learned from Kafka's K. that it is futile to participate in a legal apparatus built to take away the accused's potentiality. Instead, Mayer enacts a departure from this process altogether while, paradoxically, being trapped in the middle of it. From his dimly lit cell, the most radical aspect of the ethics of being perceived takes place in the very different decisions made by Casey's protagonist to aid even his enemies in the time leading up to his own execution.

A System of Unknown Dimensions

A final version of "La ejecución" was included as the last short story in the 1967 edition of *El regreso y otros relatos*, published by Seix Barral in Barcelona. This collection is an expanded edition of *El regreso*, which Casey had published in 1962 with Ediciones R in Havana. Casey returns to the short stories of *El regreso*, and to them he adds an edited version of a story that returns to Kafka's *The Trial*.[1] In a brief review of Kafka's *The Castle*, Casey declares from within the Revolution that there is "una literatura antes de Kafka y otra después de él" ("Kafka" 77). Thus, Kafka is at first defended as a revolutionary to be read in Cuba. Nevertheless, I analyze the 1967 version Casey circulated from exile as a critique of the hegemonic logic that by this point in Cuba had placed moralizing demands on both his writing and his sexuality. For those trapped within a regime in which the state of exception has become the rule, whether it calls itself a revolution or a democracy or something else, Casey imagines an option that restores the potential to refuse to participate in this seemingly unending cycle of power struggles from which there is no true escape.

As if the title and the epigraph were not enough to determine the unfortunate fate of Mayer, the first sentence of "La ejecución" also announces his impending arrest: "Una hora antes de que se produjera la detención, el teléfono sonó" (193). When Mayer answers the phone, no one responds; he only hears silence coming through the telephone line, until he notices that "colgaban suavemente" (194). The scene repeats itself a few minutes later, and Mayer assumes this is some sort of prank phone call. Upon hearing them hang up again, Mayer goes back to his solitary evening that the narrator describes as his "veladas a oscuras" (195). Like many of Casey's protagonists, Mayer prefers to be left alone in the dim light where no one can easily see or bother him: "Para aprovechar estas horas había cubierto con papeles opacos los cristales por donde podía filtrarse la luz de la calle" (195). In the softly lit room, Mayer goes back to his nightly routine.

The phone rings for a third time. He answers, but he does not say anything. He listens for any sound, "tratando de penetrar el silencio": "Pero el más absoluto silencio reinaba en el lugar desde donde llamaban" (196). Across the telephone lines, only absolute silence is being transmitted between an unknown entity and a seemingly unimportant protagonist who has suddenly become the focus of the fictional State. "Decidido a quitarles esa pequeña ventaja," Mayer unsuccessfully attempts to block all noises from his end, but he realizes that "los ruidos de la calle" still can be heard (197). His unknown caller creates this absolute silence from an unknown location having prepared for an unknown amount of time, whereas Mayer must improvise a response to this unexpected intrusion, establishing an asymmetry between them. Eventually, Mayer will learn the lesson that Kafka's K. does not: it is impossible to resist a system of unknown dimensions and silent, invisible agents by playing within the few rules that are barely visible to the one trapped within its all-pervading gaze. An escape may not be possible, but a line of flight along an unnoticed itinerary still is.

Clean and Modern

The silence becomes an ominous presence, signaling a sudden shift in Mayer's life: "Sin que pudiera precisar qué exactamente, creyó notar que algo había cambiado de modo imperceptible en los objetos que le rodeaban" (196). The silence penetrates and fills Mayer's home like the filtered street light. However, he does not panic: "No pudo evitar una sonrisa al comprobar que caminaba de puntillas" (196). Something about this whole situation seems ridiculous to him. Soon after noticing this imperceptible change while peering into the darkness, three police officers knock at his door, arrest him, and take him to the police station. The silent telephone calls were the harbinger of what was already underway—Mayer's arrest and prosecution after being framed.

In Casey's narrative, the legal institutions are not tucked into attics that appear to be moving always away from the protagonist; the police precinct is an imposing building filled with bright lights that blind those within it. Further foreshadowing Mayer's execution, a uniformed man walks around "con un brillante recogedor

Chapter Twelve

de basura—Mayer nunca había visto un recogedor tan brillante, posiblemente era de cobre muy pulido— [...] y con un movimiento casi imperceptible de la escobilla hacía desaparecer [...] todo lo que pudiera disminuir la limpieza del lugar" (200). All refuse is quickly collected and eliminated from the precinct, which "olía a desinfectante," leaving even the tools used to purify this space as shiny as possible (200). Here there is no room for anything or anyone labeled "filth," a visible warning written on every shiny surface of this building about the precinct's primary goal: the violent annihilation of all those considered to be operating against the sovereign.

Unlike Somers's protagonists who find something in common and then choose to expose fragments of their most intimate ideas to one another, Mayer is forcibly revealed under the blinding lights of the police precinct. Skylights and wall sconces illuminate the long corridors, and the interrogation room where he is put on trial by a panel of three civil servants and two uniformed men is located behind a glass door: "El lugar estaba tan escrupulosamente limpio como el resto del edificio; lo iluminaban altas ventanas. Todo era moderno y confortable, incluso de buen gusto" (205). This well-lit space decorated with clean, modern lines and glass gives the impression of trying desperately to insist on the transparency of the fraudulent legal proceedings taking place within it. However, no real evidence is brought to light in this place, and his accusers on the other side of the room talk in hushed tones he cannot hear as the lights begin to blind him: "El resplandor del salón le había producido un vivo ardor en los ojos" (207). As the evidence used to frame Mayer is presented, from his perspective the modern design only produces the damaging effects of being revealed under the sovereign's totalizing, yet unlocatable sources of light and absolute silence.[2]

Rewriting Kafka

Casey's narrative does not rewrite the ending of Kafka's novel; both K. and Mayer die in the end. Rather, I contend that Casey's avant-garde text returns to *The Trial* at the point at which K. failed to realize his lack of potentiality within the legal apparatus that had already decided to convict and kill him. The narrator in Kafka's novel explains K.'s attempt to remain alert while preparing his defense: "He accepted it as a fundamental principle for an accused man to be always forearmed, never to let himself be caught napping, never to let his eyes stray unthinkingly to the right when his judge was looming up on the left—and against that very principle he kept offending again and again" (*Trial* 164). K. thinks he knows what he must do to succeed: remain alert at all times in order to prepare a legitimate defense and prove his innocence. In retrospect, for the reader who learns that in the end K. will fail to perceive this institution in its totality and will be executed, K.'s heightened vigilance only marks his own delusions or misguided optimism. K.'s major failure was not that he kept offending against that principle; no degree of alertness would ever have been sufficient. Rather, K.'s failure was his inability to comprehend that his potentiality—the ability to do and to refuse to do, the capacity to make a decision—had been irrevocably blocked well before the guards knocked at his door. Despite his many clever attempts and important contacts, K. is radically prohibited from doing or refusing to do anything to save himself from the all-pervasive legal apparatus of which he only ever manages to catch a fleeting glimpse.

In reality, the sovereign, his decrees, and the logic underlying both of these trials never appear in plain sight; only their threat of violence shines bright. The difference is that Mayer recognizes that it is impossible to challenge this institution directly. Instead of repeating K.'s frantic itinerary through that maze of alleys and attics, Mayer creates brief moments of pleasure for himself that constantly disrupt the linear narrative leading to his execution. As he is being charged and arrested, the narrator describes "el placer familiar que la oscuridad le causaba" ("Ejecución" 200). Mayer even finds the silence and darkness of his jail cell to be comforting; in order to recreate his nightly routine, he covers the small window with a blanket "hasta obtener una oscuridad casi completa" (201). This allows him to fall into a deep sleep, and he enjoys the brief moments he is allowed into the empty, interior courtyard surrounded on all sides by ten-story walls. No light reaches the ground floor where he walks, but he arrives at the conclusion that "al dar los rayos sobre la inmensa superficie de los muros, pintada de blanco, producirían un resplandor molesto" (204–05). It is as if Mayer knows all too well how futile K.'s efforts were and how vulnerable K. had become under the harsh lights of the imperceptible legal apparatus that had ensnared him. Mayer seems to know he is living a repetition of those events in another time and place and that there will be no way out of this cycle. Since fighting the system by playing within its rules is futile, Mayer's only potential political gesture, a highly imperfect solution, is to reclaim his potentiality by refusing to participate earnestly in the legal process that has already banned him to a jail cell and abandoned him there. He signs any papers they give him and makes no attempt to challenge their accusations or their verdict.

From Enemies to Adversaries

This refusal by which he recuperates his potentiality is his political gesture, but if it ended here, there would be no ethics of this politics. In what I have described so far, Mayer only secures a bit of tranquility for himself by turning his dark jail cell into a temporary refuge that remains almost completely isolated from everyone else. Nevertheless, he does have frequent contact with an old man who works as his guard. The most radical aspect of the ethics of being perceived takes place when Mayer engages his guard in dialogue not as his enemy but rather as an adversary still worthy of being treated as another human being despite the institutions that very literally separate them into opposing spaces and mark them as one another's enemies.

Mouffe argues for a radical democratic politics that transforms antagonism into agonism by reframing enemies as adversaries. Instead of creating an exclusive, moral community for democracy or a naïve vision of a society without power relations, Mouffe seeks a democracy without the will to totality: "The democratic character of a society can only be given by the fact that no limited social actor can attribute to herself or himself the representation of the totality and claim to have the 'mastery' of the foundation" (*Democratic Paradox* 100). Instead, a democracy must be founded on the ineradicable and irreducible antagonism brought out by the pluralism of values. Mouffe does not attempt to eliminate different social identities nor to relegate their differences to an idealized private space; instead, she contends for the need to allow people with radically different values to engage openly in political power struggles. For this reason she calls for antagonistic struggles to be reconfigured as agonistic ones: "*Antagonism* is the struggle between enemies, while *agonism* is a struggle between adversaries" (102–03). Mouffe argues that radical democracy can only take place if the hegemonic power structures that constantly organize bodies into friends opposed to enemies is completely reconfigured: "the aim of democratic politics is to construct the 'them' in such a way that it is no longer perceived as an enemy to be destroyed, but as an 'adversary,' that is, somebody whose ideas we combat but whose right to defend those ideas we do not put into question" (102). For my purposes, the final aspect of the ethics of being perceived takes place when one person attempts to dialogue with those who had been cast as evil enemies that must be vanquished, thus turning against the current and reframing them as an adversary worthy of being engaged in dialogue. Otherwise, the dialogues I have been analyzing would be limited to those between people who already exist within the same limited community or identity group.

Casey imagines a character who achieves this dialogue with one of his guards. Long before they meet, the police state in this short story structures their relationship as that between mutual enemies. This guard is much older than the other officers, and as he takes Mayer to his cell, they have to walk slowly:

> Era evidente que el esfuerzo de andar agitaba al guardián. Al principio agarró a Mayer por un brazo; luego, cuando se hizo más fatigosa su respiración, la presión de su mano sobre el brazo de Mayer aumentó. A medida que avanzaban por el largo corredor, el prisionero sintió que el hombre se apoyaba cada vez más en él y su respiración se hacía más penosa.
> —¿Quiere que nos detengamos un momento?— preguntó Mayer.
> —Sí, por favor— repuso el guardián.
> —Apóyese en mí— sugirió Mayer cuando reanudaron la marcha.
> ("Ejecución" 201–02)

At first, it may be argued that Mayer simply follows the lead and pace of his guard, hesitant to do anything that would further harm his case. However, when the guard leans on Mayer, the interaction is narrated with the verb "apoyar," which means "to help, assist, support" in addition to "to lean on." Mayer supports his own guard. First, he offers to let the guard take a break, an offer he was in no position to actually make, and so he frames it as a request. Then Mayer tells the guard to brace himself on him, politely commanding the guard to allow his prisoner to aid him. Mayer wholly disregards the pre-established rules of their relationship. He aids his guard in a gesture that recasts his enemy as his adversary and, as a result, he recovers a bit of his own potentiality. In this unnoticed interaction, he makes the decision to slow down and commands his guard to lean on his shoulder as they hobble toward Mayer's cell locked arm in arm.

Mayer's unnoticed potentiality is only recovered during brief moments when he and his guard have the opportunity to speak in dialogues that go unnoticed by the other guards. One day, Mayer decides to ask the guard about his health when he brings him his food: "Hablaron un rato y el hombre prometió comprar ciertos medicamentos que Mayer le había sugerido" (209). Mayer advises the guard on how to improve his health. He receives no special treatment for this. In fact, the guard frequently forgets to take Mayer to the patio, and he will not intervene as the execution approaches. Nevertheless, Mayer overhears the guard say his health has improved, "gracias quizás a las indicaciones del prisionero, aunque esto no podía afirmarse con completa exactitud" (211). The guard even notes Mayer's improvement in health; here the narrator intervenes to ensure this is not interpreted as the guard's own self-congratulating gesture: "En realidad había mejorado visiblemente" (211). As a result, perhaps, of the way Mayer reconfigured their relationship, both Mayer and the guard have seen their health improve within the precinct. Casey's text only imagines this ethical gesture between the two of them, but if this type of interaction were to sweep across an entire political landscape, I like to think its effects could provoke monumental change toward the creation of a radically democratic community.

Through Casey's ethical gesture, I have returned from Filloy's massive pandemonium to the everyday scale of Somers's novel. As I approach the end of my analysis of the politics of going unnoticed, I am not convinced that a global opening in which anyone and everyone can participate in democratic institutions without being cast as the enemy is just around the corner. Such institutions and politics have not come into existence. Rather, new strategies to further partition humanity into opposing moral and political categories appear and reappear every day, and they return with ever-greater force from both above and below. It will take continual efforts like those of Somers's and Casey's protagonists to begin to pry open the space in which Filloy's pandemonium might one day take place. From my perspective, Mouffe's agonistic democracy allows for a potential merger or overlapping to take place between Somers's ethics in which one self engages another in fragmented dialogues and Filloy's pandemonium of competing people who cannot claim moral superiority over one another. This is a tall order, but one that Casey's fiction also imagines by reconfiguring the relationship between friend and enemy, good and evil, into a tense, uneven, and incomplete dialogue among adversaries. Such reconfigurations are a continual process that will break down as dialogues end, as someone chooses to close pandemonium, and as actual people choosing to engage in this form of dialogue die or are killed by others. Without these types of small gestures, another political, aesthetic, and ethical organization of the world cannot even become possible. But with them, you or I or someone else might step briefly out into the open and begin a reconfiguration of the institutional and everyday demands that constantly seek to divide us from one another in the service of political and economic inequality.

Conclusion

Re-ves la ArteletrA

> We stumble on, thinks Jaslyn, bring a little noise into the silence, find in others the ongoing of ourselves. It is almost enough.
>
> Colum McCann, *Let the Great World Spin*

In *Viajes. De la Amazonía a las Malvinas* (2014), Beatriz Sarlo recollects and relates her travels as a young woman of relative means and privilege from Buenos Aires throughout the Amazon and the Andes in the sixties and early seventies. She even visited, a year before, the same region where Che Guevara would be killed. She frequently notes her and her fellow travelers' youthful enthusiasm to find and become part of a new Latin America in the Sixties: "Sobre todo en los viajes de la década del sesenta, buscábamos un continente en curso de transformación: había que viajar por América Latina porque el desplazamiento nos llevaría hacia formas semiocultas o más o menos visibles del futuro" (95). She summarizes one of their trips, as they imagined it at the time, as follows: "Un viaje hacia un territorio de utopía donde podía vivir un sujeto no contaminado y, en consecuencia, agente de liberación. Ese gigantesco malentendido no nos atrapó sólo a nosotros" (105). Writing fifty years after these travels, more than a narrative of how they forged some sort of complete and total "comunidad imaginaria" among Latin Americans from across the region, Sarlo harshly judges and dismisses her former desires and goals at every turn (99). She constantly refers to her group of travelers and herself as "inexpertos, ignorantes," even "crédulos" (88, 111). Her frequent recourse to narrating in the first-person plural creates the effect of extending her criticism of these projects to her entire generation: "Viajábamos para conocer pero no estábamos en condiciones de entender lo que encontrábamos" (135).

Conclusion

In retrospect, Sarlo projects her disillusionment on an almost global scale to these types of naïve journeys and futile political projects from the Sixties.

In April of 2017, Sarlo was invited to the University of Maryland, College Park, to give a series of lectures that began with a discussion of *Viajes*. I had the opportunity to explain to her my surprise that she was so judgmental of her younger self and to ask why, as she reflected today on her own experiences in the Sixties, she rejected her former utopianism. Standing with both hands braced firmly on the table, her unflinching answer to me was, and I quote from what I was able to record in my notes at the time: "Éramos sumamente ignorantes y equivocados. No utópicos. No se debe llamar utópico lo que es realmente la estupidez."[1] Though she explained that she does not reject the projection of a utopian horizon, of maintaining an ethical commitment to the formation of a better world, she remained intent on rejecting the uninformed, naïve framework, the foundational ignorance, that led her and her companions to take those trips in the first place. Furthermore, she refuses to call what they did "utopian." That word will have to be left to name some other type of practice not found in her own travels or in the superficial, essentializing ideology that motivated them at the time. In this sense, what she narrates in *Viajes* are her own failures and those of certain members of her generation.

Sarlo's self-criticism might seem harsh, but her evaluation of her younger self and of her failed politics from the Sixties is convincing. For my purposes, the itinerary she and her fellow travelers took did not, either intentionally or by chance, produce the sort of unnoticed thresholds I have studied in the works of Casey, Filloy, and Somers. The politics I have studied in their texts, though not explicitly committed, resonate with the failed projects of the Left. However, these writers, their works, and their protagonists went unnoticed in the Sixties, which is a different sort of failure altogether. Almost all of the protagonists I have studied fail at the end of their narrative. Casey's anonymous narrators are jailed or executed. Filloy's Konsideransky has the details of his refuge revealed to the world, and the military conscript cannot prevent the General's coup. Somers unleashes that terrifying scorpion on the least suspecting individuals, and the last image of Rebeca Linke is of her dead, bruised body face down in the river. Perhaps this is why these stories were paid so little attention at the time.

They did not provide a clear map of a newly visible subject who would rise from the darkness, awaken the consciousness of those still chained in the shadows, and prevail over the biopolitical machines that structure their inequality and strip them of their potentiality. For precisely this reason, I suggest these writers be read today as one possible way to return to the Sixties while considering what political, aesthetic, and ethical tools could be relevant in the twenty-first century.

Despite these failures, an outright rejection of utopianism is not what I propose. In *Spaces of Hope*, David Harvey argues for the need to keep utopian thought alive: "The rejection, in recent times, of utopianism rests in part on an acute awareness of its inner connection to authoritarianism and totalitarianism [...]. But rejection of utopianism on such grounds has also had the unfortunate effect of curbing the free play of the imagination in the search for alternatives" (163). Utopian thought and the potentiality I have studied share an open character; they cannot guarantee *a priori* any particular politics, aesthetics, or ethics; yet without them, there is nowhere to turn, no alternative to imagine, no hope to build a better community. In this sense, it would be inaccurate to characterize the writings of Casey, Filloy, and Somers as anti-utopian or devoid of hope just because of the many failures they narrate.

Briefly, I would like to return to one of the final paragraphs of Casey's "Notas de un simulador." These notes that comprise the narrative are a diary written from his jail cell. Because of the narrator's proximity to all of those dying, abandoned bodies to which he attended along his errant path, he is accused of having murdered each of them. This text is his attempt to set the record straight, explaining why he was creeping around the city at night, with the hope that someday someone might stumble across his version of the events. After his failure, he explains:

> A las toneladas de papel y los ríos de tinta que narrarán mi caso, impreso junto a otras deformaciones de la verdad para que lo lean millones de ojos extrañamente ávidos de novedades, sólo puedo oponer estos párrafos que redacto con dificultad a la mala luz que llega hasta donde trabajo. Los obstáculos son tremendos pero sé que alguna vez llegarán estas líneas a conocerse. Esperemos. (90)

Conclusion

Whereas the juridical system wrongly accused him of murder and the mass media promptly circulated the official story, he writes so that future readers might read against the current of this river of ink in order to recognize him as the philanthropic caretaker he claims to be. I interpret his condemnation of the mass media as a rejection of a certain reliance on easily consumable bits of entertaining information that falsely offer easy access to the total knowledge of an other, or in this case, of an other's alleged crime. Casey's narrator writes and exposes his own version that cannot be assimilated by the mass media or the legal system. He locates, to borrow a phrase from José Esteban Muñoz, "a kernel of potentiality" after and despite this failure (173). That is, he refuses to give up, thus opening the potential to continue moving, erring, and engaging in dialogues, at least through his writing. He offers his own, externally unverifiable, narrative that he writes under the poor light of his jail cell, not under the total light of knowledge or the supposedly transparent language of the newspapers. His notes become an incomplete narrative that opens this seemingly unimportant, already closed case to further interventions and reconfigurations. Despite his failure and the unlikeliness that he will be exonerated, he remains hopeful that his version of the story, this trace of the past, will be disseminated to future readers.

The failure of the politics of going unnoticed is not an unfortunate outcome but rather the necessary condition for dissent and disagreement to continue into the future. Muñoz conceives of failure in contemporary performances by queers of color who engage in future-oriented projects as "not so much a failure to succeed as it is a failure to participate in a system of valuation that is predicated on exploitation and conformity" (174). Following Muñoz's definition of failure "as active political refusal," the tactics of those who go unnoticed is only unsuccessful when interpreted from within a normative, moralizing framework that delineates the distinction between the proper and the improper, the timely and the untimely (174). The failure of all those who go unnoticed is an active refusal to participate in exploitative or universalizing projects as well as in any identity politics that would seek to homogenize its community in the name of political expediency.

Going unnoticed was already in the first place a failure by those who arrived too late and traced untimely itineraries through the already occupied cultural cartographies of their era. The next failure of those who go unnoticed takes place as a refusal to subscribe to such normative demands. Instead of pretending to be social heroes who move in Platonic fashion from the darkness of ignorance to the light of knowledge and the good, these subjects wander along errant lines of flight that pass through the swirling shadows and lights of their era. They go about opening a space for dissent from which they write an alternative arrangement of the political in plain sight, thus becoming exposed both to others who are going unnoticed and to the vigilant eyes and violent obstacles they previously desired to evade. By being perceived, one might argue that they have failed to remain unnoticed; however, staying unnoticed, as opposed to going unnoticed, would vacate their political gestures of its ethics, of its potential to keep open a space for dialogue. Therefore, these failures become the condition of possibility for keeping the future open and stumbling into other political, aesthetic, and ethical tools that will continue to be necessary to tear down the walls constantly erected by the biopolitical machines that show no signs of slowing down today.

Reading ARTELETRA *al vesre* and *al verse*—an imperfect reversal that allows for a different, but still contingent arrangement of texts and discourses to face one another and engage in dialogue—has served as the heuristic for reading against the currents of the cultural maps of the era. Without ever leaving the space of the Sixties in Latin America, I have caught a glimpse of this cast of mostly anonymous protagonists spread throughout the works of Casey, Filloy, and Somers who go unnoticed within the cultural and political landscapes of their fictional worlds. What I have located is how this refusal to participate in a political landscape by going unnoticed within it—as even Casey attempted in his actual life in Cuba—can generate the conditions of possibility to reconfigure that inescapable space. Each of these authors has imagined and created alternative forms of political participation in the midst of an era when almost every individual and every group was vying for visibility. When almost everyone else rushes onto the stage, behind are left those who choose not to fight and shout their way into the spotlight. Instead, they may stumble on in the darkness and begin to perceive a different type of political arena that opens the potential for dialogue among adversaries.

Without a doubt, a utopian ethos underwrites this desire to imagine models for non-violent political spaces in the Sixties

Conclusion

and to attend to those discourses today; in this way, these texts appear to be very much of their own time, to be contemporary texts, and I contend that such a revival of hope is also necessary today. However, those who go unnoticed never fall into the trap of assuming that a perfect, conflict-free political space will come about simply by going unnoticed and later being perceived. Knowing that their community is always a coming community and that their individual desires are never universal sets them apart from those who would use violence to obtain a hegemonic position in the political arena. Going unnoticed opens a space in which it becomes possible to imagine alternatives that may end in failure but also have the potential to be successful.

Going unnoticed is not by necessity limited to the Sixties in Latin America, the time and place in which I was able to catch a glimpse of these practices. The politics of going unnoticed, despite its contemporaneity, was cast aside, but these gestures still can point toward possible alternatives within the contemporary political landscape today. They may become successful tools for opening paths toward that unforeseen horizon of democratic dialogues to come. They will fail to ever see that moment materialize into a static regime, but this was never their goal. Every time those who go unnoticed arrive at an end or an obstacle, it becomes necessary to turn around again. In one final, imperfect rearrangement of *vesre* and *verse*, I will end by looking at ARTELETRA from a new perspective: *re-ves la ARTELETRA*. As one unnoticed protagonist emerges, engages in dialogue, and fails to fix everything, others can go unnoticed and start over again. Their failures set in motion a radically democratic process of continually re-seeing ("re-ves, you re-see") the political landscape and the art of writing about it in order to keep walking down the errant paths toward greater social and economic equality. What I find necessary today is to shake off the disillusionment of those who saw their political projects fail in the Sixties and to take up once more this type of utopian thinking. Now is the time to ask what other futures, instead of dwelling in the tragedies of the past, are possible today. As Casey's protagonist says from his jail cell toward the end of "Notas de un simulador": "Esperemos" (90).

Notes

Introduction

1. See Jamila Medina Ríos, *Diseminaciones de Calvert Casey*, for a thorough bibliography on Casey's writings and the scattered criticism that has been written on him to date.

2. See María Cristina Dalmagro, *Desde los umbrales de la memoria. Ficción autobiográfica en Armonía Somers*. Dalmagro has compiled a bibliography that is indispensable for studying Somers.

3. See Mario Merlino, "Delantal para Calvert Casey," in *Notas de un simulador* and Ilan Stavans, "Introduction," in *Calvert Casey: The Collected Works*.

4. See Mempo Giardinelli, "Don Juan de las Siete Letras: Vida y Obra de Filloy," in Juan Filloy, *La potra. Estancia "Los Capitanejos."*

5. The examples Ángel Rama gives include: in Uruguay, Alfa and Arca; in Buenos Aires, Losada, Emecé, Sudamericana, Compañía General Fabril Editora, Jorge Álvarez, La Flor, and Galerna; in Chile, Nascimento and Zig Zag; in Venezuela, Monte Ávila; in Mexico, Fondo de Cultura Económica, Era, and Joaquín Mortiz; and in Barcelona, Seix Barral, Lumen, and Anagrama ("El 'Boom'" 66–67).

6. See Rama, "La insólita literatura de Somers: la fascinación del horror," (30); Mario Benedetti, "El derrumbamiento" (115); and Benedetti, *Literatura uruguaya siglo XX* (second expanded edition).

7. In Chapter 1, I make one exception to this in my analysis of Calvert Casey and the essays he wrote while still living in Cuba. However, my argument does not rely on whether or not his essays were read, but the extent to which he maneuvered the revolutionary public sphere in order to publish ideas that could have been considered counter-revolutionary.

8. See Julio Prieto, *Desencuadernados: vanguardias ex-céntricas en el Río de la Plata. Macedonio Fernández y Felisberto Hernández* (18–28).

9. See Andrea Giunta, *Avant-Garde, Internationalism, and Politics: Argentine Art in the Sixties*, (55–89).

10. See Vicky Unruh, *Latin American Vanguards: The Art of Contentious Encounters* (21–26).

11. Between 1968 and 1971, the well-publicized polemic between Julio Cortázar and José María Arguedas took place within this context in which writers constantly had to defend their commitment to the revolutionary cause. Both authors attempted to defend themselves from a series of broader attacks leveraged against writers in the era, but they ended up attacking one another. Cortázar felt the need to prove his cosmopolitan commitment to revolutionary causes in Latin America from Paris, and Arguedas had committed to writing from the Andes but did not achieve the same popularity and commercial success as the Boom writers. For Arguedas, Cortázar's comments only further underscored the Eurocentric dismissal of so-called

peripheral literatures—to which even Cortázar belongs—as nothing more than nationalist folklore. Laura Demaría argues that in the case of this polemic "cada autor se queda pegado a uno de los dos términos excluyentes de la oposición" (*Buenos Aires y las provincias* 51). Neither was capable of stepping fully outside of this division between cosmopolitan and peripheral literatures to reconfigure the structure of the debate itself, and so this polemic faded without achieving much at all.

PART ONE

1. The metaphors of destroying, remodeling, or constructing new buildings or houses in times of revolution are not new in the Sixties; see Víctor Goldgel-Carballo, *Cuando lo nuevo conquistó América. Prensa, moda y literatura en el siglo XIX.*

2. The Padilla Affair has been well-documented and analyzed in various studies. The multiplicity of texts in which authors publicly weighed in on the situation has been collected in Lourdes Casal, *El caso Padilla: Literatura y Revolución en Cuba. Documentos*. Heberto Padilla's collection of poetry is also compiled alongside a selection of these public texts surrounding the affair in *Fuera del juego*. For an analysis of the Affair, see Martín Chadad, "Testimonio de partes, o quién es quién," in *Polémicas intelectuales en América Latina. Del "meridiano intelectual" al caso Padilla (1927–1971)* (207–12).

Chapter One

1. See Rose Mary Sheldon, "The Sator Rebus: An Unsolved Cryptogram?" (233–50). Sheldon has compiled an annotated bibliography and summary of the state of the question surrounding the Sator Square.

Chapter Three

1. See the chapter on Somers, "Armonía Somers y el carácter obsceno del mundo," that appears in the expanded edition of Mario Benedetti's *Literatura uruguaya siglo XX*.

2. The good press brought by Rama marked a small step toward the positive reception of her works, carried out primarily by feminist critics and those studying fantastic literary traditions since the 1980s. For a thorough summary of the reception of Somers's works through the 2000s, see Cristina Dalmagro, "Armonía Somers/Etchepare: las huellas biográficas," in *Desde los umbrales de la memoria* (45–98). These articles by Monegal, Benedetti, and Rama, as well as many others, are documented in her exhaustive archival research.

3. In chapter 8, I focus on Somers's critique of the logic of immunization underlying her various metaphors of contamination in *Un retrato para Dickens* and *Sólo los elefantes encuentran mandrágora*.

4. See Rebecca E. Biron, *Murder and Masculinity: Violent Fictions of Twentieth-Century Latin America*, which includes a masterful study of masculinity in Somers's "El despojo."

PART TWO

1. See Hermann Herlinghaus and Monica Walter, *Postmodernidad en la periferia. Enfoques latinoamericanos de la nueva teoría cultural*; John Beverley, Michael Aronna, and José Oviedo, eds., *The Postmodernism Debate in Latin America*; Beatriz Sarlo, *Una modernidad periférica. Buenos Aires, 1920–1930*; and Hermann Herlinghaus, *Renarración y descentramiento. Mapas alternativos de la imaginación en América Latina*.

2. See Achille Mbembe, "Necropolitics." He forcefully expands the temporal scope of the state of exception before the camps of World War II to include the technologies of killing that existed within European colonies and on plantations that reduced native and enslaved bodies through the violence of necropower.

3. "Bare life" is the translation of Agamben's phrase, "*nuda vita*," as proposed by Daniel Heller-Roazen in *Homo Sacer*. In Giorgio Agamben, *Means without Ends: Notes on Politics*, the translators prefer the phrase "naked life" (5). It is worth noting the two possibilities, since the former connotes a certain biological simplicity and being divested of legal status, whereas the latter highlights the lack of covering or protection and being utterly exposed in addition to evoking the negative moral values associated with nudity and sexuality.

Chapter Four

1. See also, William Luis, *Lunes de Revolución: Literatura y cultura en los primeros años de la Revolución Cubana*, which provides a detailed index of each number of the journal.

2. See Manuel Díaz Martínez, "La pistola sobre la mesa," *Revista Encuentro de la Cultura Cubana* 43 (154). While the general proceedings of these conferences are well-known and frequently summarized, I have paraphrased the outcome of these events based on Díaz Martínez's essay and William Luis's previously cited work.

3. See *Conducta impropia*, directed by Néstor Almendros and Orlando Jiménez Leal. This documentary has proven controversial. For a measured criticism of the film's facile comparisons between the UMAPs and the violence of Pinochet's dictatorship or the Nazi concentration camps, see Ian Lumsden, *Machos, Maricones, and Gays: Cuba and Homosexuality*. Despite this criticism, Lumsden explains, "These were terrifying times for many homosexuals, particularly those in entertainment, culture, and education" (70).

4. According to Guillermo Cabrera Infante, it was out of fear of being sent to the UMAPs for being gay that finally prompted Casey to go into exile in 1965. Cabrera Infante relates how Casey, who did not try to hide his sexuality, had confessed his fears of these camps to Emmanuel Carballo, a Mexican writer who was invited to Cuba by *Casa de las Américas*. The next day, Carballo reported back to Haydée Santamaría, then director of *Casa*. When he learned of this, Casey took advantage of the translation of his short

stories into Polish to apply for permission to travel to Poland and from there went to Italy. See Cabrera Infante, "¿Quién mató a Calvert Casey?"

5. Castro only stated his regret of this homophobia from his death bed in the early 2000s, too little too late, and Guevara openly discriminated against queer subjects until his death. For example, Juan Goytisolo tells the story of Guevara at the Cuban embassy in Algiers hurling one of Virgilio Piñera's books across the room while shouting, "How dare you have in our embassy a book by this foul faggot" (Quiroga, "Fleshing" 168). The institutionalized homophobia of the radical left—a homophobia that was certainly not limited to Cuba—has been well documented. See Lumsden's *Machos, Maricones, and Gays: Cuba and Homosexuality*.

6. For a more detailed reading of the debates surrounding the distinctions between the *Orígenes* group and the *Lunes* group, see Duanel Díaz, "Orígenes, Lunes, Revolución," *La Habana Elegante. Segunda etapa* (29).

7. For a detailed analysis of the various positions taken in these debates ranging from Castro's "Palabras" to the polemic Padilla Affair in 1971, see Ana Serra, *The "New Man" in Cuba: Culture and Identity in the Revolution*.

8. In a May 1961 article in *Lunes*, "Los caminos a Playa Girón," Casey further proves his genuine commitment to the Revolution by collecting and presenting a series of testimonies from ten soldiers who fought in the Playa Girón/Bay of Pigs invasion. The bulk of the article is comprised of these testimonies, but he briefly introduces them explaining that these are "hombres tan complicados y armados de verdades tan simples" (34). Then, he explains that telling all of their stories would be "físicamente imposible" (34). Instead, these few, fragmented stories become for him the "pequeña muestra humana, espléndidamente humana" that allow others to begin to understand this key moment in the defense of the Cuban Revolution (34). This essay upholds Casey's broader political and aesthetic program.

9. Mouffe uses the term "politics" to refer to these consensus-building practices of various institutions and "the political" to name dissensus (101). However, I only borrow her distinction between consensus and dissensus.

10. In Part Four on ethics and the formation of a political community, I explore how Mouffe theorizes the transformation of antagonism into agonism by which an enemy is transformed into an adversary within a radical democratic politics.

Chapter Five

1. These "monodialogues," as I have chosen to translate Filloy's neologism, "monodiálogos," constitute a rhetorical structure that I will explore further in Chapter 11 in its relation to ethics, that is, to engaging in dialogue across unfathomable distances with others to form a community. While each of the seven monodialogues slightly varies in its number of speakers and interlocutors, the general structure is comprised of one person, always a man, who dominates the entire discussion while ignoring most of

what is said by the rest. The monodialogues often end in an ironic turn of events that undermines the force of the speaker who will not cede to or even acknowledge the others near him, as will be the case in "Yo y los intrusos."

2. Detailing the political landscape from 1973–76 in particular, Maristella Svampa shows that in 1973, the Peronist Héctor Cámpora is elected President and appears to make room for "la Juventud maravillosa" within Peronism ("Populismo" 395). However, upon Perón's return that same year, the situation changes drastically with the massacre of those youth at Ezeiza and Perón's speech in which the same youth are cast aside as "imberbes" and "estúpidos" (403–04). The entire drama surrounding the reappearance of the Peronists in the political arena, Perón's return to Argentina, those who dismiss Perón's ideological turn to the right with the "teoría del cerco" that assumes that Perón was being poorly advised by those around him, the violence committed by the Montoneros in order to spark a revolution, and the violence committed under Perón's orders to eliminate this "internal enemy" is not only complex, but difficult to historicize objectively. See Daniel James, ed., *Violencia, proscripción y autoritarismo (1955–1976)*.

3. See the documentary, *Ecce homo: una autobiografía de Juan Filloy*, directed by Eduardo Montes-Bradley—the last interview with Juan Filloy in which he recounts his own biography and publishing history.

4. Plato, *Republic* (232–49).

5. Derrida advances a related argument in "Plato's Pharmacy" about the impossibility of arriving at any origin outside of *logos*, and writing becomes more closely associated with myth than it does with knowledge or the truth: "And at the same time, through writing or through myth, the genealogical break and the estrangement from the origin are sounded" (74). The *pharmakon*, which in the *Phaedrus* is associated with writing, is both a remedy and a poison; it is necessary for seeking "the origin or cause of *logos*," but that external origin or cause can never be investigated outside of *logos*, that is, outside of writing (80).

6. It is not my intention here to add further commentary to the exhaustive debate provoked by David Stoll, *Rigoberta Menchú and the Story of All Poor Guatemalans*, in which he claims to disprove certain aspects of Rigoberta Menchú's testimony, ultimately reminding readers of any text's narrative construction.

7. See Tulio Halperín Donghi, *Una nación para el desierto argentino* (143).

Chapter Six

1. See Mariana Iglesias, "La excepción como práctica de gobierno en Uruguay, 1946–1963" (132).

2. Iglesias records eighteen cases in which the *medidas prontas de seguridad* were invoked in Uruguay in each of the following years: 1902, 1903, 1904, 1906, 1909, 1910, 1914, 1917, 1919, 1920, 1932, 1933, 1934, 1935, 1936, 1942, 1943, and 1945 (142).

Chapter Seven

1. See Carlos Hernán Sosa's "Ecos paródicos. Resonancias de la gauchesca en *La potra* de Juan Filloy" for an exploration of the links between the Ochoa Family Saga and the gaucho genre in the second text of the Saga.

2. Domingo F. Sarmiento's approach to the *gaucho malo* is more complex than that of Ascasubi. In Chaper II of *Facundo*, the *gaucho malo* figures in the author's gaucho taxonomy alongside three other types: *el rastreador, el baqueano, and el cantor*. Though Sarmiento develops a moral complexity in his descriptions, in particular relating to the detailed knowledge each of these gaucho types possess about the territory they roam, what characterizes the *gaucho malo* is that he steals, even if not out of malice: "roba es cierto; pero esta es su profesión, su tráfico, su ciencia" (89).

3. Filloy's Saga further dismantles Ascasubi's binary logic by including multiple sets of twins within the Ochoa family. The prologue to *Los Ochoa* mentions Octavo and Noveno (b. 1894) and Decena and Docena (b. 1921), and in "Carbunclo," Segundo and Secundina, "dos sabandijas" who assume the responsibility of caring for their ageing grandfather, but they are not moral opposites as in the case of Ascasubi's twins (35).

4. Borges and Bioy Casares also direct their critique toward Ricardo Rojas for deriving the gaucho genre from the oral tradition of the gauchos: "Rojas quiere derivar el género gauchesco de la poesía popular de los payadores; creemos que esa genealogía es errónea" (viii–ix).

5. In Canto VIII, the *Martín Fierro* reads: "Él anda siempre juyendo. / Siempre pobre y perseguido; / no tiene cueva ni nido, / como si juera maldito; / porque el ser gaucho … ¡barajo!, / el ser gaucho es un delito" (Hernández 157).

6. Even before fleeing the army, Proto explains in "El juído (El patriarca)" that he spent much of his life walking back and forth between the Postas of the Camino Real that connected, in part, Buenos Aires to Córdoba in the late colonial period and served as military posts throughout much of the nineteenth century: "Hasta me parece que n'hubiese sufrido nada yendo una y mil veces de Esquina del Lobatón a Saladillo de Ruiz Diaz, a Zanjón, a Fraile Muerto, a Tres Cruces, a Capilla de Dolores, a Esquina del Corral de Barrancas, a Arroyo Chucul y la Concepción del Río Cuarto. Saltos de langosta. Tas, tas, tas …" (9). Proto flits from one place to another, never laying down roots; even his place of birth becomes unimportant for this "satafareño, satafesino que le dicen, de Esquina de la Guardia, acordobesao en Cruz Alta y Cabeza del Tigre" (9).

7. In "Biografía de Tadeo Isidoro Cruz (1829–1874)," Borges describes Cruz's adventures in *La ida* as a story that "es capaz de casi inagotables repeticiones, versiones, perversiones" (862). It can be copied, translated, and adapted, because it is full of gaps: "En su oscura y valerosa historia abundan los hiatos" (863). See Jason A. Bartles, "Gauchos at the Origins: Lugones, Borges, Filloy."

Chapter Eight

1. Dalmagro's article also situates Somers's novel in the context of twentieth-century Montevideo "en donde la preocupación por la delincuencia juvenil y la marginalidad del niño fue motivo de interés generalizado y abordado especialmente por ella en sus trabajos como educadora" ("El revés" 177). See also in the same collection of essays Alicia Torres, "El Oliver dickensiano y la huérfana de Somers: tráfico de identidades."

2. Consult the 1969 edition of *La mujer desnuda* by Arca. Many, but not all, of these errors were mistakenly removed in the 2012 edition by El cuenco de plata.

3. As I explained in the introduction, Foucault's early writings on biopolitics demonstrate that the technologies of power are expanded from their disciplinary function toward the perpetuation of life at the collective or species level. This allows the sovereign to kill individual bodies—now little more than bare, biological material—because their so-called impurity, degeneracy, or abnormality threatens the survival of the species as a whole (*Society*).

4. See Roberto Esposito *Bíos: Biopolitics and Philosophy*. Esposito offers a brief survey of the metaphor of the body politic that I will not rehearse here as it exceeds the scope of my argument, but he explains that "it has been by far the most influential metaphor used in political discourse to represent life in society" (113).

Chapter Nine

1. See Walter Benjamin, *The Arcades Project*. Benjamin speaks of images that form constellations as follows: "image is that wherein what has been comes together in a flash with the now to form a constellation" (462).

2. "Piazza Margana" is Casey's only story to explicitly mention homosexuality, and it is only one of two texts written in English. See Gustavo Pérez Firmat, "Bilingual Blues, Bilingual Bliss." Jamila Medina Ríos further explains the strangeness of the text, and how it has been read alternately as book chapter, short story, and poem (50).

3. Cohen also provides a detailed bibliography on the subject, including a wide range of anthropological, psychoanalytical, economic, and cultural analyses of filth.

4. There is something paradoxical in Guevara's attempt to cleave unarmed intellectuals from the revolutionary process. In *El último lector*, Ricardo Piglia reflects on the photo taken of Guevara in Bolivia in which he is sitting in a tree reading and on the story of him reading a book in a hammock while waiting to begin an ambush ("Ernesto" 106–07). Piglia recalls that Guevara states his own "tendencia a aislarse, separarse, construyéndose un espacio aparte" (107). It is in this separate space where he spends his time reading, a space and an activity that shares an undeniable similarity to the paradigm of

the ivory tower intellectual. It should be recalled that the journals that were found on Guevara's body after being captured and killed in Bolivia include a long list of books that Guevara either read or planned to read, including books by G. W. F. Hegel, Friedrich Nietzsche, Fyodor Dostoyevsky, William Faulkner, Graham Greene, Rubén Darío, and Julio Cortázar, among many others (Guevara, *Diario* n.p.). In Piglia's assessment, Guevara becomes yet another intellectual in a long literary tradition who desperately wants to know "cómo salir de la biblioteca, cómo pasar a la vida, cómo entrar en acción, cómo ir a la experiencia, cómo salir del mundo libresco, cómo cortar con la lectura en tanto lugar de encierro" ("Ernesto" 127). In this way, Guevara himself is caught somewhere between the ideal armed revolutionary that he appears to embody and the intellectual that he cannot quite shed from his own life who reads and writes incessantly.

5. Recall Guevara's oft-cited phrase: "Podemos intentar injertar el olmo para que dé peras; pero simultáneamente hay que sembrar perales. Las nuevas generaciones vendrán libres del pecado original" ("El socialismo" 381). Of course, the disdain for intellectuals within the Cuban Revolution was well known before this essay. In "Guerrilla Warfare," Guevara underscores that "intensive popular work must be undertaken to explain the motives of the revolution, its ends, and to spread the incontrovertible truth that victory of the enemy against the people is finally impossible" (56). This apparently intellectual labor is not assigned to the traditional intellectuals. However, women combatants can readily fill the role of guerrilla teacher, though education remains a gendered activity to be carried out by other guerrilla fighters already within the armed struggle.

6. Reinaldo Arenas similarly praises *Mi tío el empleado*, because Meza offers "una crítica a la visión turística y romanticoide de la realidad latinoamericana" ("Meza, el precursor" 778).

7. Critics disagree as to whether the *cuna* is representative of a proto-democratic space or whether Villaverde's intention is to show that unmitigated democracy leads directly to sacrilege and the destruction of civilized society, since this is where the incestuous relationship between Leonardo and Cecilia begins. As Christina Civantos explains: "la obra exhibe la tensión entre el anhelo de proclamar una nación unida, o por lo menos factible aunque sea muy jerárquica, y el deseo de mantener muy lejos el disgusto de la mezcla, del vínculo, y hasta de la identificación, entre el yo y el otro" ("Pechos" 517–18). For her, the value of Villaverde's Realism lies precisely in representing this social tension.

8. Explaining the social significance of these different dances, Peter Manuel demonstrates that the Cuban *contradanza* stands as an example of "a popular dance form that was democratic, informal, and free from the hierarchy and rigidity of the minuet"; the *contradanza* temporarily opened some social divisions before being "undermined by the triumph of bourgeois individualism" and the popularity of "danza and danzón in Cuba, with their couples dancing independently, even intimately" ("Cuba" 103).

9. See Chapter 4 for the context in which this debate took place.

10. See Rafael Martínez Nadal, "Calvert Casey: notas a una lectura de 'Piazza Margana.'" He recounts his final meeting with Casey and how he came to be entrusted with this manuscript.

11. In "Is the Rectum a Grave?" Leo Bersani cautions against idealizing sexual practices of any sort as intrinsically democratic or ethical acts in which hierarchical distinctions fully disappear, offering the gay bathhouse as one example "of the most ruthlessly ranked, hierarchized, and competitive environments imaginable" (206). Notably, Casey's narrator does not choose sex as the event that allows for the encounter with his lover, the other man. This ethics of such an interaction with the other is elaborated in Chapter 12.

12. Cynthia L. Sears explains, "Comprised of 500 to 1000 bacterial species with two to four million genes, the microbiome contains about 100-fold more genes than the human genome and the estimated 10^{13} bacterial cells in the gut exceeds by 10-fold the total ensemble of human cells" (247).

PART FOUR

1. Virtue ethics is founded primarily upon the works of Aristotle, especially his *Nicomachean Ethics* in which he explores virtue of character as that which guides moral action. In *Leviathan*, Thomas Hobbes postulates mankind's "state of nature" as the proclivity toward violence and war, the opposite of the virtuous character. In *An Enquiry Concerning the Principles of Morals*, David Hume insists, on the contrary, on the innate goodness of humankind, thus reviving the possibility of virtue ethics in the eighteenth century. See Rosalind Hursthouse, "Virtue Ethics."

2. Jeremy Bentham and John Stuart Mill, as the founders of utilitarianism, stand as the classical figures of consequentialism. Bentham's *An Introduction to the Principles of Moral Legislation* underscores mankind's search for pleasure over pain, while Mill's *Utilitarianism* seeks to establish a sort of hierarchy among those pleasures. For both philosophers, moral actions are those which bring about the greatest pleasures for the greatest good; the consequences of actions, not the virtue of character or the intentions of the moral agent, are what determine the ethical value of an action. See Walter Sinnott-Armstrong, "Consequentialism."

3. Kant's "categorical imperative" is the classic example of deontology; moral action is a duty, an imperative, that must be carried out, and it is categorical insofar as "my maxim should become a universal law" (*Grounding* 14). In contradistinction to the previous two branches, Kant's is not founded on the innate, virtuous character of the agent, nor does it depend solely on the outcome of an agent's decisions, since neither the immediate nor the long-term effects of any actions can ever be known at the moment one makes a decision. For Kant, only the moment one makes a decision can be judged morally. See Larry Alexander and Michael Moore, "Deontological Ethics."

Chapter Ten

1. In the Introduction, I analyze this scene in more detail related to the desire of the narrator to go unnoticed. See Nicasio Perera San Martín "La intuición y los papeles. En torno a *De miedo en miedo (los manuscritos del río)*." He argues for this setting, despite the lack of stereotypical Parisian references, through a study of the original manuscript.

2. See Núria Calafell Sala, *Armonía Somers. Por una ética de lo ex-céntrico*. She has studied what she calls an ethics of the ex-centric in Armonía Somers's literature, which centers on the erotic and mystic elements of her works through a primarily psychoanalytic framework. Despite both of our attempts to construct an ethics from Somers's works, Calafell Sala's analysis shares little with my own approach, in particular for focusing on the "ex-céntrico," which means in Spanish both "eccentric, odd" and "peripheral, outside of the center."

3. See María Cristina Dalmagro, *Desde los umbrales de la memoria. Ficción autobiográfica en Armonía Somers*. She interprets the narrator's anxieties, his "vacío interior," as representative of the existentialist character through a comparison with Ernesto Sabato's *El túnel* and Jean Paul Sartre's *Being and Nothingness* (294).

Chapter Eleven

1. As I explained in Chapter 6, in "On Potentiality" Agamben defines "potentiality" as an opening for both darkness and light, for both good and evil: "To be capable of good and evil is not simply to be capable of doing this or that good or bad action (every particular good or bad action is, in this sense, banal). Radical evil is not this or that bad deed but the potentiality for darkness. And yet this potentiality is also the potentiality for light" (181). If both darkness and light are not guaranteed as potential actions or decisions, then there is no action or decision to be made, but only forced compliance with a mandate.

Chapter Twelve

1. An earlier version of Casey's "La ejecución" appeared in 1964 in *UNEAC* in Cuba. For a comparison of the two manuscripts, see the archival work carried out by Jamila Medina Ríos in the Argentine edition of *El regreso y otros relatos*.

2. The original version of "La ejecución" includes a passage that was removed in which the precinct is described as having multiple hallways filled with constant, but distant sounds: "un zumbido monótono y enorme (nada desagradable, pensó Mayer)" (187). As in other of Casey's narratives, the narrator is drawn toward the threshold spaces of swirling lights and shadows, noises and silences.

Conclusion

1. Transcribed from my personal notes, April 4, 2017.

Works Cited

Agamben, Giorgio. *The Coming Community*. Translated by Michael Hardt, U of Minnesota P, 1993.

———. *Homo Sacer: Sovereign Power and Bare Life*. Translated by Daniel Heller-Roazen, Stanford UP, 1998.

———. *Means without Ends: Notes on Politics*. Translated by Vincenzo Binetti and Cesare Casarino, U of Minnesota P, 2000.

———. *Nudities*. Translated by David Kishik and Stefan Pedatella, Stanford UP, 2011.

———. "On Potentiality." *Potentialities: Collected Essays in Philosophy*, edited and translated by Daniel Heller-Roazen, Stanford UP, 1999, pp. 177–84.

———. *The Open: Man and Animal*. Translated by Kevin Attell, Stanford UP, 2004.

———. *Stanzas: Word and Phantasm in Western Culture*. Translated by Ronald L. Martinez, U of Minnesota P, 1993.

———. *State of Exception*. Translated by Kevin Attell, U of Chicago P, 2005.

———. *The Use of Bodies*. Translated by Adam Kotsko, Stanford UP, 2016.

Agosín, Marjorie. "*La mujer desnuda* o el viaje decapitado: un texto de Armonía Somers." *Revista Iberoamericana de Bibliografía*, vol. 4, 1992, pp. 585–89.

Alexander, Larry, and Michael Moore. "Deontological Ethics." *The Stanford Encyclopedia of Philosophy*, edited by Edward N. Zalta. Accessed 8 Aug. 2013.

Almendros, Néstor. "Pasado Meridiano." *El caso P.M. Cine, poder y censura*, edited by Orlando Jiménez Leal and Manuel Zayas, Editorial Hypermedia, 2014.

Almendros, Néstor, and Orlando Jiménez Leal, directors. *Conducta impropia*. Egales Editorial, 2008.

Álvarez-Tabío Albo, Emma. *Invención de La Habana*, Casiopea, 2000.

Amar Sánchez, Ana María. *Juegos de seducción y traición. Literatura y cultura de masas*. Beatriz Viterbo, 2000.

Ambort, Mónica. *Juan Filloy, el escritor escondido*. Op Oloop Ediciones, 1992.

Andermann, Jens. *Mapas de poder. Una arqueología literaria del espacio argentino*. Beatriz Viterbo, 2000.

Antelo, Raúl. *Archifilologías latinoamericanas. Lecturas tras el agotamiento*. Eduvim, 2015.

Works Cited

Arenas, Reinaldo. "Meza, el precursor." *Revista Iberoamericana*, vol. 56, no. 152–53, 1990, pp. 777–79.

Aristotle. *Nicomachean Ethics*. 2nd edition, translated by Terence Irwin, Hackett, 1999.

———. *Politics. The Internet Classics Archive*, edited by Daniel C. Stevenson, translated by Benjamin Jowett. Accessed 9 Jun. 2017.

Ascasubi, Hilario. *Santos Vega el payador. Poesía gauchesca*, Vol. 1, edited by Jorge Luis Borges and Adolfo Bioy Casares, Fondo de Cultura Económica, 1955, pp. 304–624.

Atwood, Margaret. *The Robber Bride*. Anchor Books, 1998.

Bartles, Jason A. "La alegoría errante de la torre-cueva de Juan Filloy." *Revista Iberoamericana*, vol. 82 no. 254, Jan–Mar 2016, pp. 213–28.

———. "Calvert Casey's Wasted Narratives." *Revista Hispánica Moderna*, vol. 70.1, 2017, pp. 19–35.

———. "La ética de exponerse en *De miedo en miedo* de Armonía Somers." *La escritura de Armonía Somers. Pulsión y riesgo*. Edited by María Cristina Dalmagro, Editorial Universidad de Sevilla, 2019, pp. 63–76.

———. "Gauchos at the Origins: Lugones, Borges, Filloy." *Variaciones Borges*, vol. 40, 2015, pp. 133–52.

Beasley-Murray, Jon. *Posthegemony: Political Theory and Latin America*. U of Minnesota P, 2010.

Benedetti, Mario. "*El derrumbamiento*." *Número*, vol. 5, no. 22, 1953, pp. 102.

———. *Literatura uruguaya siglo XX*. 2nd edition, Alfa, 1969.

Benjamin, Walter. *The Arcades Project*. Translated by Howard Eiland and Kevin McLaughlin, Belknap Press, 1999.

———. "Theses on the Philosophy of History." *Illuminations: Essays and Reflections*, edited by Hannah Arendt, translated by Harry Zohn, Schocken Books, 1968, pp. 253–64.

———. *The Work of Art in the Age of Its Technological Reproducibility and Other Writings on Media*. Translated by Edmund Jephcott, Rodney Livingstone, Howard Eiland, et. al., Belknap Press, 2008.

Bentham, Jeremy. *An Introduction to the Principles of Morals and Legislation*. Clarendon Press, 1907.

Bersani, Leo. "Is the Rectum a Grave?" *October*, vol. 43, 1987, pp. 197–222.

Best, Stephen, and Sharon Marcus. "Surface Reading: An Introduction." *Representations*, vol. 108, 2009, pp. 1–21.

Works Cited

Beverley, John. "Anatomía del testimonio." *Revista de Crítica Literaria Latinoamericana*, vol. 13, no. 25, 1987, pp. 7–16.

Beverley, John, Michael Aronna, and José Oviedo, eds. *The Postmodernism Debate in Latin America*. Duke UP, 1995.

Biron, Rebecca E. *Murder and Masculinity: Violent Fictions of Twentieth-Century Latin America*. Vanderbilt UP, 2000.

Blatchford, Samuel. *Reports of Cases Argued and Determined in the Circuit Court of the United States for the Second Court*. Vol. 24, Baker, Voorhis & Co., 1888.

Borges, Jorge Luis. "Biografía de Tadeo Isidoro Cruz." *Obras Completas*. Vol. 1, Sudamericana, 2011, pp. 862–864.

———. "El escritor argentino y la tradición." *Obras Completas*. Vol. 1, Sudamericana, 2011, pp. 550–57.

Borges, Jorge Luis and Adolfo Bioy Casares. "Prólogo." *Poesía gauchesca*. Vol. 1, Fondo de Cultura Económica, 1955, pp. vii–xxvi.

Bürger, Peter. *Theory of the Avant-Garde*. Translated by Michael Shaw, U of Minnesota P, 1984.

Cabrera, Sabá, and Orlando Jiménez Leal, directors. *P.M.* 1961. *Vimeo*. Accessed 28 Mar. 2018.

Cabrera Infante, Guillermo. "¿Quién mató a Calvert Casey?" *Quimera*, vol. 26, 1982, pp. 42–53.

Calafell Sala, Núria. *Armonía Somers. Por una ética de lo ex-céntrico*. Editorial Academia del Hispanismo, 2010.

———. "Sabotaje, cuerpo y violencia en *La mujer desnuda*." *Escritural. Écritures d'Amérique latine*, vol. 9, 2016. Accessed 10 Jun. 2017.

Campodónico, Miguel Ángel, and Armonía Somers. "Diálogo." *Armonía Somers, papeles críticos. Cuarenta años de literatura*, edited Rómulo Cosse, Linardi y Risso, 1990, pp. 225–45.

Cárcamo-Huechante, Luis E., Álvaro Fernández Bravo, and Alejandra Laera. "Introducción." *El valor de la cultura. Arte, literatura y mercado en América Latina*, edited by Luis E. Cárcamo-Huechante, Álvaro Fernández Bravo, and Alejandra Laera, Beatriz Viterbo, 2007, pp. 7–40.

Carrión, Miguel de. *Las impuras*. Edited by Ángel Esteban and Yannelys Aparicio, Cátedra, 2011.

Casal, Lourdes, ed. *El caso Padilla: Literatura y Revolución en Cuba. Documentos*. Ediciones Universal, 1971.

Casey, Calvert. *Calvert Casey: The Collected Stories*. Edited by Ilan Stavans, translated by John H. R. Polt, Duke UP, 1998.

Works Cited

Casey, Calvert. "Los caminos a Playa Girón. Fotos Mayita." *Lunes de Revolución*, vol. 106/107, 1961, pp. 34–36.

———. "Carrión o la desnudez." *Memorias de una isla*, Ediciones R, 1964, pp. 45–66.

———. "Un ensayo oportuno." *Lunes de Revolución*, vol. 48, 1960, pp. 13.

———. "La ejecución." *El regreso y otros relatos*, Seix Barral, 1967, pp. 191–212.

———. "Hacia una comprensión total del XIX." *Memorias de una isla*, Ediciones R, 1964, pp. 119–31.

———. "Kafka." *Memorias de una isla*, Ediciones R, 1964, pp. 69–77.

———. "Meditación junto a caballería." *Casa de las Américas*, vol. 24, 1964, pp. 50–52.

———. *Memorias de una isla*. Ediciones R, 1964.

———. "Meza literato y los Croquis Habaneros." *Memorias de una isla*, Ediciones R, 1964, pp. 25–44.

———. "Mi tía Leocadia, el amor y el paleolítico inferior." *El regreso. Cuentos*, Ediciones R, 1962, pp. 37–50.

———. "Notas de un simulador." *Notas de un simulador*. Seix Barral, 1969, pp. 9–91.

———. *Notas de un simulador*. Seix Barral, 1969.

———. *Notas de un simulador*. Edited by Mario Merlino, Montesinos, 1997.

———. "Piazza Margana." *Calvert Casey: The Collected Stories*, edited by Ilan Stavans, translated by John H. R. Polt, Duke UP, 1998, pp. 187–93.

———. "Polacca brillante." *Notas de un simulador*. Seix Barral, 1969, pp. 93–09.

———. "El Premio Nobel y la muerte." *Lunes de Revolución*, vol. 64, 1960, pp. 24.

———. *El regreso. Cuentos*. Ediciones R, 1962.

———. *El regreso y otros relatos*. Seix Barral, 1967.

———. *El regreso y otros relatos*. Edited by Jamila Medina Ríos, Final Abierto, 2016.

Casey, Calvert, et. al. "Diez escritores cubanos conversan con Nathalie Sarraute." *Lunes de Revolución*, vol. 121, 1961, pp. 2–6.

———. "*Lunes* conversa con Pablo Neruda." *Lunes de Revolución*, vol. 88, 1960, pp. 38–43.

Castro, Fidel. "Palabras a los intelectuales." *Ministerio de Cultura de la República de Cuba*, 23 Jun. 1961. Accessed 6 Jul. 2011.

Certeau, Michel de. *The Practice of Everyday Life*. Translated by Steven Rendall U of California P, 1984.

Chadad, Martín. "Testimonio de partes, o quién es quién." *Polémicas intelectuales en América Latina. Del "meridiano intelectual" al caso Padilla (1927–1971)*, edited by Marcela Croce, Ediciones Simurg, 2006, pp. 207–12.

Civantos, Christina. "Pechos de leche, oro y sangre: las circulaciones del objeto y el sujeto en *Cecilia Valdés*." *Revista Iberoamericana*, vol. 71, no. 211, 2005, pp. 505–19.

Cohen, William A. "Locating Filth." *Filth: Dirt, Disgust, and Modern Life*, edited by William A. Cohen and Ryan Johnson, U of Minnesota P, 2005, vii–xxxvii.

Cortázar, Julio. *Rayuela*. Punto de Lectura, 2006.

Dalmagro, María Cristina. *Desde los umbrales de la memoria. Ficción autobiográfica en Armonía Somers*. Biblioteca Nacional, 2009.

———. "El revés de la inocencia: Somers, Dickens y un 'Oliver' compartido." *Charles Dickens en América Latina. Reflexiones desde Montevideo*, edited by Beatriz Vegh, Linardi y Risso, 2005, pp. 161–78.

Deleuze, Gilles, and Félix Guattari. *A Thousand Plateaus: Capitalism and Schizophrenia*. Translated by Brian Massumi, U of Minnesota P, 1987.

Demaría, Laura. "Borges y Bioy Casares, 1955 y la *Poesía gauchesca* como paradójica rebeldía." *Latin American Literary Review*, vol. 22, no. 44, 1994, pp. 20–30.

———. *Buenos Aires y las provincias. Relatos para desarmar*, Beatriz Viterbo, 2014.

Derrida, Jacques. "On Absolute Hostility: The Cause of Philosophy and the Spectre of the Political." *The Politics of Friendship*, translated by George Collins, Verso, 1997, pp. 112–37.

———. *Archive Fever: A Freudian Impression*. Translated by Eric Prenowitz, U of Chicago P, 1995.

———. "*Khôra*." *On the Name*, edited by Thomas Dutoit, translated by Ian McLeod, Stanford UP, 1995, pp. 87–127.

———. "Plato's Pharmacy." *Dissemination*, translated by Barbara Johnson, U of Chicago P, 1981, pp. 61–171.

Descartes, René. *A Discourse on Method*. Translated by John Veitch, Everyman, 1986.

Works Cited

Díaz, Duanel. "*Orígenes, Lunes, Revolución.*" *La Habana Elegante. Segunda Época*, vol. 29, 2005. Accessed 12 Mar. 2013.

Díaz Martínez, Manuel. "La pistola sobre la mesa." *Revista Encuentro de la Cultura Cubana*, vol. 43, 2006–2007, pp. 147–56.

Dickens, Charles. *Oliver Twist*. Vintage Classics, 2012.

Escudero, Víctor. "Sujetos descompuestos. Pensar la 'novela de formación' desde *El palacio de las blanquísimas mofetas* de R. Arenas, *Cicatrices* de J. J. Saer y *Un retrato para Dickens* de A. Somers." *Centro de Estudios de Literatura Argentina*, 2009, pp. 1–14. Accessed 28 May 2017.

Esposito, Roberto. *Bíos: Biopolitics and Philosophy*. Translated by Timothy Campbell, U of Minnesota P, 2008.

———. *Immunitas: The Protection and Negation of Life*. Translated by Zakiya Hanafi, Polity, 2011.

Filloy, Juan. "As de espadas." *Los Ochoa*. Interzona, 2003, pp. 21–32.

———. "Carbunclo." *Los Ochoa*. Interzona, 2003, pp. 33–71.

———. *Decio 8A*. Op Oloop Ediciones, 1997.

———. *Finesse*. Ferrari Hnos., 1939.

———. "El juído (El patriarca)." *Los Ochoa*. Interzona, 2003, pp. 9–20.

———. *Karcino: Tratado de palindromía*. El cuenco de plata, 2005.

———. *Los Ochoa*. Interzona, 2003.

———. *Op Oloop*. Paidós, 1967.

———. *Periplo*. Editorial Almagesto, 2000.

———. *La potra*. Estancia Los Capitanejos. El cuenco de plata, 2013.

———. *Sexamor*. Op Oloop Ediciones, 1995.

———. *Vil & Vil. La gata parida*. El cuenco de plata, 2005.

———. "Yo y el arquitecto." *Yo, yo y yo. (Monodiálogos paranoicos)*. El cuenco de plata, 2007, pp. 11–27.

———. "Yo y el mundo subterráneo." *Yo, yo y yo. (Monodiálogos paranoicos)*. El cuenco de plata, 2007, pp. 107–24.

———. "Yo y la madre patria." *Yo, yo y yo. (Monodiálogos paranoicos)*. El cuenco de plata, 2007, pp. 29–58.

———. "Yo y los anónimos." *Yo, yo y yo. (Monodiálogos paranoicos)*. El cuenco de plata, 2007, pp. 59–78.

———. "Yo y los intrusos." *Yo, yo y yo. (Monodiálogos paranoicos)*. El cuenco de plata, 2007, pp. 125–53.

———. *Yo, yo y yo. (Monodiálogos paranoicos)*. El cuenco de plata, 2007.

Foster, Hal. *The Return of the Real: The Avant-Garde at the End of the Century.* MIT P, 1996.

Foucault, Michel. *Discipline and Punish: The Birth of the Prison.* Translated by Alan Sheridan, Vintage Books, 1977.

———. "Nietzsche, Genealogy, History." *Language, Counter-Memory, Practice: Selected Essays and Interviews*, edited by D. F. Bouchard, Cornell UP, 1977, pp. 139–64.

———. *"Society Must Be Defended." Lectures at the Collège de France, 1975–76.* Edited by Mauro Bertani and Alessandro Fontana, translated by David Macey, Picador, 2003.

———. "What is Enlightenment?" *Ethics: Subjectivity and Truth*, edited by Paul Rabinow, translated by Robert Hurley, et. al., Penguin Books, 1997, pp. 303–19.

Fowler-Calzada, Víctor. "Casey's Nineteenth Century and the *Ciclón* Project." Translated by Jacqueline E. Loss, *CR: The New Centennial Review*, vol. 2, no. 2, 2002, pp. 187–200.

Franco, Marina, and Mariana Iglesias. "El estado de excepción en Uruguay y Argentina. Reflexiones teóricas, históricas e historiográficas." *Revistas de historia comparada*, vol. 5, no. 1, 2011, pp. 91–115.

Garibotto, Verónica. *Crisis y reemergencia: El siglo XIX en la ficción contemporánea de Argentina, Chile y Uruguay (1980–2001).* Purdue UP, 2015.

Genette, Gérard. *Paratexts: Thresholds of Interpretation.* Cambridge UP, 1997.

Giardinelli, Mempo. "Don Juan de las Siete Letras: Vida y Obra de Filloy." Introduction. *La Potra. Estancia "Los Capitanejos"* by Juan Filloy, Interzona, 2003, pp. 5–10.

Gilman, Claudia. *Entre la pluma y el fusil. Debates y dilemas del escritor revolucionario en América Latina.* 2nd edition, Siglo XXI, 2012.

Giunta, Andrea. *Avant-Garde, Internationalism, and Politics: Argentine Art in the Sixties.* Translated by Peter Kahn, Duke UP, 2007.

Goldgel, Víctor. *Cuando lo nuevo conquistó América. Prensa, moda y literatura en el siglo XIX.* Siglo XXI, 2013.

Gordillo, Mónica B. "Protesta, rebelión y movilización: de la resistencia a la lucha armada (1955–1973)." *Violencia, proscripción y autoritarismo (1955–1976). Colección Nueva Historia Argentina.* Vol. IX, edited by Daniel James, Sudamericana, 2003, pp. 329–80.

Guevara, Ernesto. *Diario de Bolivia.* Edición facsímil. "Che Bolivia." Accessed 10 Oct. 2012.

———. "Guerrilla Warfare (1960)." *Guerrilla Warfare*, edited by Brian Loveman and Thomas M. Davies, Jr., translated by J. P. Morray, U of Nebraska P, 1997, pp. 40–145.

Works Cited

Guevara, Ernesto. "El socialismo y el hombre en Cuba." *Obras 1957–1967. II. La transformación política, económica y social*, Casa de las Américas, 1977, pp. 367–84.

Habermas, Jürgen. *The Structural Transformation of the Public Sphere: An Inquiry into a Category of Bourgeois Society*. Translated by Thomas Burger and Frederick Lawrence, MIT P, 1989.

Halperín Donghi, Tulio. *Una nación para el desierto argentino*. Prometeo Libros, 2005.

Han, Byung-Chul. *The Transparency Society*. Translated by Erik Butler, Stanford UP, 2015.

Haraway, Donna J. *Simians, Cyborgs, and Women: The Reinvention of Nature*. Routledge, 1991.

Harvey, David. *Spaces of Hope*. U of California P, 2000.

Herlinghaus, Hermann. *Renarración y descentramiento. Mapas alternativos de la imaginación en América Latina*. Iberoamericana, 2004.

Herlinghaus, Hermann, and Monica Walter. *Postmodernidad en la periferia. Enfoques latinoamericanos de la nueva teoría cultural*. Langer Verlag, 1994.

Hernán Sosa, Carlos. "Ecos paródicos. Resonancias de la gauchesca en *La potra* de Juan Filloy." *Argentina en su literatura*, edited by Nilda María Flawiá de Fernández, Corregidor, 2009, pp. 313–26.

Hernández, José. *Martín Fierro*. Edited by Luis Sáinz de Medrano, Cátedra, 1979.

Hobbes, Thomas. *Leviathan: with Selected Variants from the Latin Edition of 1668*. Edited by Edwin Curley, Hackett, 1994.

Hume, David. *An Enquiry Concerning the Principles of Morals*. Edited by J.B. Schneewind, Hackett, 1983.

Hursthouse, Rosalind. "Virtue Ethics." *The Stanford Encyclopedia of Philosophy*, edited by Edward N. Zalta. Accessed 8 Aug. 2013.

Iglesias, Mariana. "La excepción como práctica de gobierno en Uruguay, 1946–1963." *Contemporánea. Historias y problemas del siglo XX*, vol. 2, no. 2, 2011, pp. 132–55.

James, Daniel, editor. *Violencia, proscripción y autoritarismo (1955–1976). Colección Nueva Historia Argentina*. Vol. IX, Sudamericana, 2003.

Jameson, Fredric. *The Political Unconscious: Narrative as a Socially Symbolic Act*. Cornell UP, 1981.

Kafka, Franz. *The Trial*. Translated by Willa and Edwin Muir, Schocken, 1956.

Kant, Immanuel. *Grounding for the Metaphysics of Morals*. Translated by James W. Ellington, Hackett, 1993.

———. "An Answer to the Question: What is Enlightenment?" *Immanuel Kant: Ethics Reference Archive*. Accessed 10 Apr. 2015.

Laclau, Ernesto. *Emancipation(s)*. Verso, 1996.

Lage, Jorge Enrique. "Epílogo." *Los supremos. Superhéroes y cómics en el relato hispánico contemporáneo*, edited by Salvador Luis, El Cuervo Editorial, 2013, pp. 37–48.

Levinas, Emmanuel. *Otherwise than Being, or Beyond Essence*. Translated by Alphonso Lingis, Duquesne UP, 1997.

———. *Totality and Infinity: An Essay on Exteriority*. Translated by Alphonso Lingis, Duquesne UP, 1969.

Levinson, Brett. *The Ends of Literature: The Latin American "Boom" in the Neoliberal Marketplace*. Stanford UP, 2001.

López Abadía, Ana María. "Terror prototípico y subjetividad. Un acercamiento a la narrativa gótica en *Un retrato para Dickens* (1969)," *Escritural. Écritures d'Amérique latine*, vol. 9, 2016. Accessed 10 Jun. 2017.

Ludmer, Josefina. *The Gaucho Genre: A Treatise on the Motherland*. Translated by Molly Weigel, Duke UP, 2002.

Lugones, Leopoldo. *El payador*. Stockcero, 2004.

Luis, William. "Exhuming *Lunes de Revolución*." *The New Centennial Review*, vol. 2, no. 2, 2002, pp. 253–83.

———. *Lunes de Revolución. Literatura y cultura en los primeros años de la revolución cubana*. Editorial Verbum, 2003.

Lumsden, Ian. *Machos, Maricones, and Gays: Cuba and Homosexuality*. Temple UP, 1996.

Mansilla, Lucio V. *Una excursión a los indios ranqueles*. Edited by Saúl Sosnowski, Stockcero, 2007.

Manuel, Peter. "Cuba: From Contradanza to Danzón." *Creolizing Contradance in the Caribbean*, edited by Peter Manuel, Temple UP, 2009, pp. 51–112.

Martínez Nadal, Rafael. "Calvert Casey. Notas a una lectura de 'Piazza Margana.'" *Quimera*, vol. 26, 1982, pp. 85–87.

Mbembe, Achille. "Necropolitics." Translated by Libby Meintjes. *Biopolitics: A Reader*, edited by Timothy Campbell and Adam Sitze, Duke UP, 2013, pp. 161–92.

McCann, Colum. *Let the Great World Spin*. Random House, 2009.

Medina Ríos, Jamila. *Diseminaciones de Calvert Casey*. Letras Cubanas, 2012.

Merlino, Mario. Introduction. "Delantal para Calvert Casey." *Notas de un simulador* by Calvert Casey, Montesinos, 1997, pp. 9–29.

Works Cited

Meza, Ramón. *Mi tío el empleado*. Vol. 1, Luís Tasso Serra, 1887.

———. *Mi tío el empleado*. Vol. 2, Luís Tasso Serra, 1887.

Mill, John Stuart. *Utilitarianism*. 2nd edition, edited by George Sher, Hackett, 2001.

Montes-Bradley, Eduardo, director. *Ecce homo: una autobiografía de Juan Filloy*. Patagonia Film Group, 2008.

Mouffe, Chantal. *Agonistics: Thinking the World Politically*. Verso, 2013.

———. *The Democratic Paradox*. Verso, 2000.

Muñoz, José Esteban. *Cruising Utopia: The Then and There of Queer Futurity*. New York UP, 2009.

Nancy, Jean-Luc. *Being Singular Plural*. Translated by Robert D. Richardson and Anne E. O'Byrne, Stanford UP, 2000.

———. *The Disavowed Community*. Translated by Philip Armstrong, Fordham UP, 2016.

———. *The Inoperative Community*. Edited and translated by Peter Connor, U of Minnesota P, 1991.

Niebylski, Dianna C. *Humoring Resistance: Laughter and the Excessive Body in Contemporary Latin American Women's Fiction*. SUNY P, 2004.

Nietzsche, Friedrich. *The Birth of Tragedy and The Genealogy of Morals*. Translated by Francis Golffing, Anchor Books, 1956.

Olivera-Williams, María Rosa. "Lo femenino delirante. *La mujer desnuda* de Armonía Somers." *Romance Quarterly*, vol. 58, no. 1, 2011, pp. 27–53.

Olivier, Florence. "Entre la vida y la muerte. Del simulacro a la indentificación en 'Notas de un simulador,' de Calvert Casey." *Encuentro de la cultura cubana*, vol. 41–42, 2006, pp. 209–19.

Padilla, Heberto. *Fuera del juego*. Ediciones Universal, 1998.

Pérez Escrich, Enrique. *El manuscrito de una madre. Novela de costumbres*. Vol. 1, illustrated by Eusebio Planas, José Astort y Compañía, 1872.

———. *El manuscrito de una madre. Novela de costumbres*. Vol. 2, illustrated by Eusebio Planas, José Astort y Compañía, 1872.

Pérez-Firmat, Gustavo. "Bilingual Blues, Bilingual Bliss: El caso Casey." *Modern Language Notes*, vol. 117, no. 2, 2002, pp. 432–48.

Perera San Martín, Nicasio. "Armonía Somers: una trayectoria ejemplar." *Armonía Somers, papeles críticos. Cuarenta años de literatura*, edited by Rómulo Cosse, Linardi y Risso, 1990, pp. 17–35.

———. "La intuición y los papeles. En torno a *De miedo en miedo (los manuscritos del río)*." *Escritural. Écritures d'Amérique latine*, vol. 9, 2016. Accessed 10 Jun. 2017.

Piglia, Ricardo. "Ernesto Guevara, rastros de lectura." *El último lector*, Anagrama, 2005, pp. 103–38.

Plato. *Republic*. Translated by Robin Waterfield, Oxford UP, 1993.

———. *Timaeus*. Translated by Donald J. Zeyl. Hackett, 2000.

Portuondo, José Antonio. "Pasión y muerte del hombre." *Los mejores ensayistas cubanos*, edited by Salvador Bueno, Editora Latinoamericana, 1959, pp. 113–23.

Premat, Julio. "Los relatos de la vanguardia o el retorno de lo nuevo." *Cuadernos de literatura*, vol. 17, no. 34, 2013, pp. 47–64.

Prieto, Julio. *Desencuadernados: vanguardias ex-céntricas en el Río de la Plata. Macedonio Fernández y Felisberto Hernández*. Beatriz Viterbo, 2002.

Quintero Herencia, Juan Carlos. *Fulguración del espacio. Letras e imaginario institucional de la Revolución Cubana (1960–1971)*. Beatriz Viterbo, 2002.

———. "'El regreso' de Calvert Casey: Una exposición en la playa." *Cuadernos de literatura*, vol. 17, no. 33, 2013, pp. 377–403.

Quiroga, José. "Fleshing Out Virgilio Piñera from the Cuban Closet." *¿Entiendes? Queer Readings, Hispanic Writings*, edited by Emilie L. Bergmann and Paul Julian Smith, Duke UP, 1995, pp. 168–80.

Rama, Ángel. "El 'Boom' en perspectiva." *Más allá del Boom: Literatura y mercado*, edited by Ángel Rama, Marcha Editores, 1981, pp. 51–110.

———. *Los gauchipolíticos rioplatenses. Literatura y sociedad*. Calicanto, 1976.

———. "La insólita literatura de Somers: la fascinación del horror." *Marcha*, 1963, pp. 30.

———. "Mujeres, dijo el penado alto." *Marcha*, 1966, pp. 50–51.

Rancière, Jacques. *The Politics of Aesthetics: The Distribution of the Sensible*. Translated by Gabriel Rockhill, Continuum, 2000.

Richard, Nelly. *Residuos y metáforas (Ensayos de crítica cultural sobre el Chile de la Transición)*. Cuarto Propio, 1998.

———. *La insubordinación de los signos (Cambio político, transformaciones culturales y poéticas de la crisis)*. Cuarto Propio, 1994.

Rodríguez Monegal, Emir. "Onirismo, sexo y asco." *Marcha*, vol. 679, 1953, pp. 14.

Rodríguez-Villamil, Ana María. *Elementos fantásticos en la narrativa de Armonía Somers*. Ediciones de la Banda Oriental, 1990.

Rojas, Rafael. *La vanguardia peregrina. El escritor cubano, la tradición y el exilio*. Fondo de Cultura Económica, 2013.

Works Cited

Sabato, Ernesto. *El túnel.* Booket, 2005.

Sarlo, Beatriz. *El imperio de los sentimientos. Narraciones de circulación periódica en la Argentina (1917–1927).* Catálogos Editora, 1985.

———. *Jorge Luis Borges: A Writer on the Edge.* Edited by John King, Verso, 1993.

———. *Una modernidad periférica. Buenos Aires, 1920–1930.* Ediciones Nueva Visión, 1999.

———. *Viajes. De la Amazonía a las Malvinas.* Seix Barral, 2014.

Sarmiento, Domingo Faustino. *Facundo. Civilización y barbarie.* Edited by Roberto Yahni, Cátedra, 2008.

Sartre, Jean-Paul. *Being and Nothingness: A Phenomenological Essay on Ontology.* Translated by Hazel E. Barnes. Washington Square Press. 1984.

———. *Sartre on Cuba.* Ballantine Books, 1961.

Scarpaci, Joseph L. "Environmental Planning and Heritage Tourism in Cuba During the Special Period: Challenges and Opportunities." *Environmental Planning in the Caribbean*, edited by Jonathan Pugh and Janet Henshall Momsen, Ashgate, 2006, pp. 73–92.

Scarpaci, Joseph L., Roberto Segre, and Mario Coyula. *Havana: Two Faces of the Antillean Metropolis.* Revised edition, U of North Carolina P, 2002.

Sears, Cynthia L. "A Dynamic Partnership: Celebrating Our Gut Flora." *Anaerobe*, vol. 11, no. 5, 2005, pp. 247–51.

Serra, Ana. *The "New Man" in Cuba: Culture and Identity in the Revolution.* UP of Florida, 2007.

Sheldon, Rose Mary. "The Sator Rebus: An Unsolved Cryptogram?" *Cryptologia*, vol. 27, no. 3, 2003, pp. 233–87.

Sigal, Silvia. *Intelectuales y poder en la década del sesenta.* Puntosur, 1991.

Sinnott-Armstrong, Walter. "Consequentialism." *The Stanford Encyclopedia of Philosophy*, edited by Edward N. Zalta. Accessed 8 Aug. 2013.

Snook, Margaret L. "Who's Pulling the St(r)ing? Gender and Class in Armonía Somers's 'Muerte por alacrán.'" *Ciberletras*, vol. 13, 2005.

Somers, Armonía. *De miedo en miedo. (Los manuscritos del río).* Arca, 1965.

———. "Muerte por alacrán." *Todos los cuentos. 1953–1967.* Vol 2. Arca, 2006. pp. 109–22.

———. *La mujer desnuda.* Arca, 1990.

———. *La mujer desnuda.* El cuenco de plata, 2009.

———. *Un retrato para Dickens.* Arca, 1969.

———. *Un retrato para Dickens*. El cuenco de plata, 2012.

———. *Sólo los elefantes encuentran mandrágora*. El cuenco de plata, 2010.

———. *Todos los cuentos. 1953–1967*. 2 Vols. Arca, 2006.

Stavans, Ilan. Introduction. *Calvert Casey: The Collected Works* by Calvert Casey, edited by Ilan Stavans, Duke UP, 1998, pp. vii–xx.

Stoll, David. *Rigoberta Menchú and the Story of All Poor Guatemalans*. Westview, 1999.

Svampa, Maristella. "El populismo imposible y sus actores. 1973–1976." *Violencia, proscripción y autoritarismo (1955–1976). Colección Nueva Historia Argentina*, vol. IX, edited by Daniel James, Sudamericana, 2003, pp. 381–438.

Terán, Oscar. *Nuestros años sesentas. La formación de la nueva izquierda intelectual en la Argentina 1956–1966*. Punto Sur Editores, 1991.

Torres, Alicia. "El Oliver dickensiano y la huérfana de Somers: tráfico de identidades." *Charles Dickens en América Latina. Reflexiones desde Montevideo*, edited by Beatriz Vegh, Linardi y Risso, 2005, pp. 179–91.

Trigo, Abril. *Caudillo, estado, nación. Literatura, historia e ideología en el Uruguay*. Gaithersburg, Ediciones Hispamérica, 1990.

Unruh, Vicky. *Latin American Vanguards: The Art of Contentious Encounters*. U of California P, 1994.

Villaverde, Cirilo. *Cecilia Valdés, o la loma del Ángel*. Plaza Editorial, 2013.

Vitier, Cintio. *Lo cubano en la poesía*. Instituto del Libro, 1970.

Wright, Thomas C. *Latin America in the Era of the Cuban Revolution*. Revised edition, Praeger, 2001.

Zanetti, Susana. "El arte de narrar en los cuentos de Armonía Somers." *Orbis Tertius*, vol. 9, 2002–2003, pp. 1–13.

———. *La dorada garra de la escritura. Lectoras y lectores de novela en América Latina*. Beatriz Viterbo, 2002.

Zayas, Manuel, and Orlando Jiménez Leal. "Un baile de fantasmas." *El caso P.M. Cine, poder y censura*, edited by Orlando Jiménez Leal and Manuel Zayas, Kindle ed., Editorial Hypermedia, 2014.

Index

aesthetics
  revolutionary, 158–63
  of writing in plain sight, 109–11
Agamben, Giorgio
  anthropological machine, 100–101
  bare life, 59–60, 100–103, 211n3
  biopolitics, 22–23, 100–105
  the contemporary, 24–25
  ethics, 188–89
  homo sacer, 58–60
  Oedipus and the Sphinx, 132–33
  potentiality, 97–98, 218ch11n1
  state of exception, 58–60
  totalitarianism, 103
allegory, 75–89, 110
"Allegory of the Cave" (Plato), 20, 80–86, 92–93
al vesre/al verse, 1–4, 8, 12, 17, 31
anonymity, 9–10, 44–46
Argentine desert, 85–86
Arguedas, José María, 209n11
Aristotle, 97
ARTELETRA, 1–2, 35–38
  See also palindrome
avant-garde, 13–15

bare life. *See* Giorgio Agamben
Batista y Zaldívar, Fulgencio, 5, 62, 65–66
Bay of Pigs (Playa Girón), 62–63
Beauvoir, Simone de, 16
being-with, 169–71
Benjamin, Walter, 2, 14, 36, 144, 215n1
binaries
  against, 2, 14, 16, 28, 166–67, 171, 178, 188
  biopolitics and, 4, 24–26
  examples of, 5, 8–9, 20, 30, 58, 86–87, 114–15, 162

biopolitics, 4, 22–25, 101–4, 138–40, 215ch8n3
  See also Giorgio Agamben, Roberto Esposito, Michel Foucault
Bioy Casares, Adolfo, 118
Boom, El, 7, 11–12, 16, 29
Bordaberry, Juan María, 5, 94, 139
Borges, Jorge Luis, 118, 214n7
Bürger, Peter, 13–14

Cabrera, Sabá. *See P.M.*
Cabrera Infante, Guillermo, 6, 11, 62–63, 211ch4n4
Carrión, Miguel de, 154–58,
Casa de las Américas (editorial), 5, 45–46, 63–64
Casey, Calvert
  biography, 5–6
  "Carrión o la desnudez," 154–58
  "La ejecución," 193–201
  "Un ensayo oportuno," 65–67
  "Hacia una comprensión total del XIX," 143, 147–50
  homosexuality and exile, 18, 65, 211n4
  "Meditación junto a Caballería," 145–47, 162–63
  Memorias de una isla, 144, 147
  "Meza literato y los Croquis Habaneros," 150–51
  "Mi tía Leocadia, el amor, y el paleolítico inferior," 144–45, 152–54
  Notas de un simulador, 18
  "Notas de un simulador," 39, 44–47, 205–6, 208
  "Piazza Margana," 160–63, 215ch9n2
  "Polacca brillante," 17–19
  "El Premio Nobel y la muerte," 61, 71–73

Casey (*continued*)
  El regreso, 194, 218ch12n1
  El regreso y otros relatos, 194, 218ch12n1
  translations of, 6
Castro, Fidel, 4–5, 16, 18, 62–65, 160, 212n5
Cecilia Valdés (Cirilo Villaverde), 155–57
Certeau, Michel de, 23–24, 39–40
Cold War, 16, 30, 86–87, 94
commitment without dogma, 28
community, 28, 57, 68, 103–7, 139–40, 165–67, 169–71, 178–79, 188, 198–200, 205, 206, 208
Consejo Nacional de Cultura, 63
consequentialism. *See* ethics
contamination. *See* immunity
cookbook, 128–29
Cordobazo, 78, 84, 87
Cortázar, Julio, 13, 29, 35, 209n11
costumbrismo, 150–51, 158
Cuban Revolution, 6, 16–18, 29–30, 62–67, 77–78, 143–45, 148–50, 158–63
  homophobia and, 6, 65, 212n5
Cuban Romantics, 148–50
cultural markets, 11–13

Deleuze, Gilles, and Félix Guattari, 10, 37–38, 42–43, 55, 92
  becoming, 42–43, 92
  going unnoticed, 10
  lines of flight, 37–38, 55
  rhizome, 37
  zones of indiscernibility, 42
deontology. *See* ethics
Derrida, Jacques, 64, 81–83, 117, 213n5
Descartes, René, 20–21
dialogue, 4–5, 10, 26–28, 70, 81–82, 169–179
  See also monodialogues, pandemonium
Dickens, Charles, 27, 128–29
disagreement, 19, 69, 91, 101, 106–7, 127, 167–68, 179, 192, 206,
disillusionment, 3–4, 37, 204, 208
dissensus. *See* Chantal Mouffe

Ediciones R (editorial), 6, 62, 144, 194
editoriales culturales. *See* cultural markets
enigma, enigmatic, 32–34, 50, 56, 98, 102, 106, 110, 128–42
errancy, errant, 26–27, 29–38, 44–46, 75–89, 179
Esposito, Roberto, 138–40, 215n4
essentialism, essentialist, 2–3, 27, 107, 110–11, 113–14, 116, 118, 123, 125
Etchepare, Armonía, (pseud. Armonía Somers)
  biography, 7
  feminist readings of, 7, 11, 210n2
  De miedo en miedo (los manuscritos del río), 9–10, 50–52, 169–179
  "Muerte por alacrán," 52–56
  La mujer desnuda, 7, 27, 49, 91–93, 95–107
  Un retrato para Dickens, 128–29
  Sólo los elefantes encuentran mandragora, 128, 133–142
  Todos los cuentos. 1953–1967, 7
  translations of, 7
ethics
  of being perceived, 165–68, 171, 176–79, 189, 194, 198–99
  branches of, 166
  as opposed to morals, 166–67

everyday, 19, 39–40

face-to-face encounter, 3, 177
family, 26, 29–30, 45–46, 119–22
family romance, 128–29
fascism, 4
feminist criticism, 7, 11, 178, 210n2
Filloy, Juan
   biography, 6
   "Carbunclo," 115, 124–25
   Decio 8A, 6, 113
   Finesse, 6
   "El juído (El patriarca)," 119–20, 123–24, 214n6
   Karcino. Tratado de palindromía, 1, 6, 31–38, 113, 127, 143
   Los Ochoa, 6, 113–15, 120–24, 214n3
   Op Oloop, 6
   Periplo, 6
   as rural writer, 7, 116
   Vil & Vil (La gata parida), 6, 27, 80, 181–192
   yomismo, 79, 89, 105, 165, 182
   "Yo y los intrusos," 75–77, 80–89, 184
   Yo, yo y yo (Monodiálogos paranoicos), 75, 87, 184–85
   palindromes, 1, 6, 26–27, 31–38, 83–84, 113, 127, 143
filth. *See* waste
Foster, Hal, 14–15
Foucault, Michel, 22, 122, 167, 215ch8n3
fragments, fragmented texts, 8, 39, 41, 62, 71, 128–29, 152, 173, 175–79, 186, 201

Gaceta de Cuba (editorial), 6
gaucho, 113–25
   gaucho jodón, 114–16
   good and bad gauchos, 123–24, 214n2
   as national allegory, 116–19
   poetry, 115–17
gender and sexuality, 37
Genette, Gérard, 187
globalization, 4, 58
going unnoticed, 1–4, 9–28, 30, 39–47, 57–60, 69–73, 81, 88–89, 97–101, 105–7, 109, 165–66, 169, 171, 177, 206–8
   becoming and, 10, 41–43, 81
   identity and, 24, 43,
   as material practice, 44
   politics of, 3, 19–20, 57–61, 65, 69–71, 73, 75, 77, 79, 82, 86, 89, 99, 101, 105–7, 165–66, 178, 183, 200, 206–8
   as process and movement, 42–43, 81,
   visibility and, 3, 10, 24, 109
Guevara, Ernesto "Che," 6, 16, 73, 148, 191, 212n5

Habermas, Jürgen, 57–58
Han, Byung-Chul, 22–23
Haraway, Donna J., 140
Harvey, David, 205
house, 44–47, 210n1
   See also revolutionary house

ICAIC (Instituto Cubano de Arte e Industria Cinematográficos), 63
identity, identity politics, 7, 19–26, 43, 68, 103, 166, 169–71, 178, 188, 206
immunity, 138–142
   See also Roberto Esposito
impuras, Las (Miguel de Carríon), 145, 154–55, 157

individualism, 4, 71, 157, 181
inoperative, inoperativity, 4, 14, 24–26, 28, 43, 52, 101, 107, 170, 172
  See also Jean-Luc Nancy
invisible, invisibility, 3–4, 9, 12, 23, 35, 41, 57–59, 68, 81, 109
itinerary, 3, 5, 10, 14, 19, 24, 29–30, 31, 34–35, 38, 44–45, 46, 51–52, 56, 117, 135, 195, 197, 204, 206

Jameson, Fredric, 110
Jiménez Leal, Orlando. *See P.M.*

Kafka, Franz, 193–98
Kant, Immanuel, 20–21, 22, 167, 217n3

Laclau, Ernesto, 119
Left Turn, 4
Levinas, Emmanuel, 3, 175–78, 184, 191
Ley de Seguridad, 87
Lugones, Leopoldo, 116–25, 131, 144
Lunes de Revolución (editorial), 5, 13, 27, 61–65, 69–70, 73, 144, 160, 211ch4n1, 212n8
Lunfardo, 1–2

Mandrake Syndrome. *See* Armonía Etchepare
manuscrito de una madre, El (Enrique Pérez Escrich), 134–35
Martín Fierro (José Hernández), 117–120, 190–91, 214n5
"*medidas prontas de seguridad*," 59, 93–94, 213n2
mercado cultural. *See* cultural markets

Meza, Ramón, 145, 150–53
Mi tío el empleado (Ramón Meza), 145, 150–53
modernismo, 14, 79
modernity, 29, 58
monodialogue, 75, 84–85, 88, 181–92, 212n1
Montoneros, 78
Mouffe, Chantal, 19, 67–68, 198–99, 201, 212n9
  agonism, 198–99, 201
  dissensus, 19, 67–68, 212n9
  pluralism, 68
Movimiento Revolucionario 26 de Julio (MR-26-7), 62–63
Muñoz, José Esteban, 206

Nancy, Jean-Luc, 169–70, 172, 179
neoliberalism, 4, 22, 29
Neruda, Pablo, 69–70, 191
Nietzsche, Friedrich, 122, 166–67, 188
norms, normativity, 3, 8, 13, 23, 26–27, 97, 145–46, 166, 206–7

Padilla, Heberto (Padilla Affair of 1971), 5, 30, 63, 70, 144, 210pt1n2, 212n7
"Palabras a los intelectuales" (Fidel Castro), 63–64, 70, 159–60, 212n7
palindrome, 1–2, 29–38, 64, 77, 83–84, 113, 127, 132, 143, 173, 179, 183
  going unnoticed and, 30, 36–37, 179
  hermeneutics of, 33
  as heuristic, 1, 26, 31, 36, 207
  Sator Square, 32–34, 110, 132, 176, 210n1
Pandemonium, 181–192, 200–1

Pasternak, Boris, 61, 64, 72–73, 75, 88, 105, 150
payador, El (Leopoldo Lugones), 116–17
perception, 10, 32, 35–36, 41–43, 97, 110, 125, 165, 170–71
Pérez Escrich, Enrique, 27, 134–35, 139
peripheral modernity, 58, 209n11
Perón, Juan, 5, 77–78, 86–87, 182, 213ch5n2
Peronism, 4–5, 77–80, 86–87, 118, 213ch5n2
Plato, 20, 25, 27, 75, 80–86, 92–93, 100, 167, 207
pluralism. *See* Chantal Mouffe
P.M., 27, 63–64, 144–45, 158–60
politics
    Greek public sphere and, 57–60
    of visibility, 3, 19–25, 68–69
    See also going unnoticed
postmodernism, postmodernity, 24, 58, 68, 158
Portuondo, José Antonio, 66–67
privacy, private, 9–10, 21–23, 25, 58–59, 198
pseudonyms, 7, 10, 43
public sphere, 3, 20–23, 57–60, 71, 73

Quimera (editorial), 6

Rama, Ángel, 7, 12–13, 49, 115, 209n5
Rancière, Jacques, 21, 68–69
Republic (Plato), 20, 81–82
Revolución (editorial), 62–63, 160
revolutionary house, 26, 29, 46–47
Richard, Nelly, 23, 133–34, 159
Rosariazo, 78

Sarlo, Beatriz, 14, 116, 203–4
Sarraute, Nathalie, 69–71

Sartre, Jean-Paul, 16–18, 191
Sator Square. *See* palindrome
Schmitt, Carl, 64
scorpion, 52–56
Seix Barral, 6, 194
Sixties
    literary-political arena of, 7–8
    periodization and, 4–5, 29–30
Somers, Armonía. *See* Armonía Etchepare
sovereignty, 22
Soviet Union, 16, 61, 158, 187
space, 3, 19–20, 22–23, 58, 82, 96–98
state of exception. *See* Giorgio Agamben
surface reading, 110
surveillance, 9–10, 18, 22, 24–25, 30, 40, 43, 45–46, 57

testimonio, 84–85
totality, totalizing, 8, 16, 26, 29–30, 68, 81, 127, 133–35, 176–78, 198
transparency, transparent, 22–23, 134
Tupamaros, 5, 94, 139

UMAP (Unidades Militares de Ayuda a la Producción), 6, 64, 144
Unión de Escritores y Artistas de Cuba, 63
Uruguayan Civil Code, 95–97
utopia, 5, 156, 204–5, 207–8

Villaverde, Cirilo, 155–57, 216n7
virtue ethics. *See* ethics
visibility, 2–3
    discourse of, 24
    metaphors of, 20
    production of knowledge and, 24
    politics of, 19

Index

waste, 143–163
    body and, 161–63
    filth and, 146–47
    sewers and, 145–47
wasted narratives. *See* waste
Woolworth sit-in, 152
writing in plain sight, 10–11,
    109–11

About the Book

ArteletrA analyzes the Sixties in Latin America in order to revisit the core claim of literary and cultural studies to political relevancy in the contemporary world: the task of making visible the invisible. Though visibility can secure rights for the disenfranchised, it also risks subjecting them to the biopolitical and capitalist arrangements of space. What is at stake in this book is a series of aesthetic and ethical tools for engaging in politics—defined here as the potential to disagree—without first passing through visibility. These tools cohere around a practice Bartles calls "the politics of going unnoticed," which he derives from an archive of three noteworthy, though under-appreciated, authors who wrote during the Sixties: Calvert Casey (1924–69), Juan Filloy (1894–2000), and Armonía Somers (1914–94). For the first time ever, Casey, Filloy, and Somers are put in dialogue with one another to further demonstrate the unique contributions of Latin American writers to contemporary debates about the crossroads of literatures and politics. What unites them is their shared investment in stories about those who go unnoticed. As a practice, going unnoticed creates space and opportunities for queer, rural, and female subjects, among others, to step back from unjust institutions. As a political discourse, going unnoticed deactivates the binary structures of biopolitics (e.g., visible/invisible, pure/filthy, friend/enemy) that divide humans from one another in the service of power and economic inequality. Though the politics of going unnoticed was ignored during the Sixties for its apparent individualism, these three writers work through alternatives to the politics of visibility that has animated political discourse on the left for the last half-century. More than a self-interested critique, going unnoticed opens new possibilities for engaging in the messy business of politics while imagining and creating better communities.

About the Author

Jason A. Bartles is an associate professor at West Chester University. He received his BA from Gettysburg College and his MA and PhD in Latin American Literatures and Cultures from the University of Maryland, College Park. His research explores the political, aesthetic, and ethical discourses that restore the possibilities for utopian thinking in the fiction and essays of twentieth and twenty-first century Latin American and Latinx writers. He has published articles in *Aztlán, Revista Iberoamericana, Variaciones Borges, Revista Hispánica Moderna*, and *Revista de Estudios Hispánicos*. His fiction has appeared in *Punchnel's, Here Comes Everyone, Boned, The Metaworker*, and in the collection, *My Utopia*, at Cambridge Scholars Publishing.

Jason Bartles's *ArteletrA* offers a unique, innovative framework for reading an era in Latin American cultural history that seemed foreclosed to further literary or political readings. By providing a heuristic for reading against the currents of the cultural maps of the 1960s, Bartles not only helps us revisit this decade by attending to works and writers other than the ones we commonly associate with the period, but he also opens up a much-needed space today for alternative forms of utopian thinking. Creating a dialogue between works by Calvert Casey (Cuba, 1924–69), Juan Filloy (Argentina, 1894–2000), and Armonía Somers (Uruguay, 1914–94) proves the value of comparative analysis when examining a time in the production of Latin American literatures and politics that makes sense only transnationally. The politics of going unnoticed enacted by the various characters analyzed by Bartles compels us to see this crucial period in Latin American politics outside the logic of success and failure. Instead, *ArteletrA* unsettles and interrogates this binary, as it does those between visibility and invisibility, transparency and opacity, that structure the political up until today.

Mariela Méndez, University of Richmond

CPSIA information can be obtained
at www.ICGtesting.com
Printed in the USA
LVHW082048050421
683485LV00015B/514